mlr
Marxist Left Review

Number 24 – Winter 2022

Editor
Omar Hassan

Editorial Committee
Mick Armstrong
Sandra Bloodworth
Omar Hassan
Louise O'Shea

Reviews Editor
Alexis Vassiley

© Social Research Institute

Published by Socialist Alternative
Melbourne, August 2022

PO Box 4354
Melbourne University, VIC 3052

www.marxistleftreview.org

marxistleftreview@gmail.com

Contributions to *Marxist Left Review* are peer-reviewed

ISSN 1838-2932
rrp. $17

Subediting and proofreading
Tess Lee Ack
Diane Fieldes

Layout and production
Oscar Sterner

Cover
Oscar Sterner

Printed by IngramSpark

Marxist Left Review is a theoretical journal published twice-yearly by Socialist Alternative, a revolutionary organisation based in Australia.

We aim to engage with theoretical and political debates on the Australian and international left, making a rigorous yet accessible case for Marxist politics. We also seek to provide analysis of the social, political and economic dynamics shaping Australian capitalism.

Unless indicated otherwise all articles published reflect the views of the individual author(s).

We rely on our readers' support to continue publication.
You can help by subscribing at *marxistleftreview.org*

Marxist Left Review

Number 24 – Winter 2022

FEATURES

1   OMAR HASSAN
    Editorial: Inflation intensifies class war

13 MICK ARMSTRONG
    Chifley: Extinguishing the light on the hill

41 PHOEBE KELLOWAY
    Private profit vs public access: How class struggle shaped Australia's health care system

83 RICK KUHN
    Left populism versus revolutionary Marxism: Debating economic strategy in Australia

123 VASHTI FOX
    Stalinism's failure to fight fascism

157 DUNCAN HART
    Draper, Lenin and the dictatorship of the proletariat

REVIEWS

187 JORDAN HUMPHREYS
    Indigenous people vs "settler" migrants?

199 LIZ ROSS
    Nuclear secrets and racist lies

207 ALEXIS VASSILEY
    Breaking Things at Work

OMAR HASSAN

Editorial: Inflation intensifies class war

Omar Hassan is the editor of *Marxist Left Review*. He has been active in anti-fascist and Palestine solidarity work, and has written extensively on the Middle East.

THE WORLD IS IN THE MIDST of the biggest inflationary episode since the 1970s. The costs of goods and services have gone up across the board, with increases concentrated in the most essential sectors of food, energy and housing.

This price shock has forced down the real purchasing power of working-class people. In Australia, workers have lost a decade's worth of wage rises in the space of a few months. Meanwhile, politicians, economists and business owners are preparing to punish workers even more. Indifferent to the collapse in living standards that millions are facing, the media are instead focused on the hypothetical danger of real wage rises that are facing...well, nobody.

The pandemic days when essential workers were feted have been relegated to the history books, along with concern for public health and decent welfare payments. We now face escalating assaults on living standards that, if not resisted, could set us back decades.

To understand this situation, we have to look at recent shifts in the global economy.

When the pandemic first swept the world, most economists predicted that it would result in economic catastrophe as lockdowns destroyed industries and impoverished millions of workers. Although economies did collapse in the first half of 2020, governments in the advanced capitalist world quickly stepped in with huge spending designed to prop up the system. Stimulus measures were far more substantial than those deployed in the Global Financial Crisis of 2007–09. For instance, the US government alone had spent more than $5 trillion by November 2021,[1] not including the varied and vast stimulatory actions taken by the Federal Reserve. Broadly speaking, these emergency measures staved off the predicted catastrophe.

Corporations found new ways to make money as governments provided relatively generous support to both consumers and businesses. Economic fortunes revived almost as quickly as they had cratered. The blood of millions of unnecessary pandemic casualties was sacrificed to accelerate this recovery, as governments prematurely abandoned attempts to contain COVID-19.

But the rapid rebound created new problems. There was a huge rise in household savings[2] as workers banked cash usually spent on restaurants and holidays, and, in countries like Australia, as payments increased to the unemployed and to small business owners. As the immediate fear of collapse receded, workers used their increased funds to improve their household amenities, driving a boom in furniture, whitegoods and home renovations.

But lockdowns and labour shortages restricted supply and disrupted supply chains that make world trade possible. Big manufacturers had also scaled down their capacities in the early days of the pandemic, preparing for a long recession. They were unprepared when the economy snapped back, and took months to catch up. While there has been an increase in capital expenditure in recent months, driven in part by onshoring and "friend-shoring" of strategic sectors, there can be long delays between investment and new capacity coming online.

In a classic example of how the free market fails in every crisis, these shortages led to eye-watering price rises. For instance, the cost of international shipping increased dramatically through 2020 and early 2021, by up to 1,250 percent on some lines.[3] In many countries, trucks and drivers were in short supply and waiting times at ports blew out.

---

1. Statista Research Department 2022.
2. Remes et al 2021.
3. Daily Sabah 2021.

The global boom in manufacturing, paired with the more localised booms in home renovations in the West, led to dramatic increases in the cost of necessary inputs such as timber, coal, iron ore and steel, which are only starting to ease as we go to print. Companies desperately tried to fill orders and restock their inventories, adding further pressure to supply chains. Being good capitalists, those who paid these higher prices passed on the cost to retailers, who in turn passed them on to workers.

Notably, this all preceded the war in Ukraine, which is often used by Western governments to explain away inflation. Putin's war and Western sanctions undeniably have placed additional strain on energy and food supplies, especially damaging for states in Europe and the Middle East that rely on Ukrainian and Russian exports. As well, the risk of a wider European war cannot be ruled out, however unlikely. But far from being an outlier, political shocks such as this are an inevitable feature of a world market that is simultaneously unified by trade and fragmented by geopolitical rivalries. In other words, inflation and supply shortages reflect the insanity of a world economy organised around markets and profits rather than human need.

There has been much debate about the cause of inflation. Monetarists insist that it is caused by governmental largesse and cheap credit. Keynesians prefer to blame supply shocks and lack of investment in productive capacity.

Neither of these theories can explain the current crisis. Cheap credit and quantitative easing have been in place since 2008, so why did inflation remain so low until last year? Clearly the shocks generated by lockdowns and opening-ups – involving both supply and demand – are factors. Yet the Keynesian argument, which insists that the problem can be fixed by increasing supply, fails too. The failure to sufficiently invest in new productive capacity for decades is not some accident, or bad policy choice. It reflects that the world already produces far more goods than we need, and certainly far more than can be sold profitably. No amount of subsidies, handouts and cheap credit can convince companies to build unprofitable and unnecessary projects, or to provide the necessary resources to the growing ranks of the global poor.

Central banks have proven uninterested in the nuances of these discussions. With the exception of Japan, central banks across the advanced world have discarded the "easy money" policies in place since the Global Financial Crisis, in favour of old-school monetarism. They hope to rein in inflation by tightening access to credit through raising interest rates and withdrawing support for the bond market, the main source of funds for governments and big corporations.

The immediate impact of this new policy has been to pop a number of asset bubbles. Years of cheap credit led to rampant speculation[4] in cryptocurrencies, unprofitable tech start-ups, stocks more broadly, real estate and other speculative "assets". Tightening conditions will see them all decline in value, to a greater or lesser extent. A recent newsletter by economist Adam Tooze noted that the sell-off in equities and bonds, since the peak in late 2021, has resulted in $15.5 trillion in losses,[5] equivalent to about 60 percent of US GDP in 2019.

Meanwhile Australian investors in crypto have already lost around 70 percent of their real money, with more pain to come as the ponzi schemes unravel. Housing will take longer to be impacted, but could fall by 20 percent or more. To some extent these corrections reflect a necessary return to reality: the price/earning ratio of many stocks was off the charts, housing is beyond unaffordable, and crypto is essentially worthless. Soaring stock markets have also drawn increasing amounts of capital, far surpassing investment in the real economy. Disorderly crashes in any of these sectors could bring down the whole house of cards. So even from a capitalist point of view, these bubbles posed a risk to the health of the broader economy, and an orderly correction could prove positive in the long run.

But the risks go well beyond the financial sector. A report by Bloomberg found that roughly one-fifth of America's top 3,000 firms don't earn enough profit[6] to cover the interest payments on their debts. Forcing some of these companies to the wall could be the basis for a new round of growth and accumulation, if it doesn't send the whole economy spiralling downwards.

There is also a global element to this process of cannibalisation. US corporations enjoy a significant advantage in the world markets,

---

4. Parlin 2020.
5. Tooze 2022.
6. Lee 2022.

given the dominance of their currency and the economic, political and military institutions of their home state. This gives the US ruling class a unique capacity to shape the global economy, defending key industries and interests while passing on higher costs and risks on to weaker competitors.

Many low- and medium-income countries have enormous debts, mostly denominated in US dollars. US economist Michael Spence has described the combination of rising interest rates, higher energy and food prices, and a strengthening US dollar as a "nightmare scenario" that threatens to destabilise these countries. Protests have broken out in Panama, and nuclear-armed Pakistan is at risk of defaulting on its debts. The crisis in Sri Lanka[7] is the most developed, and could be a taste of what is to come elsewhere: terrible suffering for workers and the poor, and new opportunities for the vulture capitalists to penetrate new markets. Even middle-income countries, such as Argentina, Turkey and South Africa are facing political crises underpinned by these economic shocks.

There is more than a little echo of the early 1980s in the policies of the US Federal Reserve today, even if under different conditions. Then, as now, forcing interest rates up was partly motivated by a desire to cull inefficient corporations and strengthen US capital for an imperial power play.[8] This is one element of the competition that is perpetually taking place between capitalists, supported by the institutions of their state.

Having said that, smashing workers' living standards was the key goal of the ruling class in the 1980s, just as it is today. Neoclassical economic theory says that inflation is largely a product of a vicious circle of wage rises leading to generalised price rises – what it terms a "wage-price spiral". This supposed problem can be "fixed" by driving up unemployment and reducing working-class purchasing and bargaining power.

US Federal Reserve chief Jay Powell made this point explicitly in a press conference on 4 May, explaining that, by slowing economic growth, the US could "get wages down and then get inflation down".

---

7. Morley 2022.
8. Callinicos 2006.

Australian Reserve Bank head Phillip Lowe has insisted that wages must be cut substantially: "Three-and-a-half [percent annual wage rise] is the anchoring point that I want people to keep in mind. I know it's difficult when inflation is higher than that".[9]

What we are currently seeing, however, is not a wage-price spiral, but a profits-profits spiral. Workers are collateral damage in this process, rather than the factor driving it. Inflation has nothing to do with workers being greedy or wages being too high. In research conducted for the American Economic Policy Institute, Josh Bivens found that more than 50 percent of US inflation[10] has been driven by corporations seeking to maintain or expand their profit margins, with wages accounting for just 8 percent.

Yet the capitalist media are campaigning hard to provide ideological cover for this new ruling-class offensive. When the Fair Work Commission handed down a pitiful one dollar an hour increase in the minimum wage, journalists fretted[11] about whether this trivial increase would be passed on to other workers, thus ruining the economy.

So workers are being set up to pay for this crisis through serious attacks on our living standards. Real wages are falling fast, with the *Australian* newspaper estimating that NSW public servants will lose $7,200[12] this year due to wage caps. However shocking the data, simplistic inflation-adjusted income comparisons undersell the scale of the coming fall in working-class living standards. For one thing, prices of essential goods and services are rising much more than headline inflation figures indicate. At the same time, rising interest rates and higher unemployment will lead to more pain, as servicing outstanding debts on mortgages and credit cards gets harder and harder. If that weren't bad enough, governments are now looking to reduce spending on social services and welfare to balance budgets and "reduce demand".

It is for all these reasons that discussions of an economic crisis and world recession have come to dominate the media. It is hard to say, as we go to print, how soon a recession will arrive or how deep it might be.

---

9. Quoted in Mizen 2022.
10. Bivens 2022.
11. Evans 2022.
12. McLeod 2022.

But all signs point to some sort of contraction, and a sharp drop in world growth. The most visible of these is the data on US GDP, which has fallen for two consecutive quarters, which by some definitions means it is in a technical recession. To some extent this is a statistical quirk generated by its status as the world's main importer of goods, and it is partially ameliorated by continuing growth in the manufacturing and services sectors in that country. But even in the US, the trend is downwards.

Europe is in a qualitatively worse position, being more reliant on vulnerable energy and food imports. Its inflation rates are now roughly equal to those in the US, while it enters the crisis with substantially higher unemployment. A recent survey of retail spending in Germany in June reported a reduction of 9.8 percent from June 2021, the highest fall since 1980. The cuts were driven largely by reductions in spending on non-essential goods, a sure sign that workers are already feeling the squeeze. Data from the Manufacturing Purchasing Managers' Index indicates production in Europe is already contracting due to decreased demand and fears of a downturn.

Australia is facing a similar scenario, albeit somewhat delayed. Inflation rates here are lower, and are rising more slowly than elsewhere. This means the fall in living standards, while substantial, has been less drastic than in many other countries. For instance, while the savings rate is falling fast, household savings continued to rise in the first quarter of 2022. Along with low unemployment, and high commodity prices, these are real buffers to an imminent collapse in living standards. This will probably start to change.

One decisive factor that will impact on Australia, and the rest of the world, is the fate of the Chinese economy. China carried much of the world on its shoulders during the GFC, but enters this new economic phase in a much weaker position. Its economy has been hit by repeated lockdowns and a debt crisis driven by failing real estate ponzi schemes. Any substantial slowdown there could drag the Australian economy – and the wider world – down in its wake. Growing tensions between a renewed and expanded NATO and China add to the economic and wider political risks, and that's before the possibility of a disastrous conflict over Taiwan is factored in.

In this situation, bosses are already preparing for a possible downturn, and their resolve to make workers pay will only intensify as the turmoil continues.

Politics is moving fast to accommodate the new reality. President Biden has had his signature progressive policies delayed and then gutted, the sense of relief initially generated by Trump's defeat long since replaced by frustration with yet another feeble Democratic administration. A small win on a pared-back reform bill that will hand billions to fossil fuel and automotive giants will not help, notwithstanding histrionic attempts by the liberal press to turn a legislative molehill into a mountain. Buffeted by political paralysis and economic turmoil, Biden is flapping helplessly in the political wind, waiting to be put out of his misery by an insurgent Republican party.

His main successes lie in the realm of foreign policy, where Biden has been able to ground Trump's anti-China aggression in a strengthened network of imperial alliances. Pelosi's provocative visit to Taiwan, and China's dangerous overreaction, illustrate how easy it would be for relatively minor incidents to escalate into all-out war between economic and military superpowers. In the meantime, the decoupling and fragmentation of the world market will make inflation worse.

The combination of high inflation and world recession, and the bitter social sentiments they will generate, will likely throw much of the global south into political turmoil. Latin America is the most hopeful region for left-wing social struggle, and continues to see left-wing mobilisations and important electoral victories against the right. But the heightened mobilisations of that continent reaffirm the urgency of rebuilding a revolutionary left, as victorious centre-left parties have repeatedly failed to enact positive reforms.

In Australia, the dark clouds are gathering. Despite campaigning on wages growth, the Australian Labor Party is now arguing that pay cuts will be necessary[13] and ongoing, right through to 2024. Prime Minister Anthony Albanese and Treasurer Jim Chalmers are also signalling that government spending will be reduced in the October budget update,

---

13. Mizen and Marin-Guzman 2022.

an austerian attitude foreshadowed in their initial refusal to extend pandemic leave payments. It's too early for any of this to have blunted their political honeymoon, with government spokespeople largely successful in blaming the previous Liberal government for the various crises. But this excuse will not last, especially as the cost-of-living crisis grows more acute. If unions do not lead actions to defend conditions, dissatisfaction with a right-wing Labor government could provide fuel for the Liberals and the far right.

Repeated strike action by teachers, nurses and railway workers in New South Wales shows that workers will jump at the chance to fight if given a lead. This is reinforced by the popularity of the rail strikes in the UK, which have won widespread support, especially from younger workers who have moved to the left in recent years. A successful mobilisation on 18 June by the Trades Union Congress, the union federation in England and Wales, drew tens of thousands of unionists onto the streets to demonstrate against the cost-of-living crisis. More generally, there is a real uptick in struggle across the UK, as workers fight to defend their living standards.

Objectively, the conditions for an uptick in industrial action by workers here in Australia are just as present. A tight labour market made worse by constant COVID disruptions means workers have more leverage than usual. Rising cost of living means workers will be motivated to fight for more.

Yet aside from NSW, there is no sign of a pulse in the union movement. Indeed, the strikes in NSW reflect that it is the only major state with a Liberal government. Elsewhere, the unions have refused to fight, concerned not to embarrass the state and now federal ALP governments. The experience in the teachers' union in Victoria is indicative. The Andrews government refused to lift its pay cap above the paltry 1.5 percent figure established years ago and the officials of the AEU caved in immediately, without calling a single industrial action or even mass meeting. Thousands have now left the union in protest, and the pay cap remains in place.

As economic conditions worsen, there will be growing pressure on union leaders and their members to be "reasonable" and to "tighten our belts" for the good of the economy. Already, the ACTU has suggested that it will seek wage agreements lower than the inflation rate, essentially committing to supporting cuts to workers' wages. Yet there will also be pressure the other way. This was seen in a mass meeting of the NSW nurses' union, where a motion moved by socialist activists for a 7 percent wage rise received majority support despite bitter opposition from officials who were preparing to settle for 3 percent. Following this meeting, the railway union, also involved in ongoing bargaining, quietly increased its pay claim to 7 percent, an indication of how resistance can spread.

Workers should not agree to sacrifice a single dollar at the altar of corporate profits. The fact that the ALP is committed to maintaining tax cuts for the rich and further expanding the bloated military budget is evidence that the money exists to fund a better society. Workers should instead insist that funds be spent on dramatic improvements to the health and welfare systems and the modernisation of public infrastructure, including public transport and housing. We will also need price controls and public investment in a range of areas to protect workers from inflation, if that proves to be lasting. None of this will be possible unless we build a socialist movement that can stand up to the rich and their representatives in government.

References

Bivens, Josh 2022, "Corporate profits have contributed disproportionately to inflation. How should policymakers respond?", *Economic Policy Institute*, 21 April. https://www.epi.org/blog/corporate-profits-have-contributed-disproportionately-to-inflation-how-should-policymakers-respond/

Callinicos, Alex, 2006, "Making sense of imperialism", *International Socialism*, 2:110, Spring. https://www.marxists.org/history/etol/writers/callinicos/2006/xx/reply.html

Daily Sabah 2021, "Pre-pandemic container prices now 'a dream' as bottlenecks deepen", 14 October. https://www.dailysabah.com/business/transportation/pre-pandemic-container-prices-now-a-dream-asbottlenecks-deepen

Evans, Jake 2022, "Minimum wage rise will 'flow up' to all workers and fuel inflation, businesses warns", *ABC News*, 16 June. https://www.abc.net.au/news/2022-06-16/business-warns-minimum-wage-rise-fuel-inflation/101156548

Lee, Lisa 2022, "Zombie Firms Face Slow Death in US as Era of Easy Credit Ends", *Bloomberg*, 31 May. https://www.bloomberg.com/news/articles/2022-05-31/america-s-zombie-firms-face-slow-death-as-easy-credit-era-ends

McLeod, Catie 2022, "NSW public sector workers face $7200 real wages cut every year, analysis finds", *The Australian*, 21 July. https://www.theaustralian.com.au/breaking-news/nsw-public-sector-workers-face-7200-real-wages-cut-every-year-analysis-finds/news-story/7b2e25cb038fdd1912b19f41cb76375a

Mizen, Ronald 2022, "RBA puts 3.5pc lid on wages", *Financial Review*, 21 June. https://www.afr.com/policy/economy/rba-puts-3-5pc-lid-on-wages-20220621-p5avg4

Mizen, Ronald and David Marin-Guzman 2022, "Labor bows to RBA real wage cut", *Financial Review*, 22 June. https://www.afr.com/policy/economy/labor-bows-to-rba-real-wage-cut-20220622-p5avs1

Morley, Eleanor 2022, "Crisis of Sri Lankan capitalism provokes a popular uprising", *Red Flag*, 29 May. https://redflag.org.au/article/crisis-sri-lankan-capitalism-provokes-popular-uprising

Remes Jaana, James Manyika, Sven Smit, Sajal Kohli, Victor Fabius, Sundiatu Dixon-Fyle and Anton Nakaliuzhnyi 2021, "The consumer demand recovery and lasting effects of COVID-19", *McKinsey Global Institute*, 17 March. https://www.mckinsey.com/industries/consumer-packaged-goods/our-insights/the-consumer-demand-recovery-and-lasting-effects-of-covid-19

Parlin, Andrew 2020, "This US stock bubble could rank among the biggest in history", *Financial Times*, 7 September. https://www.ft.com/content/9d12ae03-2f6b-4028-8464-e305269e7ee3

Statista Research Department 2022, "Value of COVID-19 stimulus packages in the G20 as share of GDP 2021", 5 August. https://www.statista.com/statistics/1107572/covid-19-value-g20-stimulus-packages-share-gdp/

Tooze, Adam 2022, "The Fourth Estate, Stagflation & Wealth Destruction", *Chartbook Newsletter*, 22 June. https://adamtooze.substack.com/p/the-fourth-estate-stagflation-and?utm_source=email

MICK ARMSTRONG

Chifley: Extinguishing the light on the hill

Mick Armstrong is the author of numerous pamphlets and articles on revolutionary organisation and the Australian labour movement, including *The Industrial Workers of the World in Australia*, *The Labor Party: A Marxist analysis* and (with Tom Bramble) *The Fight for Workers' Power: Revolution and Counter-Revolution in the 20th Century*.

BEN CHIFLEY HAS FOR DECADES BEEN HELD UP as one of the all-time great Labor leaders, famous for his widely repeated claim that the labour movement represented the striving and aspirations for a better world: "the beacon, the light on the hill". He was a man who supposedly never betrayed his working class roots, "who gave his all and his life to uphold the dignity and to improve the lot of the humble common man".[1]

Chifley was Australia's last blue-collar working-class prime minister; a man who lived throughout his parliamentary career in a small weatherboard workers' cottage and who spoke with a harsh, working-class Australian accent that shocked polite middle-class society when first heard on the radio. He cuts a starkly different image from today's overwhelmingly middle-class Labor politicians, whose career path has commonly been university student Labor club member, to well paid party or union staffer, to MP, and who after retiring from parliament are rewarded for their services to business with a plum job in the private sector.

Chifley campaigned against conscription in World War I and was victimised by his bosses for his prominent role in the great mass strike

---

1. As Melbourne Catholic Archbishop Daniel Mannix wrote to deputy Labor leader Doc Evatt on the announcement of Chifley's death; quoted in Crisp 1963, p.413.

that rocked Australia in 1917. In 1947 he outraged the business establishment when he attempted to nationalise the banks, and in the early 1950s he invoked his Irish heritage, declaring that, as "the descendant of a race that fought a long and bitter fight against perjurers, pimps and liars", he stridently opposed the Menzies government's legislation to ban the Communist Party of Australia (CPA).[2]

Yet this supposed working-class hero was, as Labor prime minister between 1945 and 1949, the decisive figure holding the line on behalf of the capitalist class against the magnificent working-class offensive that rocked Australia in the immediate post-World War II years. In spite of his working-class roots he adopted a boots and all approach to crush the great miners' strike of 1949, including jailing union officials and sending in troops to mine coal. Indeed, in a keynote speech in June 1949 Chifley declared:

> I make this challenge here this morning. No government in the history of Australia has ever given to private industry so much assistance and advice and help as has been given by the Commonwealth Labour [sic] government.[3]

This article will explain Chifley's political evolution from rank-and-file working-class activist to servant of the bourgeoisie. Far from being an outlier, Chifley's political course reflects the fundamental conservatism of Labor's reformist project, an analysis that still has implications for socialists in Australia today.

Early years

Chifley was born in 1885 in Bathurst NSW, a relatively posh country town riven by intense class divisions. As one of Chifley's biographers, David Day, writes:

> Around the hospital stood the expansive houses of the wealthier Bathurstians... Even grander houses were plonked about the surrounding countryside, mimicking with their architecture

---

2. Day 2001, p.509.
3. Sheridan 1989, p.36.

and landscaping, as well as the gracious lifestyles of their inhabitants, the country homes of England. Likewise, these local notables, some of whom traced their holdings back to the original crossing of the mountains, dominated the politics of the town. "Class distinctions were clear cut," wrote a local historian, "and snobbery rampant". On the one hand, there was "the glitter and respectability of the fortunate", while on the other was "the almost incredible squalor in which some of the citizens of Bathurst existed".[4]

These class divisions had been intensified by the great strikes of the early 1890s and the impact of the very deep depression of that decade, from which the Australian economy did not fully recover until the early years of the twentieth century.

Overlaying and further sharpening these divisions were the racial and sectarian tensions between the predominantly Anglo-Protestant establishment and Irish Catholics who made up a third of the town's population. The strong Bathurst branch of the viciously anti-Irish Orange lodge, which for many decades had the largest membership of any organisation in Australia, celebrated the English victory of 1690 over the Irish at the Battle of the Boyne well into the twentieth century. Or take the case of Chifley's own marriage in June 1914. Not a particularly religious Catholic, Chifley agreed to marry Lizzie McKenzie in a Protestant church. Her father – a train driver like Chifley – was a leading figure in the Masons, who were beginning to take over from the Orange Lodge as the main bigoted Protestant organisation. Nonetheless Lizzie's family refused to attend the wedding, simply because Chifley was an Irish Catholic. The intensity of feeling on the Irish side is reflected in this prayer, commonly recited in the Bathurst district about the ill NSW Premier Henry Parkes, a reactionary who had sponsored the anti-Irish Treason Felony Act:

If he's bad today, may he be worse tomorrow,
may he be dead, damned and into Hell rammed,

---
4. Day 2001, pp.41–42.

> *and may the hearthstone of Hell be his eternal pillow
> and that is my prayer for him this blessed and holy day.
> Amen.*[5]

From the late 1880s onwards the newly emerging labour movement rapidly penetrated deep into numerous rural areas of NSW, including the shearing sheds of the Bathurst district. The message of unionism was being spread by dedicated organisers such as the then socialist but later Labor renegade Billy Hughes. Unionism also found a resonance in the small towns of the area. This included Bathurst itself (population just 9,578 in 1901), which developed into a major railway junction, as well as nearby Lithgow with its coal mines and steel works, Portland with its large cement works and Wallerawang with its railway workers. In 1908 there was a large eight-hour day procession in Bathurst, led by the railway engine drivers' union. The town had two local papers; one of these, the *National Advocate*, of which Chifley was to become a board member in 1922, developed into being effectively the local voice of the unions and the Labor Party.

From an early age Chifley seems to have been intent on becoming a Labor MP. He spent nine years of his youth on a small farm at Limekilns, owned by his Irish-speaking grandfather Patrick, who railed against the banks for their role in the 1890s depression and against the English establishment. Along with many of his neighbours, his grandfather was sympathetic to the newly emerging Labor Party. Then, back in Bathurst in 1899 after the death of his grandfather, Chifley came under the influence of his father, also Patrick, a blacksmith and strong Labor supporter. Chifley read the radical literature prominent at the time in Labor circles – George Bellamy's utopian socialist novel *Looking Backwards* and the works of George Bernard Shaw and Jack London.

After finishing primary school at age 15 Chifley initially worked as a cashier's assistant in Meagher's department store. After failing in an attempt to improve the "sweated" conditions of the juniors he

---

5. Crisp 1963, p.7.

quit the job. According to his biographer LF Crisp, this experience left a lasting impression on Chifley and strengthened his Labor sympathies:

> Long afterwards he often said that this employer and two others – three of the most prosperous merchants of the city and pillars of their respective churches – were in fact three of the greatest exploiters of labour he had ever known and that this reality behind their Sunday facades was one of the most damaging influences he had known to the link between organised religion and the common people of Bathurst.[6]

After briefly working in a tannery Chifley got a job in 1903 in the railway yards of South Bathurst, initially as a shop boy, then as a cleaner, and eventually obtaining his driver's certificate in March 1912. He became active in both his union and the ALP. As early as 1912 he represented the railway drivers' union before the NSW Industrial Court. Though never a full-time union official, Chifley "was the union" in the Bathurst sheds, along with W Shanks, the Bathurst secretary. However, as his glowing biographer Crisp is at pains to emphasise, Chifley "was himself no 'militant', but rather the man who negotiated a beneficial settlement or a constructive compromise with firmness and tenacity softened by a certain sweet reasonableness".[7]

The Great Strike[8]

The World War I anti-conscription campaign sharply divided Bathurst along class and religious lines, with the Church of England bishop heading the pro-conscription forces. Pro-conscription meetings were continually disrupted by militant protests in which working-class women played a prominent role. In 1916 Bathurst voted against conscription by more than three to one, well above the national anti-conscription vote of 51.6 percent.

Chifley never volunteered for the army and was prominent in the anti-conscription campaign, though on the moderate/right wing of the

---
6. Crisp 1963, p.7.
7. Crisp 1963, p.13.
8. For an overview of the Great Strike of 1917 see Bollard 2013 and Armstrong 2015.

movement. The moderate anti-conscriptionists proclaimed they were loyal Australians who were not opposed to the imperialist war as such, but insisted that the army be volunteer-based. They raised the racist bogey that conscription would undermine the White Australia policy and lead to the mass importation of coloured labour to take white workers' jobs.

In August 1917 the furious build-up of class tensions – brought on by the imperialist war and the immense sacrifices demanded of workers, with wages falling well behind escalating inflation – exploded in the Great Strike. This sweeping mass movement from below spread from industry to industry in defiance of the trade union bureaucracy, rocking Sydney and all the industrial centres of NSW. Within weeks rank-and-file workers had spread the strike to Melbourne and then on to involve workers in every state. The core sections of the strikers were out for five weeks, and some workers, including the coal miners, Broken Hill miners and seafarers, for another month. The defiant Melbourne wharfies stayed out until 4 December 1917.

The Great Strike erupted first amongst the skilled engineering workers of Sydney's tramway and railway workshops on 2 August 1917. It quickly spread to the engineering workers employed in Bathurst's locomotive sheds – which with over 400 workers was easily the largest employer in the city. However the maintenance workers striking on their own could not immediately stop the trains leaving Bathurst. A key question was whether the train drivers would come out in solidarity.

The drivers' union was industrially conservative and had never been on strike. Driving a train, along with other highly skilled occupations such as printers and engineers, was an elite blue-collar working-class job. Drivers were the "aristocrats" of the working class, a cut above "mere labourers". It was a job that you had to work your way up to over a period of many years, going from labourer in the workshops to cleaner to fireman to assistant driver to driver, and passing numerous exams along the way. But the drivers had their own grievances. Their elite position was being undermined. It was highly dangerous work on poorly maintained country train lines, involving night work, long 12–14-hour shifts and lengthy periods away from home. Moreover the drivers had been infected with the rebellious mood that was sweeping the working class during the war years. So within days the Bathurst drivers voted overwhelmingly and enthusiastically to strike. Solidarity was strong in a close-knit railway community like Bathurst, with only five out of 150 drivers scabbing.

Chifley, who had been a union activist since 1907 and was close to the drivers' union officials in Sydney, played a prominent role in the strike. His was, however, very much a moderating influence that helped ensure that the strike and picketing in Bathurst remained peaceful, in contrast to the riots that swept through the central business district of Melbourne and the mine invasions in Broken Hill.

On 9 September the union leadership in Sydney called for the ending of the strike on utterly degrading terms that didn't even guarantee workers their jobs back. There was shock, outrage and strident hostility from the rail workers in Bathurst, including the previously conservative drivers, over this sell-out. According to the *National Advocate*:

> [T]he full text of the terms accepted by the Central Defence Committee (Sydney) fell like a bombshell amongst the railway unionists in Bathurst yesterday. It completely electrified the atmosphere in union circles and caused an almost unanimous expression of disapproval... For the first time during the strike the members got out of hand (at union mass meetings) and were disorderly.[9]

Chifley was to play a decisive role in carrying the union officials' line and undermining the solidarity of the strikers. He cajoled the drivers to break ranks with the other Bathurst workers and sign the management's forms to return to work. There was great reluctance amongst the drivers to do so, but without an alternative proposal or leadership, Chifley was able to browbeat the drivers into submission. The *National Advocate* reported:

> But it was a hard task to induce many of the men, whose one

---

9.   Crisp 1963, p.20.

ambition was to fight on. Messrs. Chifley and Shanks had all their work cut out and only succeeded after exerting much eloquence.[10]

Even as Chifley and Shanks led the other hundred or so drivers to the office to sign on, the situation remained touch and go. According to the *Bathurst Times*:

> Mr. Chifley appeared to be "laying down the law" to his brother driver. He was busily engaged in thumping his right hand with his left until the pair neared the Inspector (McGuiness) who received them in front of his office.[11]

Despite his moderating role Chifley, like numerous other union activists, was victimised by management. He appealed against his sacking, correctly claiming that he had "endeavoured to prevent any semblance of violence, disorder or unlawful tactics".[12] He was eventually re-employed but in a substantially lower-paid job, and it took years to regain his position as a permanent driver.

The hopes of the Great Strike had been thrown away. No militant democratic leadership had emerged to take the revolt forward to victory. In the absence of such an organised socialist leadership the conservative union officials, who had initially been sidelined by the elemental revolt, were able to reassert their authority and utterly betray the great fighting spirit of the mass of rank-and-file workers. Workers had suffered a bad but needless defeat. Numerous unions, including the drivers' union, were deregistered. Its membership collapsed and Chifley was one of the few who tried to hold the union together in Bathurst.

"Revolution has absolutely no appeal"

Despite his victimisation by railway management, the defeat of the Great Strike had only served to confirm Chifley in his moderate, pragmatic approach. Strikes in his view should only be used sparingly

---

10. Crisp 1963, p.21.
11. Crisp 1963, p.21
12. Day 2001, p.144.

and workers needed to look to parliament, rather than their own organised industrial strength, to achieve change.

Chifley established a profile in Bathurst by his activities in numerous local committees like the hospital board and in sporting activities. However Chifley was defeated when he first stood for Labor preselection for the Bathurst seat in the NSW state parliament in 1922 and again in 1924. He persisted and in 1925 gained preselection for the federal seat of Macquarie that covered Bathurst and the coal-mining town of Lithgow, but also considerable rural areas closer to Sydney and the conservative tourist towns of the Blue Mountains. He lost narrowly despite having substantial majorities in working-class towns like Lithgow and Portland and to a lesser extent Bathurst itself.

In the wake of the slaughter of World War I, the ongoing revolt in Ireland and the 1917 Russian revolution, a radical wave had swept the Australian working-class movement. This saw mass support surging for the syndicalist-inspired One Big Union movement and the formation in 1920 of the Communist Party. Chifley, however, stood determinedly against the radical tide, declaring: "I stand entirely for the principles of arbitration... I say frankly that the policy of revolution, other than the revolution of thought, makes absolutely no appeal to me".[13]

Chifley ran again for Macquarie in 1928, this time successfully. He doubled down on his ultra-moderate rhetoric, ironically proclaiming, given his subsequent bitter hostility to Jack Lang, that:

> [T]he Lang [NSW Labor] Government had achieved more for the workers in two years by legislation than general strikes had achieved in 20 years, while the Fisher [federal Labor] Government had done more to improve the lot of the workers than all the strikes that ever occurred in the history of Australia.[14]

Chifley made a central point of his campaign a blatant appeal to racism. He declared that "Australia was supposed to be a white man's country, but Mr Bruce [the conservative prime minister] and his Government

---

13. Day 2001, p.197.
14. Day 2001, p.229.

were fast making it hybrid".[15] His scapegoating attacks were specifically directed against southern European migrants who, he claimed, were flooding in and cutting Australian workers' wages. The *National Advocate* backed him up with an article on 10 November 1928 calling for a vote for Chifley to protect White Australia.[16]

By the time of the October 1929 election, when Chifley was re-elected with a massively increased majority, Labor had been out of office federally for 13 years. The capitalist class had had no use for them. But that was now to change. The economic downturn which was to become the Great Depression had hit Australia early and hard, polarising society along class lines. The right-wing Nationalist Party government had been severely discredited and seemed to have no answers to the unfolding economic crisis. Industrially, key sections of the working class on the waterfront and in the timber industry had suffered demoralising defeats in lengthy strikes resisting assaults on their pay and conditions. The miners on the northern NSW coal fields were still battling a lock-out by their bosses, determined to slash their wages, that was to last for 16 months.

Scullin's government

Workers now turned to Labor en masse in the hope that it would defend them from the ruling class assault and the ravages of the developing Depression. Labor was led by James Scullin, who had moved the successful motion to expel all the pro-conscriptionists from the ALP in 1916 and who was one of the architects of Labor's Socialist Objective, but by 1929 was very much on the moderate wing of the party. Scullin was swept into office on a wave of working-class euphoria, but workers were to be profoundly disappointed.

Labor promised to resolve the growing crisis by appealing to both workers and bosses. Scullin pledged to maintain the federal arbitration system for settling industrial disputes that the Bruce Nationalist government had proposed to abolish. Chifley played a leading role in the Labor defence of arbitration, arguing that what was needed was a system "where reason and moral suasion can operate in the direction

---
15. Day 2001, p.231.
16. Day 2001, p.231.

of bringing together the parties...under conditions that are conducive to a reconciliation of difference of opinion".[17] Labor also promised to provide support for farmers and pledged to intervene to end the lock-out of the NSW coal miners. It would raise tariffs on imported goods to promote manufacturing industry and provide jobs – an approach some sections of capital backed.

These measures were to prove completely ineffectual in stemming the surge of unemployment, from 13.1 percent of union members in late 1929 to 23.4 percent at the end of 1930 and peaking at 30 percent in the second quarter of 1932.[18] With the world depression devastating the economy, the ruling class consensus hardened. Business confidence, the establishment proclaimed, had to be restored, and that necessitated sharp cuts to government spending to balance the budget. Wages and pensions had to be slashed. Workers in Australia, the bankers and the business elite declared, had had it way too good for way too long and must be made to bear the burden of the crisis.

Rather than defending working-class living standards, the Scullin government increasingly accommodated to this ruling class agenda. It abandoned its pledge to end the lock-out of the NSW coal miners and imposed the Premiers' Plan, a vicious austerity policy demanded by the bankers that cut government spending by 20 percent and served to compound the already massive job losses.

A significant minority in the parliamentary Labor caucus voiced opposition to the Premiers' Plan, but Chifley was not one of them. Indeed, his parliamentary speech in favour of endorsing the Premiers' Plan was hailed by Opposition conservatives as "a simple and manly speech".[19] Chifley, who was appointed defence minister in March 1931, was very much on the conservative wing of the Scullin government. He was even offered the position of treasurer in a new conservative government headed by Joe Lyons, the former Tasmanian Labor premier who split from Labor to the right, helping to bring down the Scullin government in November 1931. Chifley stridently opposed NSW Labor Premier Jack Lang (returned to office with a massive majority in November

---

17. Crisp 1963, p.48.
18. Louis and Turner 1968, p.89.
19. Crisp 1963, pp.60–62.

1930), who had launched a populist campaign denouncing the bankers and who called on Scullin to use the army to break the lock-out by the mining magnates.

Lang was no left-winger but he was prepared to ride the tiger of working-class discontent. In opposition to the draconian Premiers' Plan, he launched the Lang Plan, which "called for the suspension of interest payments on governments' overseas debt, lower interest rates and an end to the gold standard (the valuation of the Australian pound in terms of a specific quantity of gold)".[20] Under left-wing pressure, and to head off the threat to his control of the party posed by the rapidly growing Socialisation Units that called for a three-year plan to introduce socialism, Lang was more than willing at times to engage in socialist-sounding rhetoric.[21] But Lang's essential appeal was as the "Great Man" – the mighty, powerful leader standing up for all the little people and the defender of the genuine national interest against a nefarious band of financial conspirators.

Meanwhile the Scullin government was tearing itself apart. Its working-class supporters were becoming increasingly demoralised. Joe Lyons and a coterie of right-wingers in the Labor caucus argued that Scullin was not sufficiently committed to bourgeois financial orthodoxy and split away. In late 1931 these Labor rats backed a no-confidence motion (also backed by Lang's supporters in the federal parliament) that brought down the Scullin government. In October 1931 Chifley had been expelled from his own union, the Australian Federated Union of Locomotive Enginemen (AFULE), for supporting the Premiers' Plan and opposing the Lang Plan. Even his local Bathurst AFULE branch had turned against him. There was strong support for Lang's radical populism in Chifley's electorate, especially in Lithgow, the industrial heart of the district. Chifley's own Bathurst Labor branch voted to oppose the Premiers' Plan. With the Labor vote split between Chifley, the federal Labor candidate, on 28.1 percent, Tony Luchetti, Chifley's former campaign manager and now Langite candidate, on 21.6 percent and the Communist Party on 1.3 percent, Chifley lost his seat at the October 1931 election landslide against the Scullin government.

---

20. Bramble and Kuhn 2011, p.48.
21. For the Socialisation Units see Cooksey 1976.

Labor was reduced to a tiny minority of just 14 seats in the federal parliament, with Lang Labor holding another four. Labor had utterly failed to protect workers' interests during the crisis. It had not even softened the blows. Its austerity measures had simply lengthened the dole queues. Labor had served the bosses well by demoralising workers and helping to frustrate a concerted fightback. But the bosses showed no gratitude, turning sharply against Labor in favour of the new Lyons-led United Australia Party (UAP).

Another long period of opposition followed for Labor federally. Labor had discredited itself in the eyes of many workers and was severely split in NSW. However, unlike after the fall of the Hughes Labor government, there was no swing to the left by the federal ALP after its defeat. Scullin was re-elected leader and – in an attempt to prove his credentials to the powers that be – backed the coup by the NSW state governor Sir Philip Game that overthrew the Lang Labor government in May 1932.

Lang Labor

In NSW the great mass of Labor supporters had split away to back Lang Labor, rallying to the slogan "Lang is Right". Busts of the "great man" proliferated on the mantelpieces of working-class families all across the state. Lang's radical-sounding rhetoric terrified the business establishment and the respectable middle class. For the conservatives any talk of repudiation of the debt to the British bankers reeked of national disgrace and repudiation of the links to the Empire. The banks and a virtual *Who's Who* of company directors and military officers mounted a furious campaign to bring down Lang, even orchestrating the rise of well armed and well funded far-right and fascist mass forces – the Old Guard and the New Guard. Under this intense ruling-class pressure, and having been given the nod from the King in London, the state governor, Sir Philip Game, orchestrated a coup to remove Lang.

Lang retained mass working-class support, reflected in a rally of anywhere between 200,000 and 750,000 in Sydney after his dismissal. And it was not just in Sydney that workers mobilised to oppose the coup, but in towns all across the state. In Bathurst there was a large demonstration in support of Lang, with talk by railway workers of revolution. In the subsequent state election the Langite candidate Gus Kelly held the largest election rally ever seen in Bathurst – more than 2,000, over a quarter of the town's population. But Lang, like Gough Whitlam decades later, refused to mobilise workers to overturn the coup. With Lang and his union backers refusing to act, a decisive opportunity to turn the tide against the ruling-class assault was thrown away. Tragically, the Communist Party also did its bit to frustrate the development of a fighting left alternative by simply denouncing Lang as a "social fascist" and the left reformist leaders of the Socialisation Units as "left social fascists" and refusing to mobilise resistance to the coup.[22]

The NSW branch of the federal ALP, of which Chifley was elected leader in June 1931, disgracefully backed Sir Philip Game's coup:

> We declare our faith in the integrity and the honour of Sir Philip Game as the representative of His Majesty the King in this State… it was only Mr. Lang's characteristic unintelligent obstinacy which left him unmoved after His Excellency had pointed out the plain duty of any man fit to occupy the position of Premier of the State.[23]

Despite the backing of the right-wing Australian Workers Union (AWU) and financial support from interstate Labor branches, the tiny anti-Lang federal ALP made little headway in NSW throughout the 1930s. This left Chifley without a seat in parliament for the rest of the decade, though he was cajoled in 1935 into an unsuccessful attempt to stand against Lang himself in his state seat of Auburn. It was only with the fragmentation of the Langite forces in the late 1930s that Chifley regained any hope of furthering his parliamentary career.

It is worth highlighting the relative strength of the union movement and Labor in working-class communities in NSW in these pre-war decades, compared to their ossified state today. Both the unions and the Labor Party had a genuine array of rank-and-file worker activists and a penetration into working-class life incomparably greater than

---

22. For the role of the CPA in these years see Bramble and Armstrong 2021, chapter 9.
23. Crisp 1963, pp.87–88.

anything that has existed in recent decades. Country towns such as Bathurst and Lithgow held large Labor election rallies. Unions held regular eight-hour day or May Day rallies in town after town. Even a town of just a couple of thousand like Oberon had an active ALP branch, whose large annual ball Chifley attended in the course of his 1928 election campaign. Labor preselection battles were often intensely fought affairs, with large numbers of rank-and-file union members voting. There were widely circulated union papers such as the miners' *Common Cause* and the AWU's *Australian Worker*, as well the pro-Lang *Labor Daily* that reached a peak circulation of over 160,000 at the time of the coup against Lang.[24]

The second imperialist war

After a bitter preselection battle in the now reunited Labor Party, Chifley was returned to parliament in October 1940. He rose quickly through the ranks, becoming treasurer and a key offsider to John Curtin after Curtin was installed as prime minister a year later. Labor had been in opposition for a decade. The deeply conservative Lyons government had well suited the bourgeoisie. However following the death in April 1939 of Lyons, who was replaced by Menzies, the United Australia Party government limped from crisis to crisis, exacerbated by the outbreak of war. It only retained office at the 1940 elections thanks to the support of two independents – one of whom was Arthur Coles, the managing director of Coles stores and the former lord mayor of Melbourne. When Coles crossed the floor in October 1941 to install Curtin as prime minister it was a clear sign that Labor had been given the nod of approval by an important section of the establishment. Indeed the ultra-conservative *Sydney Morning Herald* subsequently went on to praise Curtin in gushing terms:

> John Curtin has...become Australia articulate... In every race, someone arises at its direst extremity, with the gift of the very best in that race. Sometimes he is a poet, but rarely. Today we are fortunate in having him a Prime Minister.[25]

---
24. Walker 1980, p.69.
25. McMullin 1991, p.226.

There was a feeling in ruling circles that Labor would be better placed to galvanise the working class into an all-out war effort. The conservative parties were bitterly divided and too publicly associated with the interests of the rich to inspire workers to sacrifice their lives in the tens of thousands on the battlefields, and to work incredibly long and exhausting hours in the munitions factories. On top of that, the conservatives had little credibility to make the argument that all Australians had to unite to fight a supposedly heroic war against fascism when they had championed the fascist cause in Europe in the 1920s and 1930s, and funded the far-right Old Guard and New Guard in Australia.

Workers' long memories of the terrible slaughter of World War I meant there was little enthusiasm in 1939 for another war. Indeed as unemployment fell with the pickup of industry following the outbreak of the war, there was a surge of strike action in 1940 as key sections of the workforce sought to regain the losses they had suffered during the cruel Depression years.

In the late 1930s the only significant pro-war current in the labour movement was the CPA and their Popular Front supporters, some of whom had secretly entered the ALP. The CPA-led Movement Against War and Fascism had essentially become a movement *for* war against fascism and at the outbreak of the war advocated sending an Australian expeditionary force to Europe. The mainstream of the broader labour movement and especially the Langites held to an Australian nationalist, isolationist standpoint. Irish Australians in particular had little appetite to die for King and Empire, and they now made up a decisive majority of the rank-and-file membership of the ALP. Further to the left was a principled anti-imperialist current influenced by syndicalism and Marxism.

The parliamentary ALP, reflecting in part their closer connections to the capitalist state, had immediately backed the war, though it took somewhat longer to pull the leading union officials into line.

This all changed in 1941, when Japan entered the war and Labor was elected to office. On the left, Hitler's invasion of Russia meant the world communist movement abandoned its effectively pro-German stance in favour of a strident pro-Allies and pro-war posture. The voices against the war were now few and far between. By 1942 the war was no longer some far away event in Europe, and Curtin, with Chifley's backing, could appeal to traditional racist, anti-Japanese "Yellow Peril" sentiment to whip up pro-war support. Curtin, the onetime international socialist and opponent of racism and imperialism, did not rely on half measures. A week after the attack on Pearl Harbour in December 1941 Curtin assured parliament of his government's

> determination that this country shall remain forever the home of descendants of those people who came here in peace [!] in order to establish in the South Seas an outpost of the British races. Our laws have proclaimed the principle of White Australia... We intend to maintain that principle.[26]

Then in March 1942, after the fall of Singapore to Japanese forces, the Labor government launched its infamous "Hate" campaign, essentially calling for the genocide of the Japanese population. Government newspaper advertisements screamed: "We've always despised them, NOW WE MUST SMASH THEM".[27]

Conscription, however, remained a flashpoint. Opposition to conscription for overseas service had become an article of faith in the ALP following the experience of the First World War. Curtin's move to impose conscription in late 1942 thus faced bitter opposition from rank-and-file party members and from the Langites, though it was stridently backed by the Communist Party.[28] However Curtin, again backed by Chifley, was able to use their authority as anti-conscription campaigners in World War I to defeat the opposition led by Labor traditionalists like Arthur Calwell and Labor leftists like Eddie Ward.

At the height of the racist hysteria about the supposed threat of a Japanese invasion in 1942 the number of strike days fell substantially. But by 1943 they had rebounded, and by 1945 they were surging. Amongst the militants in the most politically advanced sections of the class, especially the coal miners and seafarers, there was a genuinely anti-imperialist sentiment. CPA miners' union officials complained that they had difficulty convincing militants that the supposedly

---

26. Griffiths 1990, p.50.
27. Griffiths 1990, p.51.
28. Ross 1973, pp.288–308.

anti-fascist war wasn't simply just another imperialist war like World War I. But with the CPA being aggressively pro-war there was no political force capable of organising and cohering these militants to influence broader layers of organised workers who might not yet have opposed the war outright but did not see why they should sacrifice their living standards for the sake of the bosses' profits.

Right from the moment that Curtin and Chifley took office they made it clear that their overwhelming priority was waging the war on behalf of the capitalist class, not advancing working-class living standards. Chifley's first budget essentially copied that of the previous conservative Treasurer Fadden and was initially rejected by the Labor caucus for not sufficiently increasing old-age pensions. Chifley subsequently went on to systematically raise income taxes on low and very low income earners. Even the moderate NSW union leader Jim Kenny described Chifley as "hysterical about the war effort…completely indifferent to the requests of the trade unions".[29]

In an attempt to quieten union discontent, Eddie Ward, widely seen as the most left-wing member of the Labor caucus, was appointed minister for labour and national service. But to back up Ward's velvet glove approach, the Curtin/Chifley government employed the iron fist, with harsh national security regulations aimed in particular against the militant coal miners who continued to strike despite the pleas of their union leaders. Any miner who struck in defiance of the union hierarchy was to be expelled from the union and face conscription into the army. In 1944 Chifley condemned the rank-and-file miners for not working hard enough to meet wartime production targets, declaring that "the miners had been treated [by the Commonwealth and State Labor Governments] with a consideration and a generosity amounting to indulgence, and that this liberality had been shockingly requited".[30]

Post-war industrial upsurge

Despite considerable internal tensions, Labor was able to ride out the wartime working-class unrest without a major split in its ranks, as had occurred during World War I. But with the war coming to an end,

---
29. Crisp 1963, pp.155–56.
30. Crisp 1963, p.215.

the pressure on the Labor government mounted as the mood in the working class shifted further. It was one thing, the feeling went, to accept sacrifices during the war but now we have to fight to improve our lot – win shorter hours and much better wages before another recession hits. There was a widespread view that things had to fundamentally change. There could be no return to the 1930s with its mass unemployment, poverty and misery, the rise of fascism and then the sacrifices of another murderous war.[31] Capitalism had been massively discredited in workers' eyes. As a leading business magazine, *Rydge's*, acknowledged in April 1944:

> If I were asked to *debate* the proposition that state ownership is preferable to the system of private enterprise I would prefer to argue on the side of state ownership if I wished to take the less difficult side in the debate. It is so very easy to put forward powerful compelling reasons which would promise so very much more to the community than is possible under private enterprise.[32]

Labor, however, had absolutely no intention of challenging the capitalist market. Chifley had taken over as prime minister after Curtin died on 5 July 1945, and maintained his conservative approach. With the capitalists widely discredited, the Chifley government, in alliance with the union bureaucracy and the Arbitration Courts, was to prove to be the key bastion of defence of capitalism against an insurgent working class. Chifley saw his task as holding the line as long as possible against even workers' most basic demands – the 40-hour week and improved wages. In a letter to the peak union body, the ACTU, in November 1945 he stated:

> My Government is greatly disturbed by the prevailing industrial unrest throughout the Commonwealth and is most anxious that this unrest should be replaced by a spirit of harmony and co-operation that will enable both Employers and Employees to

---
31. For an overview of this period see Bramble and Armstrong 2021 and Sheridan 1989.
32. Sheridan 1989, p.81.

work together in the solution of the Industrial and Productive tasks which face Australian industry.[33]

By trickery and clever manoeuvres Chifley exploited workers' illusions in the good intentions of the Labor government to maintain the stringent wartime wage-pegging controls. He was ably abetted by the arbitration courts, which dragged out hearings of workers' claims for months, and a union bureaucracy which put loyalty to the ALP and the stability of the capitalist system well above the interests of its rank-and-file members. Nonetheless pressure from below was building. Strike after strike broke out, with nearly five and a half million working days lost between 1945 and 1947.[34] Even the bosses acknowledged that there was widespread public sympathy for striking workers, especially in 1946 and 1947.

Eventually the pressure was too much and workers crashed through Chifley's wage-pegging barriers. The 1946–47 Victorian metal trade dispute was a decisive battle. In response to overtime bans and other limited industrial action in support of a wage claim, the bosses locked out 20,000 workers in Victoria in November 1946. From there the battle spiralled. When on 20 January 1947 the employers lifted the lock-out, the workers bluntly refused to go back to work. They were determined to teach the bosses a lesson.

The skilled metalworkers of the Amalgamated Engineering Union (AEU) were at the forefront of the struggle. They constantly pushed their officials, some of the most militant in the country at the time, to pull out more and more workers, including the apprentices on the railways and in the power plants and the vital maintenance workers in a broad swath of industries. Not one of Melbourne's 49 suburban AEU branches voted to accept a compromise offer from the Arbitration Court. Their determination and defiance of arbitration delivered them a path-breaking victory – the biggest gains ever in the long history of their proud and militant union.[35] This was but one of the many major strike battles of this era – two of the most famous being the victorious

---

33. Johnson 1989, p.29.
34. O'Lincoln 1985, p.53.
35. The best account of the strike is in Sheridan 1989, pp.125–48.

1948 Queensland rail strike against the Hanlon Labor government and the defeated seven-week long coal miners' strike of 1949.

Workers made some very important gains from these militant struggles, including the long sought goal of a 40-hour week. However it remains the case that Chifley's relentless delaying measures paid off for the ruling class at a time when they were in a very difficult situation during the most turbulent phase of post-war economic and social reorganisation. The Labor government set the Australian capitalist class up to profit enormously at workers' expense from the post-war boom.

Part of the reason that the Labor government was able to hold the line as struggle rose sharply in the last year of the war and the immediate post-war years was the role of the Communist Party, which had substantially strengthened its position in the unions during the war years. After Hitler's invasion of Russia the CPA had adopted a win the war at all costs approach, stridently opposing strikes and backing the Labor government virtually uncritically. At war's end the CPA leadership shifted somewhat; its rank-and-file members were able to play an active role in the strikes that broke out as the party became marginally less hostile to workers' struggle. But as a party they did not radically change course between 1945 and 1947, and did not attempt to seriously radicalise and lead the strike movement forward. Indeed party members were urged to oppose any attempt to use strikes to break Labor's wage controls, and CPA leaders were particularly concerned not to unduly embarrass the Chifley government in the lead-up to the 1946 federal elections.

However as the Cold War deepened the line from Moscow changed. From about the end of 1947 the Communists became more hostile to Labor. This flowed through to more industrial aggression, but the shift came too late. The wave of militancy had already peaked. The bosses were beginning to regain their confidence and the red-baiting Cold War atmosphere had made the CPA much more isolated politically. The media, the Liberals and the Chifley government blamed any strike that occurred on a Communist conspiracy to sabotage the economy. In reality the strikes overwhelmingly reflected genuine working-class grievances, not sinister Communist manipulation. CPA union officials, even after the party's left turn, were not as a whole more industrially militant than Labor left union leaders such as the AEU's Joe Cranwell, who played a central role in the victorious 1946–47 metal trades struggle and in the 1948 Queensland rail strike. Indeed Australia's most prominent Communist union leader, Jim Healy, head of the Waterside Workers Federation (WWF), did all he could to fulfil his promise to Chifley "that the Federation would do all in its power to keep the waterfront working prior to the [1949] election period".[36]

Nonetheless a crunch was coming, and it was the coal miners who were to feel the full weight of the Cold War anti-Communist crusade. The miners were the most militant and politically advanced section of the Australian working class. Rank-and-file miners were commonly more militant and defiant than their Communist and left Labor union officials. They had long endured extremely harsh working conditions and were determined to win shorter hours and longer leave. The miners had the power to shut down all the core sections of industry, as coal was then central not just to electricity generation but to shipping, the railways, the manufacture of gas and much else.

Chifley was determined to teach both the miners and the Communist Party a lesson. He feared that if the miners broke through, their gains would quickly flow on to wide sections of the working class. In the sharply intensifying Cold War atmosphere, Chifley was also determined to demonstrate that Labor was tough on the reds. He introduced draconian legislation to seize strike funds, jailed the miners' union leaders and ordered police raids on Communist Party offices. But it was not simply repression that broke the strike. Chifley rallied the ACTU and the other key union leaders behind him, and the miners were left isolated, to be starved back to work. Chifley floated the threat of destroying the miners' union by bringing in AWU members as scabs. To emphasise his determination, he became the first Labor leader in peace time to send in troops to break a strike by working some of the open-cut mines. After seven weeks the miners, with their backs to the wall, folded and returned to work.

---

36. Sheridan 1989, p.174.

It was not simply on industrial relations that Chifley fought to advance the interests of Australian capitalism. In 1946 he won Labor endorsement of the Bretton Woods Agreement which created the International Monetary Fund (IMF) and the International Bank for Reconstruction and Development (later the World Bank). This came about despite bitter opposition from Calwell and Ward, who denounced it as leading to a dictatorship of finance capital over the population. Then in 1949, under pressure from both the British and US governments, Chifley established the red-baiting spy agency ASIO. Even Chifley's seemingly most radical measure, his 1947 attempt to nationalise the banks, was not motivated by some socialist desire to undermine big capital. Instead he believed the private banks were an irresponsible vested interest whose financial policies were holding back the rapid expansion of a profitable manufacturing sector and other industries key to the rounded development of Australian capitalism.

However by the late 1940s Labor had served its purpose from a ruling-class perspective. The conservative political forces had been reorganised in a new, highly aggressive Liberal Party with a mass middle-class membership. The intensifying Cold War atmosphere had pushed back post-war radicalism and Robert Menzies had launched a "reds under the beds" anti-Communist crusade. A very well funded reactionary mobilisation was unleashed to bring down the "socialist" Chifley government at the 1949 elections. This involved the banks, who paid off large numbers of their staff to campaign against Labor, the overwhelming bulk of the media, the doctors' associations and the full array of capitalist and middle-class forces. Menzies narrowly triumphed, with 51 percent of the two-party-preferred vote; though the great majority of blue-collar workers remained loyal to Labor, which received 46 percent of the first preference vote.

After the elections Chifley was re-elected unopposed as Labor leader, but within 18 months he was to die of a heart attack. The new Menzies Liberal government was determined to push society sharply to the right by whipping up a Cold War frenzy with talk of a new world war. One of Menzies' key immediate objectives was to ban the Communist Party. He understood that this would sharply divide the ALP.

As his draconian measures to smash the 1949 miners' strike demonstrated, Chifley was not in any sense favourable to or soft on the Communists. He had no hesitation in strongly backing the Korean War in 1950. However he was critical of McCarthyism and of the US's extreme Cold War approach, and was hostile to Menzies' proposal to ban the CPA. Chifley saw the ban as an unproductive means of fighting Communist influence in the unions and he feared that this attack on democratic rights would set a precedent for similar measures to be taken against the trade unions and the ALP itself. However the ALP federal executive, under pressure from a hysterical right-wing media campaign and the growing far-right "Movement" inside the party, capitulated. It narrowly voted to overrule Chifley and Labor waved the ban through the Senate, which it still controlled. In defiance, ALP deputy leader Doc Evatt then headed a successful legal challenge by Communist-aligned unions to the ban as unconstitutional. The ban was eventually narrowly defeated in a referendum. By then Chifley was dead.

The Cold War atmosphere had aided the rapid growth of a new right-wing, stridently anti-Communist faction in the ALP associated with BA Santamaria's Catholic Social Studies Movement, which backed outlawing the CPA. The fanatical new Movement leaders viewed traditional Labor moderates and fellow Catholics like Chifley as too soft on the communists in the workers' movement. The old Labor power brokers in turn saw the Movement activists as "too Catholic for their own good". Chifley despised newly elected Movement-aligned Labor MPs such as Stan Keon, declaring: "Remember, the religious fanatic is always far worse than the political fanatic".[37] The scene was being set for the bitter split in the ALP in 1955, leading to the formation of the right-wing Democratic Labor Party (DLP) that was to keep Labor out of office federally for 23 years.

37. Crisp 1963, p.384.

Conclusion

Ben Chifley, unlike his friend and fellow Labor Prime Minister John Curtin, had never been a radical socialist. But nor, unlike so many Labor politicians today, was he some middle-class careerist. As a young worker he became active as a rank-and-file member of his union and of the ALP, though he never held a full-time union position. He was ambitious and talented, and saw himself as advancing the interests of his fellow workers and the people of his home town Bathurst. But these advances were to be achieved via the official channels of capitalist society – through arbitration courts, lawful union bargaining, through parliament, the local shire council, the local hospital board and myriad other local committees. Chifley did not set out to challenge the existing power structures of capitalist society. Even before his election to parliament he saw strikes very much as a last resort. They should be run in an orderly way and not "get out of hand" by inflaming class tensions, let alone lead to workers imposing their own power on society.

To operate successfully within the framework of the official parliamentary and legal channels you have to adapt more and more to the rules of the game. And those rules were not set by the workers of Bathurst and Lithgow who voted Chifley into office, but by those with the real power and wealth in society – the capitalist class. Having chosen this reformist path of relying on the official channels Chifley necessarily came to accept the constraints that the legal system, the financial markets, the bosses and the bourgeois media impose upon the class struggle. Even in the best of times that means being prepared to compromise the interests of working-class supporters so that capitalist profitability is not seriously undermined. In times of war or economic crisis, a commitment to reformism means a willingness to impose harsh measures – the slashing of living standards and compelling workers to sacrifice their lives on the battlefields.

But more than that, Chifley, like the overwhelming majority of Labor politicians before and after him, increasingly came to identify with the interests of the Australian capitalist nation state rather than with the interests of workers. He became a servitor of the bourgeoisie.

That is the whole logic of Labor's reformist politics that has been played out time and time again over the last 120 years. Socialists should be under absolutely no illusions that the new Albanese government, coming to office at a time of deepening economic volatility, will in any way break with this pattern. To defend, let alone advance their living standards and social conditions, workers are going to have to fight the Albanese government just as they had to fight all the Labor governments that Chifley was a part of. That also sharply poses the vital need to build a militant socialist party that is prepared to forthrightly oppose Labor's betrayals; a party that is determined to lead the struggle to get rid of the capitalist system that Labor leaders like Ben Chifley have so long defended.

References

Armstrong, Mick 2015, "How World War I led to class war", *Marxist Left Review*, 9, Summer. https://marxistleftreview.org/articles/how-world-war-one-led-to-class-war/

Bollard, Robert 2013, *In the shadow of Gallipoli. The hidden history of Australia in World War I*, NewSouth.

Bramble, Tom and Rick Kuhn 2011, *Labor's Conflict. Big business, workers and the politics of class*, Cambridge University Press.

Bramble, Tom and Mick Armstrong 2021, *The Fight for Workers' Power. Revolution and Counter-Revolution in the 20th Century*, Interventions.

Cooksey, Robert 1976, *Lang and Socialism. A study in the Great Depression*, Australian National University Press.

Crisp, LF 1963, *Ben Chifley: A Political Biography*, Longmans.

Day, David 2001, *Chifley*, Harper Collins.

Griffiths, Phil 1990, "Australian Perceptions of Japan: The History of a Racist Phobia", *Socialist Review*, No.3, https://marxistleftreview.org/articles/australian-perceptions-of-japan-the-history-of-a-racist-phobia/

Johnson, Carol 1989, *The Labor Legacy. Curtin, Chifley, Whitlam, Hawke*, Allen & Unwin.

Louis, LJ and Ian Turner 1968, *The Depression of the 1930s*, Cassell.

McMullin, Ross 1991, *The Light on the Hill. The Australian Labor Party 1891–1991*, Oxford University Press.

O'Lincoln, Tom 1985, *Into the Mainstream. The decline of Australian Communism*, Stained Wattle Press.

Ross, Lloyd 1977, *John Curtin. A biography*, Sun Books.

Sheridan, Tom 1989, *Division of Labour. Industrial Relations in the Chifley Years, 1945–49*, Oxford University Press.

Walker, RB 1980, "The fall of the Labor Daily", *Labour History*, No.38, May, pp.67–75.

PHOEBE KELLOWAY

Private profit vs public access: How class struggle shaped Australia's health care system[1]

Phoebe Kelloway is a socialist, historian, and a member of the Public Service Association. She wrote this article in a personal capacity.

THE HEALTH CARE SYSTEM IN AUSTRALIA today is commonly described as being in "crisis". New South Wales nurses and midwives on strike in February and March this year carried home-made placards contradicting Health Minister Brad Hazzard's claims that hospitals were "coping". One midwife attested that the previous few months had "been absolute hell".[2]

Although the main immediate cause of the dire strain the system is under is the Covid-19 pandemic, it is widely recognised that health care was under severe pressure before that. This article does not analyse how the present situation arose, but aims to provide the reader with an historical perspective on the health system confronting this crisis, by examining the key battles that formed its structures in the twentieth century. A study such as this is important because the health care system is not only essential social infrastructure, but a major industry: it employed 1.1 million people in 2021, and has made up 10 percent or more of Australia's GDP since 2015–16.[3] Health and health

1. Special thanks to Wren Somerville for research assistance, Liz Ross and Janey Stone for sharing ideas and information, and Omar Hassan and Louise O'Shea for feedback on earlier drafts.
2. Holcombe 2022.
3. Australian Bureau of Statistics 2022; Australian Institute of Health and Welfare 2021.

care in any given society are shaped first and foremost by that society's economic system.

Capitalism prioritises profit-making over human life and everything else, and therefore it produces illness: it makes working-class people, in particular, sick.[4] Whether the health of any population – or for that matter, any individual – is generally good, average or poor is shaped by numerous factors. Fundamental ones include reliable access, or lack thereof, to nutritious food and good-quality shelter, essentials which are not guaranteed for the majority of humanity in a system run for profit. From the late nineteenth century in industrialised countries, construction of sewerage systems and provision of clean drinking water contributed to improved health among city dwellers. But working conditions often undermined health, and continue to do so. Economic disadvantage is closely correlated with worse health outcomes. In short, access to health care and medicines is only one of the factors that shape health. While the economic system produces conditions detrimental to health, the health care system is supposed to prevent and cure illness and treat injury. The health care system is not expected to maximise good health, but rather to serve the interests of the ruling capitalist class. The standards this requires will vary depending on specific contexts and factors, including unemployment and profit rates, expectations of the population, the pressure the working class may bring to bear, and more. However, its implicit minimum requirement is for enough of the population to be sufficiently healthy to maintain the status quo. In particular, the capitalist class needs most of the working class to be healthy enough to work and to raise the next generation of workers, and sufficient numbers to be fit for military service. It also needs most of the middle classes to be in good enough health to fulfil their specific roles (ranging from shop keepers to managers to doctors).

Within the capitalist framework, health care can be organised in different ways, with varying levels of public and private sector involvement. Drawing on health systems expert Gwendolyn Gray's outline of distinct types of systems, it is useful to distinguish between the financing and delivery of health care, and identify whether they are in private

---

4. Haynes 2009.

or public hands.⁵ In a national health service system, both are publicly controlled: hospital and medical services are publicly financed and provided. Doctors are generally salaried employees or contracted to the state, rather than operating private practices, and hospitals are publicly owned. Everyone can access the medical and hospital treatment they need, free of charge (or at a low cost), with services funded through tax revenue. Health systems close to that model operate, for example, in Sweden and Britain.

By contrast, where private insurance predominates, both the delivery and financing of health care are in the hands of private operators. Doctors are generally in private practice, hospitals are privately owned, and providers charge patients fees. Private health insurance, in theory, provides a means for individuals or their employers to prepay the costs of health care. However, fees tend to be high, even for those with insurance. Where private insurance is the main means of health financing, a proportion of the population is uninsured – usually over 15 percent in industrialised countries – because they cannot afford the premiums, and a further proportion is under-insured. It is not the case that public finance plays no role – indeed, Gray noted that private health insurance systems cannot operate without being heavily subsidised by taxpayers – but governments have little control. The system in the United States operates along those lines. In a national health insurance system, provision of health care is likewise private, but the financing is under public control. Services are generally funded by residents' contributions to public insurance, or otherwise through taxation. Governments can exercise a high level of control over costs, as the dominant or sole payer. Costs to patients, and therefore financial barriers to care, are usually eliminated or kept low. The health systems of Canada and most European countries are closest to that model.

Health care in Australia today is delivered by a mixture of private and public providers, and financed predominantly by public funds. We do not have universal health care, but a system of health insurance that fits somewhere between the private insurance and public insurance models. Medicare, administered by the Health Insurance Commission,

---

5. Gray 2004, pp.18–22.

is a less-than-universal national health insurance scheme.[6] Alongside it operates a large private insurance sector, which is heavily publicly subsidised. Private insurance is fostered through a "carrot-and-stick" approach: those who purchase cover receive a public rebate for a proportion of their premiums, while higher income earners without sufficient hospital cover must pay a Medicare levy surcharge.[7] As of March 2022, 55 percent of Australia's population has private insurance for general treatment, and about 45 percent for hospital treatment.[8] Thus, although public funds consistently comprise over two-thirds of health care expenditure, there is less public control than in a national health service.[9]

Most health care providers are private enterprises, from general practitioner (GP) clinics to pharmacies to specialists. Hospitals are the major exception: most of them are public, and run by the states and territories. In some instances, a public entity competes with private operators, for example in pathology in South Australia, with SA Pathology narrowly escaping privatisation amidst the Covid pandemic. Adding complexity, the responsibility for funding hospitals and other public health services is split between the state and federal governments. The emergence of this jumbled organisation is briefly outlined below. It is important to recognise that health care is treated as a commodity in this country, not as a human or civic right. Although Medicare obscures and somewhat mitigates this fact, access to health care is nonetheless shaped by a person's ability to pay for it. Profits, by contrast, are all but guaranteed in this system, underpinned by generous public subsidies to capitalists, large and small.

The shape of the health care system is often discussed as the product of conflict between contending interest groups.[10] That conceptual framework provides a reasonable starting point, but such

---

6. Medicare covers most people living in Australia, but not everyone. Those eligible include Australian and New Zealand citizens, and permanent residents of Australia. Notably excluded are prisoners, many asylum seekers, and most international students. Biggs 2016.
7. Biggs and Cook 2018.
8. Australian Prudential Regulation Authority 2022, p.2.
9. Australian Institute of Health and Welfare 2021.
10. Sax 1984 called it "a strife of interests" in the title of his book.

analyses at worst elide the fundamental matter of the class positions of those groups. This article instead applies a Marxist analysis and examines how class struggle shaped the modern health care system. To contain the scope of the subject, it concentrates on the role of the main players in the conflicts – namely, the major political parties and doctors' organisations – and also gives attention to interventions of the organised working class. As such, the article omits the part played by the supporting cast: insurance companies, hospital boards, the public service and state governments in the federal political sphere. The main actors considered here are: the Liberal Party, which defends the interests of the capitalist class; the Australian Labor Party (ALP), which is understood as a "capitalist workers' party", that is, a party with a base in the working class but that is committed to governing Australia in the interests of the nation's capitalists; and the organised medical profession, which protects doctors' interests as a middle-class group.[11]

The article considers how the modern health care system developed from when federal governments became involved in the 1940s. It deals mainly with fights at the federal political level, starting with the reform efforts of the Curtin and Chifley governments and the resistance they met. Taking a leaf out of Rob Watts' book, it resists the narrative of a heroic struggle of the ALP against reactionaries.[12] The first part accounts for why Australia does not have a national health service. Secondly, the article covers struggles over health insurance policy, which explain how the current system emerged. It concentrates on the late 1960s to 1983: Whitlam's introduction of Medibank, Fraser's destruction of it and union resistance, and Hawke's reintroduction of universal health insurance as part of the Accord. The article's focus shifts to the state level for its final part, about nurses' industrial action, to explore how organised workers can have an impact on the system.

While struggles at the federal level have largely decided the health system's structures, and particularly the matter of who pays for health care, equally fierce battles have been waged at the state level. Those fights have been over the resources the states provide for health, particularly for hospitals. The levels of funding and of staffing, and pay

---

11. Bramble and Kuhn 2011, pp.6–24 (chapter 1).
12. Watts 1987.

and conditions for staff, have been key matters in recurring struggles. A brief overview is provided of the most outstanding such battle to date – the 50-day strike in 1986 of Victorian nurses – as well as their industrial action in 2000. Those actions had structural implications in terms of both professionalisation and nurse-patient ratios. Fights against the privatisation of particular institutions, and significant structural changes that were introduced without major political struggles – such as organising hospitals around efficiency targets – are beyond the scope of this article. Before delving into the 1940s events, a summary is given of today's health care structures in terms of how patients access care, followed by an outline of the system's evolution up to the mid-twentieth century.

Today's health system

The first point of contact for anyone seeking medical care is usually a GP, who provides primary care for ill health. Treatment sought from a GP may involve a range of other medical professionals. A GP may, for example:

– order diagnostic tests, which require the skills and equipment of pathologists or radiographers;

– prescribe medication, which the patient must buy from a pharmacy;

– refer the patient to an allied health professional or a medical specialist.

If a serious illness is diagnosed, the patient may need specialist treatment in a hospital. If the patient needs surgery, but their life will not be endangered if they do not receive it, it is categorised as elective surgery and they will generally be put on a waiting list. A person suffering a life-threatening medical episode usually goes directly to hospital, often under the care of paramedics in an ambulance.

Each of those elements of care is treated as a commodity that must be paid for, and a patient typically pays out-of-pocket for at least some of their treatment. Even a Health Care Card holder who goes to a bulk-billing doctor for a script will have to pay the chemist for medicine, although most of the cost is paid by the federal government through Medicare, which is funded by tax revenue. Importantly, Medicare also promises that those it covers are eligible for free hospital services as public patients in public hospitals. Services that the government subsidises are itemised on the Medicare Benefits Schedule (MBS), which also lists a nominal cost (known as the schedule fee) for each service. Medicare pays providers some or all of the schedule fee: 75 percent for services in hospital, 85 percent for most services out of hospital, and 100 percent for GP consultations.[13] Bulk-billed services are free to the patient, as the provider accepts the Medicare benefit as their whole payment. The Pharmaceutical Benefits Scheme works in a similar way. Patients pay a co-payment (which is lower for concession card holders) and the Australian government pays the rest.[14] The rebate system has a catch for patients: providers do not have to limit their charges to the MBS schedule fee, indeed they can and do charge far higher fees. Those who have bought private cover may be insured for some or all of the gap between the Medicare rebate and the actual cost.

The parallel operation of public and private insurance effectively entrenches a two-tiered system of health care. Those who rely on Medicare are not insured for all health services they may need: for example, most dentistry is not covered by Medicare. Public patients face excessively long waiting times for elective surgery, as a result of long-term cost-cutting to public hospitals. Private patients, however, can pay to avoid the worst queues. To access dental care or surgery as a private patient, for example, anyone without private insurance will face large out-of-pocket costs. This makes access extremely difficult, if not impossible, for low income-earners. Those who are privately insured – and generally wealthier – thus have better access to care, though they too usually also have to pay out-of-pocket costs, as well as insurance premiums.

Emergence of the system, up to 1940

In the nineteenth century, various practitioners provided primary health care services in Australia, generally on a fee-for-service basis. Medical practice was not particularly scientific until the later decades of that century; there was little to differentiate doctors from quacks.

---

13. Biggs 2016.
14. Grove 2016.

But with breakthroughs in medicine, the profession gained prestige.[15] The question of equitable access to medical services did not become an issue until a random patient consulting a random doctor had a better than 50/50 chance of benefiting from the consultation, a milestone estimated to have been reached in 1912.[16] While fee-for-service remained the predominant method of paying doctors, from the 1870s to the mid-twentieth century many working-class people accessed medical services through associations of mutual aid called friendly societies.[17] Members effectively prepaid for basic medical care by regular contributions to the friendly society, which contracted doctors to provide services for an annual per-person payment. That system came under great strain in the economic depressions of the 1890s and 1930s, which provided the impetus for states to intervene to subsidise services.[18] Those who could not afford to subscribe to a friendly society but needed a doctor's care either sought treatment as a charity case at a hospital's outpatient department, or went without.

Hospitals began as small institutions. The purpose of public hospitals was to care for the sick poor, but they could provide little in terms of curative treatment.[19] In NSW and Victoria, most were founded as charities to which wealthy contributors subscribed, while some were established by religious orders. Even in their early days, subscriptions did not provide enough funds to sustain these hospitals, so colonial authorities contributed public funds. As hospital care improved, demand for treatment and hence operating costs grew. Hospitals were brought under public ownership as they became increasingly reliant on public funds, although independent boards that ran them retained a high degree of control. In the less populous states, colonial and subsequently state authorities played a greater role in establishing and running hospitals from the outset.

From around the 1920s, public hospitals were transformed and grew into large institutions. The transformation was brought

---

15. Sax 1984, pp.7–13.
16. Scotton and Macdonald 1993, p.5.
17. Sax 1984, pp.13–14, 19–21; Crichton 1990, pp.18–20; Gray 1991, p.52; Gillespie 1991, pp.7–15.
18. Crichton 1990, p.25; Sax 1984, pp.31–32; Gillespie 1991, p.60.
19. Crichton 1990, pp.13–17; Sax 1984, pp.21–26.

about by advances in surgical practice, medicines and technology.[20] Techniques developed in military hospitals, and equipment such as x-ray machines, were brought into public hospitals after the First World War. Public hospitals became the sites where the medical profession's emerging specialisations were practiced and taught, and where the most advanced care was delivered. Until that juncture, public hospitals admitted as patients only those who needed charity, judged by a strict means test. Patients were not charged fees and doctors provided their services on an honorary basis (free of charge). But the improvements in treatment brought new demands for access to be extended to patients who would not seek or be eligible for care as charity cases, and responses to it differed between states.[21]

In NSW and Victoria, hospitals allowed doctors to admit their private patients on a fee-paying basis, while charity treatment continued for means-tested patients. The high cost was a barrier to hospital treatment for those whose means ruled out charitable admission, but could not afford private fees. By contrast, in Tasmania and Queensland state governments intervened to take greater control of public hospitals in response to systemic financial shortfalls, and expanded access while excluding private practice and abolishing stigmatising charity treatment. The state takeover of hospitals was carried out by Labor in Queensland, but in Tasmania non-Labor governments also took part, and all did so for pragmatic rather than ideological reasons. In Queensland, all means testing and patient fees were ended in 1945.

The federal government did not become significantly involved in hospitals until the 1940s. At Australia's federation, health care remained mainly with the states, while the federal government was put in charge of quarantine. States also kept administering taxation after 1901. This only changed in 1942, when the Curtin Labor government succeeded in gaining uniform taxation powers as part of strengthening the war effort.[22] This created a vertical fiscal imbalance: while states remained responsible for the large expenditure hospitals needed, the

---

20. Gray 1991, pp.53–54; Gillespie 1991, pp.15–29.
21. Scotton and Macdonald 1993, p.6; Gillespie 1991, pp.57–86 (chapter 3); Gray 1991, pp.54–60; Sax 1984, pp.42–44.
22. Crisp 1961, pp.156–57.

Commonwealth had taken over their former revenue-raising power.[23] The split responsibility set the stage for each level of government to continually blame the other for under-funding of hospitals. The Chifley government extended free public hospital treatment beyond Queensland to all states and territories in 1946, but did so without implementing a nationally coherent and unified health system. Federal involvement in health care thus continued and entrenched the mixed private-public structure of the health system that persists to this day.

1940s health system battles

Welfare and the Second World War

The health reforms introduced by 1940s Labor governments came in the context of widespread expectations of far-reaching changes following the misery of the Depression and the Second World War. Far from being a product of Labor's supposed radicalism, they fulfilled a longstanding intent on both sides of politics for the federal government to provide welfare. By the outbreak of the Second World War, the major political parties agreed that the Commonwealth should provide social security, including expanding access to health care, although they disagreed on how to organise it. Non-Labor governments favoured contributory national insurance schemes, and twice tried to introduce one, in 1928 and 1938. The first was set aside as the economic depression began.[24]

The 1938 scheme was to cover health care, sickness and disability benefits, old age and widows' pensions, and be financed by employee and employer contributions and government.[25] Labor had opposed contributory schemes since 1912, arguing that social security should not be a charge on workers' wages but paid for by the whole community through general revenue. The 1938 scheme had multiple shortfalls and produced objections from all sides (including farmers as well as unions and the ALP), but most notably from the medical profession. Leaders

---

23. Swerissen and Duckett 2002, pp.15–16, 20–24.
24. Sax 1984, pp.35–37.
25. Sax 1984, pp.39–42; Watts 1987, pp.1–24 (chapter 1); Gillespie 1991, pp.87–112 (chapter 4).

of the main doctors' organisation, the British Medical Association (BMA) initially agreed to it, but a revolt by its members forced them to withdraw their support, on the basis that the proposed payments would be insufficient.[26] The 1938 legislation was dropped largely because of doctors' opposition.

The Second World War provided greater impetus for welfare reforms, to help secure support for the war effort. The major parties recognised the lack of popular enthusiasm for the war when it began: working-class people had in recent years borne the brunt of the 1930s Depression and, moreover, remembered the devastation wrought by the last war.[27] There was bipartisan agreement on making post-war social services a major objective. Conservative Prime Minister Robert Menzies established the Joint Parliamentary Committee on Social Security (JPCSS) to plan for them in July 1941.[28] Historians of the health and welfare systems, Sidney Sax and Rob Watts, have disputed the idea that social services were intended to buy social peace.[29] But it is hard to believe that popular sentiment did not factor into governments' calculations, and Watts cites one account of concern over civilian morale influencing Labor Prime Minister John Curtin to introduce a reform.[30] Throughout 1942, Curtin's government successfully galvanised support for the war by encouraging fear of Japanese invasion, despite knowing that was not going to happen.[31] The following year though, increased strike action indicated that working-class discontent was again rising. When the war ended, the strike rate exploded as fear of a new depression lent urgency to workers' demands for better wages and conditions.[32] A widespread sentiment that ordinary people deserved substantial improvements after their wartime sacrifices, plus the industrial unrest, clearly contributed to welfare reforms remaining on the government's agenda.

---

26. BMA branches were founded in Australian colonies from the late nineteenth century. They merged to become the Australian Medical Association (AMA) in 1962.
27. O'Lincoln 2011, pp.119–24.
28. Sax 1984, p.48.
29. Sax 1984, pp.33–34; Watts 1987, pp.26–27.
30. Watts 1987, pp.110–11.
31. Bramble and Kuhn 2011, pp.56–57; O'Lincoln 2011, pp.139–44.
32. Sheridan 1989.

In addition, as Watts' study shows, Australia's welfare state was developed as "part of novel taxation and fiscal policies" crucial to the war economy.[33] The Curtin government secured the financial basis for both greater wartime expenditure and future social services by expanding the federal tax base. Against opposition from the states, it established uniform taxation by seizing tax-raising powers from them in mid-1942. It then extended taxation to most wage earners, who had not previously been subject to income tax. In late 1942, Ben Chifley as treasurer was under pressure to find extra tax revenue, both to fund the war and curtail civilians' spending to head off inflation.[34] The Labor government did this by significantly lowering the income tax threshold, which immediately raised the number of direct taxpayers from 800,000 to two million in 1943, to raise funds from all but the poorest workers.[35] To make this reactionary policy palatable, it was linked to the foundation of the National Welfare Fund which would receive 30 percent of the new revenues.[36] Thus the ALP abandoned its previous position that social services should be funded by the rich, to institute a system largely paid for by workers. Independent labour MP Maurice Blackburn criticised it as "steal[ing] a sheep and giv[ing] the trotters away in charity".[37] The welfare system amounted to income redistribution within the working class, not from bosses to workers.[38]

Anticipation of a national health service

In relation to health care specifically, it was widely expected that Labor would introduce a free, comprehensive health service. The party's platform included the nationalisation of "public health" (as well as banking and other sectors).[39] Curtin, when in opposition, had said the ALP believed that "national health services should be treated, in principle, in the same way as education. They should be free to all

---

33. Watts 1987, p.26.
34. Watts 1987, pp.94–95.
35. Crisp 1961, pp.156–58; Watts 1987, pp.98–99.
36. Watts 1987, pp.96–103.
37. Quoted in O'Lincoln 2011, p.147.
38. Bramble and Kuhn 2011, p.62.
39. Australian Labor Party 1942.

members of the community".[40] Within days of Labor forming government in October 1941, new health minister EJ Holloway indicated that he wanted to nationalise medical services.[41] Such statements were basically understood to mean that the government would run a national network of medical clinics and hospitals, which would be available free of charge, staffed by salaried doctors. Proposals along those lines came not only from Labor, but equally from public sector entities. The National Health and Medical Research Council (NHMRC) recommended a national health service in 1941; likewise a JPCSS subcommittee drafted detailed proposals for a salaried medical service two years later.[42] Since doctors' organisations later made the question of compulsion a major theme of their campaigning against Labor's health reforms, it is important to note that these proposals did not involve compulsory participation. On the contrary, they expected that private medical practice would continue for doctors and patients who wanted it.[43] It was recognised that the Commonwealth lacked the constitutional authority to run a national health service, but this was not seen as an insuperable obstacle.[44]

From the start of the decade, the medical profession anticipated a far-reaching overhaul of the health system, and it looked like it would cooperate with it. In discussion on the future of Australia's health system in the BMA's publication, the *Medical Journal of Australia*, from 1940, all contributors thought a national medical service was inevitable. Most expected it would be a salaried service, which some were in favour of, although most wanted the more lucrative fee-for-service model.[45] GPs who had established commercially successful practices, and wealthy specialists, were generally wary of becoming government employees. However, doctors in working-class areas who mainly treated friendly society patients appreciated the stable income of contracts and were generally more open to a salaried system. In late

---

40. Quoted in Sax 1984, p.49.
41. "Has Big Health Proposal", *Sun (Sydney)*, 8 October 1941, p.2. http://nla.gov.au/nla.news-article230957786
42. Gillespie 1991, pp.131–54; Sax 1984, pp.48–52; Gray 1991, pp.65–69.
43. Sax 1984, pp.49, 52.
44. Gray 1991, p.66.
45. Gillespie 1991, pp.176–82.

1942, the Victorian branch of the BMA drafted a proposal for a salaried medical service, reasoning that a system drawn up by medical professionals would be better than a government-conceived scheme.[46] Even Menzies indicated he favoured a salaried service, as late as 1948, albeit in a private meeting.[47] In short, Labor said it intended to nationalise health services, and everyone in the early 1940s expected it would. So what went wrong?

Action postponed and powers denied
Initially, the new Labor government deferred the anticipated major changes. In January 1942, Holloway promised doctors that "no complete salaried [medical] Service [would] be inaugurated during the war".[48] That commitment was probably motivated by the government's need for the medical profession's cooperation: with up to one-third of Australia's doctors in the military, the rest had to make up the shortfall in civilian services. Although Holloway's undertaking did not rule out any new initiatives (as the BMA later claimed), it precluded setting up the structures of a national service so that doctors leaving the military could directly enter it. In 1943, the BMA's attitude towards reforms shifted from reluctance to opposition, and the government set aside its plans for a national service.[49]

The Curtin government, re-elected in August 1943, tried to lay the basis for post-war health care reforms in the meantime. Since it would be more straightforward for the federal government to implement a national health service directly, it tried to obtain the power to do so through a constitutional referendum. In August 1944, it sought to extend the additional powers the Commonwealth had temporarily gained during the war. But the "Yes" campaign was poorly organised and faced concerted opposition. Labor's conservative opponents used "red scare" themes and accused the government of authoritarian overreach.[50] Their objection to centralisation of powers was probably mainly because

---

46. Gillespie 1991, pp.181–82.
47. Gillespie 1991, p.243.
48. Quoted in Gillespie 1991, p.144.
49. Sax 1984, p.53.
50. Griffen-Foley 1995.

the proposal came from a Labor government. After its failure, the ALP abandoned the project of far-reaching health care restructure, in favour of cash payments to subsidise existing services.[51] Whether the referendum result should have prompted that response is a matter we will return to. First, it is necessary to examine the extraordinary fight over pharmaceutical benefits, which began around the same time.

The battle over pharmaceutical benefits

The government believed that a Pharmaceutical Benefits Scheme (PBS) was one element of health reform it could implement without major controversy. Yet the proposed PBS generated an unprecedented political storm. The BMA waged a fierce fight with the Labor government over the scheme, which it saw as a proxy for the broader issue of "socialised medicine".[52] It involved two High Court challenges to the legislation, a propaganda campaign by the BMA, and a near-unanimous doctors' boycott of the scheme.

The government did not anticipate opposition from doctors, as a PBS would have only a minimal impact on their practice. Labor hoped to provide patients with prescription medicines free of charge. Medications eligible for subsidy would be on an extensive list called the formulary, which would include all pharmaceuticals that GPs regularly prescribed. (But unlike in New Zealand, the government would not subsidise every medicine because it feared a cost blowout.) The doctor would fill out a government-issued prescription form for the patient, who would obtain the medicine from a pharmacy, and the government would pay the pharmacist. The Curtin government secured in-principle agreement from the Pharmacy Guild. In December 1943, it provided the BMA with details of the scheme, which worked similarly to one doctors already participated in, a limited benefit scheme for war veterans.[53] But doctors with a range of views on other health reforms were basically united in objecting to the PBS.

This allowed BMA leaders to mobilise opposition to the PBS with little risk of internal dissent, on the grounds that they opposed

---

51. Gillespie 1991, pp.156–58.
52. Hunter 1965; Gillespie 1991, pp.209–32 (chapter 9); Gray 1991, pp.69–72.
53. Gillespie 1991, pp.214–15.

government interference in medical practice. Some doctors were initially concerned about limits to the formulary, but even when it was clear most medicines would be covered, the BMA painted its limits as symptomatic of flaws of state-controlled medicine. As the campaign progressed, anti-socialist themes became more prominent, as the BMA railed against public control over medicine and public employment of doctors.

A boycott was declared in October 1945: the BMA instructed all members to return the new prescription forms and copies of the formulary unopened.[54] Only about 180 doctors – less than two percent – joined in the scheme to provide free medicine.[55]

BMA leaders were keen to challenge the constitutional validity of the legislation, but Menzies convinced them to wait until after the August 1944 referendum. If they had challenged it earlier and won, that could well have helped the government win the referendum. Thus the High Court heard the challenge in November 1945, and it overturned the *Pharmaceutical Benefits Act*.[56] By implication its decision also threatened Commonwealth welfare payments such as maternity allowances and unemployment benefits. This set the stage for another constitutional referendum.

The next referendum was held in September 1946, at the same time as the federal election, which Labor won. The government put three separate questions to electors in the constitutional referendum: the one relevant here asked for the Commonwealth to be given power over social services. The initial draft included a clause to safeguard against "industrial conscription", but Menzies convinced Attorney-General HV Evatt to amend it to "civil conscription", a detail that later became significant.[57] The referendum question on social services power had bipartisan support, and it was successfully carried. This allowed the government to bring in new legislation for a PBS.

In mid-1947, a new *Pharmaceutical Benefits Act* came into effect and the BMA's battle against it resumed. The BMA fought in three ways:

---

54. Gillespie 1991, p.221.
55. Hunter 1965, p.418.
56. Sax 1984, p.54; Gray 1991, pp.63–64; Gillespie 1991, pp.222–23.
57. Wilde 2005, pp.43–46.

through propaganda, a boycott and another High Court challenge. The PBS was a very popular measure, for obvious reasons, so the BMA cynically declared it had no objection to free medicine. Yet in private correspondence the BMA's president suggested an agreement might be reached if patients were required to pay part of the cost.[58] Meanwhile in newspaper advertisements, the Victorian BMA secretary made the ludicrous claim that any doctor who used government forms to write prescriptions would "immediately place his private practice under Government control".[59] Some doctors thought of the fight against the PBS as one front in a broader battle against the "socialistic tiger".[60] The boycott continued: in March 1949 there were just three doctors participating in Queensland and eleven in NSW, although in Victoria 111 participated.[61] Doctors, as a group of middle-class professionals, were taking reactionary collective action to defend their narrow interests.

The government's response to the BMA's assault was inept. It barely responded to BMA propaganda: health department officials were frustrated that the only literature supporting the PBS came from the Communist Party of Australia.[62] When the Australian Council of Trade Unions (ACTU) offered to launch a campaign in support of the PBS, the new health minister, Nick McKenna, demurred, insisting that it would be counterproductive.[63] Building trade unions raised the prospect that they might ban work on buildings owned or occupied by doctors who did not comply with the free medicine scheme, but they did not follow through.[64] Thus union opposition to the propaganda and boycott was essentially limited to passing worthy resolutions. In May 1948 the government introduced penalties for doctors who refused to participate in the scheme. This gave the BMA – and its reactionary allies in the judiciary – grounds to once again challenge the legality of the Act.

---

58. Gray 1991, p.70.
59. Hunter 1948.
60. Quoted in Gillespie 1991, p.221.
61. Gillespie 1991, p.228.
62. Gillespie 1991, p.229; Communist Party of Australia 1948.
63. Gillespie 1991, p.236.
64. "Unions Threaten Doctors on Free Medicine Stand", *Herald (Melbourne)*, 3 June 1948, p.2. http://nla.gov.au/nla.news-article247302635

The High Court made its ruling in October 1949, finding in the BMA's favour. It found that that requirement to use the government's prescription form, backed by penal sanctions, amounted to "civil conscription". This dubious decision, like its rejection of bank nationalisation around the same time, reflected the deep anti-Labor sentiment sweeping through the ruling class. The ruling did not invalidate the entire *Pharmaceutical Benefits Act*, only one particular clause. Labor postponed any decision on what to do about it until after the upcoming election, which it lost to Menzies, who dismantled Labor's health reforms. The High Court's finding was thus decisive, marking an end to the battles of that era over the health system.[65] Doctors, organised collectively, had succeeded in denying patients access to free medicine. A similar government subsidy scheme was eventually established by the Liberals, but it required a co-payment from patients. That received no opposition from doctors. However, it was restricted to a narrow list of drugs: it was not until a decade later, in March 1960, that the scheme was expanded to cover the full range of medicines.[66]

Watered-down reforms

While its first attempt at the PBS was being challenged, the Labor government introduced its *Hospital Benefits Act* 1945, which established a Commonwealth subsidy of six shillings per day for each occupied hospital bed.[67] Through the subsidy, universal access to free treatment as a public patient in a public hospital was guaranteed nationwide.[68] This was done by means of conditional grants from the Commonwealth to the states: the funding was provided on the condition that no means test be applied to public patients. The subsidy was similarly provided for private patients on the condition that their fees be reduced by six shillings per day. This was a progressive achievement: it significantly expanded free access to advanced medical care, while lowering costs for all patients. Yet it was a substantially diluted

---

65. Gillespie 1991, pp.229–30.
66. Hunter 1965, pp.423–25; Gillespie 1991, pp.256–64.
67. Gillespie 1991, pp.196–208 (chapter 8); Gray 1991, pp.72–74; Sax 1984, pp.56–57.
68. "Public Ward Fees Go", *Sydney Morning Herald*, 13 September 1945, p.5 http://nla.gov.au/nla.news-article17953158

version of Labor's earlier policy. The government ignored the advice it had sought from the NHMRC and JPCSS, which had both strongly recommended substantial capital expenditure to expand the capacity of public hospitals.[69] It did not want to embark on a program of big spending, so it settled for improving access to the existing system. This meant essentially abandoning any attempt at public planning for service provision. The bill also entrenched a split in welfare provision between civilian and war veteran schemes, with repatriation hospitals providing better quality services than were available to the rest of the population.[70]

The hospital scheme was the one element of health reform that succeeded because it dodged all the major issues, and essentially preserved the status quo.[71] And since the subsidy was granted equally to private patients, it did not threaten private practice.[72] The expansion of free treatment was expected to put an end to the honorary system and result in specialists becoming hospital employees, a change some doctors were against. However, the BMA's state branches were divided on the question – Queensland hospitals had already moved to a salaried system by 1938 – so it did not oppose it.[73] In fact, the honorary system was only ended in Tasmania as a result.[74] Doctors reported by the end of 1946 that the abolition of the means test had not significantly affected their practices.[75] Another advantage in subsidising existing services was that the government avoided having to confront the Catholic church, which controlled a substantial proportion of hospitals, and still does to this day. There was some resistance from state governments, but increased Commonwealth funding attracted them.

The scheme began operating at the start of 1946, and all states had passed enabling legislation by July of that year. But it was a short-lived reform: it lasted only until 1952. After that, the Menzies government used new funding agreements to force the re-introduction of means

---

69. Gillespie 1991, pp.196–97.
70. Gillespie 1991, pp.199–200.
71. Gillespie 1991, pp.207–8.
72. Gray 1991, p.73.
73. Gillespie 1991, p.200.
74. Gray 1991, p.73.
75. Sax 1984, p.57.

testing and axe universal free treatment. Only Queensland refused to comply and kept hospital treatment free for patients.[76]

The third and final element of the Labor government's health reforms was a medical benefits scheme to subsidise out-of-hospital care.[77] This was legislated towards the very end of Chifley's government, in late 1949, instead of a national health service. The scheme was barely a shadow of its earlier ambitions. It provided for the patient and the government to share the costs of treatment, with no requirement for doctors to participate, and no role for the government in any planning of services. This minimal measure never got off the ground; the Menzies government was elected a few weeks later and mothballed it.

The failure of the 1941–49 Labor governments to inaugurate a national health service warrants further comment. Their defenders would undoubtedly point to the 1944 referendum result and the BMA's hostility to explain it. The first of these arguments is unsatisfactory, because the referendum's failure did not rule out implementing a medical service through tied grants, the means by which the government successfully introduced hospital benefits and a program to control tuberculosis.[78] Gray and Gillespie both suggested that the federal government could have reshaped the health system that way. Gray identified that there was the basis for the beginnings of a national service: three states had salaried medical services in rural areas which might have been expanded. She also noted that hospitals had successfully recruited salaried staff, especially in Tasmania and Queensland.[79] Gillespie pointed to the fact that Queensland Director-General of Health Raphael Cilento advocated using conditional grants to pursue health reforms; the option was on the table, but the government did not take it up.[80] Obstruction by the medical profession would have presented a greater obstacle. However, there were differences of opinion among doctors, who were not always united behind the BMA.

---

76. Gillespie 1991, pp.277–78; Gray 1991, p.94.
77. Gillespie 1991, pp.246–49; Gray 1991, pp.76–79.
78. Gray 1991, pp.74–76.
79. Gray 1991, p.78.
80. Gillespie 1991, pp.196–97.

For example, in a dispute over hospital staffing in Tasmania in 1918, the BMA was not able to control its own members: many accepted salaried posts against its instructions.[81] Gillespie's history highlighted the divisions within the profession over prospects of a future medical service.[82] Some were in favour of a national service, and those who were not would likely have adapted over time, as they adjusted to other changes.

The biggest problem was that the government essentially surrendered after the 1944 referendum defeat. Sally Wilde, writing about the 1946 referendum, was probably right to remark that Labor "had no plans to...nationalise medicine".[83] Although the government's lack of intention is impossible to prove, it may be stated categorically that a national health service was not one of its priorities, as it focused instead on attempts to nationalise banking and airlines. Thus it was not that the government was defeated in its effort to fundamentally reform health care, but that it did not seriously fight to do so. The BMA's victory over the PBS was the final nail in the coffin of any hopes for a free, comprehensive health service in Australia. Labor had aimed to establish a strong public health system, to guarantee medical treatment as a right for its working-class base and the wider population. But faced with concerted opposition from a section of the middle class, it simply gave up: the opportunity to transform the health system was squandered without a serious fight.

Struggles over health insurance

Inequity under Menzies, and the alternatives

Since the late 1960s, the main battles over the health system have concerned health insurance. After the December 1949 election of the Liberal government, federal funding for health care continued, but for the ensuing 23 years it was directed towards bolstering the private market. The new health minister Earle Page – a surgeon and BMA member – overturned Labor's reforms and established a scheme with

---

81. Gray 1991, pp.57–58.
82. Gillespie 1991, pp.166–95 (chapter 7).
83. Wilde 2005, p.46.

private fee-for-service practice at its centre, and publicly-subsidised health insurance playing a major role.[84] Universal access to care was no longer a consideration; instead, health care was treated as an individual responsibility, and free publicly-funded services made up only a residual part of the system. Only pensioners were eligible to receive care and medications free of charge; everyone else had to pay out-of-pocket. Even those with insurance still had significant co-payments for care outside of hospital, at least one-third of the treatment cost. Page's scheme was originally meant to include a system for working-class patients to prepay for care with doctors in contract practices, as per the friendly society arrangements, but opposition from the medical profession meant that element was scrapped.[85]

Health care became increasingly expensive for patients, who were effectively divided into three classes: pensioners, the insured and the uninsured.[86] The latter, predominantly lower income earners, were by far the worst off as cost barriers restricted their access to care. To make matters worse, the Page scheme only offered public subsidies for health care for those with private insurance; the uninsured received no support. That is, public funds assisted the wealthier patients.

Through the 1960s there was growing criticism of the health system and calls for reform.[87] Working-class expectations and confidence were rising across the board despite long-standing Liberal rule, as the growing number of economic and political strikes indicated. Under Page's scheme, the proportion of uninsured was never below 17 percent of the population, and by the mid-1960s it was about one-third.[88] Serious illness could spell financial ruin for many working-class people. As opposition leader, Gough Whitlam railed against not only the inequity of this situation, but also the "national waste".[89] Such remarks pointed to the fact that reforming health care to improve access would be beneficial for Australian capitalism.

---

84. Scotton and Macdonald 1993, pp.11–13; Crichton 1990, pp.42–47; Sax 1984, pp.59–68; Gillespie 1991, pp.253–279 (chapter 11); Gray 1991, pp.83–103 (chapter 4).
85. Gillespie 1991, pp.267–73; Gray 1991, pp.89–91.
86. Scotton and Macdonald 1993, p.13.
87. Gray 1991, pp.96–99.
88. Scotton and Macdonald 1993, pp.10–13; Boxall and Gillespie 2013, p.33.
89. Quoted in Boxall and Gillespie 2013, p.42.

Initially, there were three camps in the debate over how to fix the health care system.[90] Political conservatives, including many doctors, thought minor improvements that did not alter the main structures would suffice. On the left of the unions and the ALP, there were proponents of a publicly-run national health service. They included Labor MPs who were medical doctors, notably Moss Cass, opposition health spokesperson, who had earlier outlined a plan for such a service.[91] ALP leader Whitlam and the party's right favoured the public health insurance scheme that would become Medibank, and later Medicare. Whitlam quickly made clear that universal health care was off the table, despite being Labor's long-standing policy. Instead, he got the Labor Party to adopt the national insurance proposal, which would renew the public-private system.[92]

As with Curtin and Chifley's earlier plans, Whitlam's universal insurance hoped to improve health care access by removing financial barriers, but not to disturb the basic structures of a system organised for private profit. Whitlam had concluded that Labor's earlier objective of nationalising health was an outdated relic, whereas public insurance was a viable alternative to the existing system.[93] He made the Medibank proposal the main health policy that the ALP took to the 1969 and 1972 federal elections. After Labor lost in 1969, a sub-committee of its parliamentary caucus that included Cass and four other doctors argued the party should ditch the Medibank proposal and instead pursue its national health service policy. Whitlam, however, would not countenance that recommendation as he saw Medibank as a vote winner, central to the party coming close to victory. He railroaded objections from his party and parliamentary colleagues to keep his policy, then and after winning the 1972 election.[94] Thus, while class struggle expanded, the main fight over the health system shifted to narrower terrain, centred on whether it should be based on private or public insurance, where it has basically remained since.

---

90. Swerissen and Duckett 2002, pp.28–29.
91. Cass 1964.
92. Boxall and Gillespie 2013, pp.36–45.
93. Whitlam 1985, pp.332–36.
94. Boxall and Gillespie 2013, pp.44–45, 48.

The fight to set up Medibank[95]

Medibank was not a universal health care system, but a national health insurance scheme that would further subsidise existing services. Yet despite its relatively modest aims, this too took a major fight to establish.[96] Academic economists Richard Scotton and John Deeble developed the scheme that Whitlam advocated during the 1969 election campaign.[97] The multiple existing insurance funds would be replaced by one Commonwealth fund, which would extend health cover to Australian citizens and residents. Taxpayers would contribute 1.25 percent of their taxable income to the fund. All residents would receive free hospital care, and would be reimbursed for 85 percent of doctors' fees if they paid them upfront. If their doctors chose to bill the fund, they would not pay anything. Whitlam was at pains to emphasise the fact that Medibank was not modelled on the British National Health Service (NHS), a state-run system which at the time provided free and comprehensive health care.[98]

The Labor government once again faced enormous opposition from the Australian Medical Association (AMA, formerly the BMA) and a hostile Senate. The AMA argued against the universal insurance scheme from 1969, and fought for increased medical fees in the first half of the 1970s.[99] It launched an unprecedented lobbying effort to ensure that non-Labor MPs opposed the legislation, backing it up with an extensive publicity campaign.[100] Private hospitals and private insurance funds also campaigned against Medibank, and their influence was probably decisive: the AMA alone may not have convinced politicians, because of its poor public image from its aggressive pursuit of higher fees.[101] In mid-October, the Liberals committed to opposing

---

95. The Medibank discussed here was the public health insurance scheme that operated from 1975 to 1981 – not to be confused with the private health insurance company, Medibank Private.
96. Sax 1984, pp.108–18; Gray 1991, pp.132–47; Boxall and Gillespie 2013, pp.36–77 (chapters 2–4); Scotton and Macdonald 1993.
97. Sax 1984, pp.79–80; Boxall and Gillespie 2013, p.43; Scotton and Macdonald 1993, pp.20–27.
98. Boxall and Gillespie 2013, p.45.
99. Sax 1984, pp.110–11; Scotton and Macdonald 1993, pp.44–49, 79–86.
100. Scotton and Macdonald 1993, pp.28–29, 96–102.
101. Sax 1984, pp.114–15.

Labor's legislation, on the grounds that it would "lower the quality of care" and "be the first stage of nationalisation of health and medical care in Australia".[102]

When the Medibank bills were first introduced in December 1973, the reactionary Democratic Labor Party voted with the opposition to defeat them in the Senate. This made it clear to the ALP that none of its contentious legislation would pass. The government fought back by using the second rejection of the Medibank bills as grounds for a double dissolution election.[103] This was a political gamble that only partly paid off: after the May 1974 election, Labor still lacked a Senate majority. When the Senate voted against the Medibank bills for a third time, the government convened a joint sitting of both houses of Parliament – a constitutional provision never used before or since – in August 1974, which passed the bills. However, supporting legislation (which could not be considered at the joint sitting) was subsequently rejected by the Senate. This meant the government could set up Medibank, but not the income tax levy to finance it.[104] Nevertheless, Medibank was rapidly established: it began on 1 July 1975.[105] The federal government secured agreements with the states to operate the hospital side of it by offering increased funding, with costs shared between the Commonwealth and states on a 50/50 basis. The new agreements all came into effect by October 1975, just weeks before the Kerr coup.[106]

Doctors' organisations campaigned vociferously against Medibank from 1973, and specialists resisted its implementation. AMA advertising equated the scheme with "nationalised medicine", pushing the idea that it would be an authoritarian system in which each patient would be seen as simply a number.[107] Medibank's opponents claimed the freedoms of patients and doctors were under threat, and the AMA

---

102. Quoted in Scotton and Macdonald 1993, p.110.
103. A provision in the Australian constitution allows a parliamentary deadlock to be resolved by dissolving both houses of parliament, to proceed to elections for the House of Representatives and the full Senate (in general elections, only half of the Senate is elected).
104. Boxall and Gillespie 2013, pp.49–51.
105. Scotton and Macdonald 1993, pp.197–215 (chapter 11).
106. Boxall and Gillespie 2013, pp.52–63 (chapter 3); Scotton and Macdonald 1993, pp.152–72 (chapter 9), pp.186–95, 219–22.
107. Scotton and Macdonald 1993, pp.99–100.

asserted that the scheme was only the start of Labor's "socialisation" plans.[108] The General Practitioners' Society in Australia (a small organisation that gained outsized prominence) went the furthest, comparing Labor's health program to Nazi control in a poster depicting Bill Hayden, social security minister, in an SS uniform.[109] A minority of doctors who were in favour of Medibank organised themselves into the Doctors Reform Society to speak out in support of it, but the extent of their impact is unclear.[110] Market research showed that the AMA had got its message about nationalisation across, but that more people supported "nationalised medicine" than were opposed to it.[111]

GPSA poster, September 1973

---

108. Boxall and Gillespie 2013, p.68.
109. Scotton and Macdonald 1993, pp.102–3.
110. Scotton and Macdonald 1993, p.104; Boxall and Gillespie 2013, pp.68–71.
111. Scotton and Macdonald 1993, p.101.

Once the legislation had passed, the AMA moved to delay Medibank coming into effect, and tried to undermine it by advising members not to bulk bill.[112] In April 1975, the AMA recognised it would have to "live with Medibank" although it was still against it.[113] However, specialists working in hospitals actively resisted. Faced with the new requirement that they be employed on a contract rather than fee-for-service basis, large numbers refused to cooperate. In September 1975 in Victoria, they performed only emergency surgical procedures in public wards, on an honorary basis as per the old system. NSW and Victorian surgeons threatened a complete strike, including emergency services. Even after Whitlam was sacked, hospital doctors' boycott actions continued. At the same time though, the uptake of bulk-billing (doctors invoicing Medibank and not the patient for their services) was increasing.[114] So by early 1976, Medibank had started, but it was not yet functioning smoothly.

Defending Medibank against Fraser

The dismissal of the Whitlam government was a monumental attack on democracy and the labour movement. In the context of renewed economic crisis, the governor-general intervened because Australia's ruling class feared Labor would not govern in its interests. This was despite the 1975 budget, which indicated that Labor would comply with the monetarist trend towards slashing social spending and attacking workers' living standards.[115] Regardless of its accommodation to ruling-class orthodoxy, working-class people were livid that "their" Labor government had been ousted. Many trade unionists wanted to wage an industrial fight to reverse the coup, but ALP and union leaders instead told them to "cool it". Having abandoned the extra-parliamentary fight, Labor was easily defeated by Malcolm Fraser's Liberal Party. In that context, all of the Whitlam government's reforms were potentially under threat. Although Medibank had not fundamentally transformed the health system, it had nonetheless improved the standard of living

---

112. Scotton and Macdonald 1993, pp.177–86.
113. Quoted in Scotton and Macdonald 1993, p.179.
114. O'Lincoln 1993, pp.37, 58.
115. Bramble and Kuhn 2011, pp.94–100.

for the Australian working class. It was the union movement, rather than the ALP, that took the lead in defending it.

The Fraser government did not immediately launch a frontal attack on Whitlam's health scheme, but dismantled it in stages before ending it completely, despite Fraser earlier promising to maintain it.[116] The Liberal government first ended one of Medibank's core features, its universality, by encouraging those who could afford to buy private insurance to opt out, expecting about half of all taxpayers to do so. In 1977, it cut hospital funding without consulting or notifying the states, reducing the Commonwealth's share to 45 percent.[117] It stopped bulk-billing (except for pensioners) in May 1978, and abolished the last of Medibank in 1981 when it ended free hospital care (except in Queensland).[118] Anne-marie Boxall and James Gillespie contended in *Making Medicare* that Fraser did not intend to destroy Medibank, but did so due to financial pressures and ineptitude in health policy-making.[119] However, the Fraser government's intentions were far less important than its actions. It destroyed Medibank, so the union movement was right not to trust it.

Sections of the union movement came to Medibank's defence and pushed for a nationwide fightback.[120] In the wake of the Kerr coup, union militants were spoiling for a fight with the Fraser government and the undemocratic ruling class it represented. Its May 1976 mini-budget (widely seen as an attack on labour) introduced a 2.5 percent Medibank levy, but allowed those who bought private health insurance to opt out and avoid it. This attack on Medibank led labour movement activists to fight back. Unionists on the NSW South Coast, with long traditions of militancy, kicked off the industrial action. Some 40,000 workers in the Illawarra joined in a 24-hour stoppage on 7 June, with thousands rallying in Wollongong, vowing to take further industrial action. Post office workers voted to ban the government's pamphlets about the Medibank changes from their counters. The trades

---

116. Boxall and Gillespie 2013, pp.78–113 (chapters 5–7); Sax 1984, pp.127–73; Gray 1991, pp.147–51.
117. Gray 1991, p.148; Sax 1984, p.136.
118. Sax 1984, pp.151–53, 170; Gray 1991, p.150.
119. Boxall and Gillespie 2013, pp.96–98, 102–13 (chapter 7).
120. O'Lincoln 1993, pp.57–66.

and labour councils of Queensland and South Australia demanded the ACTU lead nationwide resistance to changes to Medibank, with the latter calling for a 24-hour strike. Leaders of the Victorian left-wing unions likewise pressed for an industrial response. In *Years of Rage*, Tom O'Lincoln recounted the anger at a Melbourne meeting of 1,500 shop stewards, who saw the Victorian Trades Hall Council (VTHC)'s proposal for a four-hour stop-work as utterly inadequate.[121] They voted instead for a 24-hour stoppage. Despite that, the VTHC called only a four-hour strike for 16 June. Of the 350,000 who struck, some 150,000 remained out after the official 1pm end of the VTHC stoppage.[122] Faced with rank-and-file outrage, union leaders then called a 24-hour strike for 30 June, which involved some 400,000, or 90 percent of Victoria's blue-collar workers.[123] Bob Hawke, leader of the ACTU, successfully delayed its decision on a national strike until early July.

The ACTU eventually called a national one-day political strike on 12 July, the only such strike it has ever held.[124] But the strike did not advance the campaign to defend Medibank, undermined as it was by the union bureaucracy. By stalling for weeks, Hawke, who preferred negotiations with the Fraser government to industrial resistance, had effectively dissipated the energy of the movement. The ACTU did not call central rallies on the strike day, and 12 July was a Monday, which made the stoppage feel like a "long lazy week-end", rather than a militant action.[125] This made the strike a relatively harmless way for unionists to register their objections, rather than a declaration of war. Such a timid approach could not reverse the government's measures, though it probably contributed to delaying further changes.

121. O'Lincoln 1993, pp.61–62.
122. "Now...all day stop bid", *The Age (Melbourne)*, 17 June 1976, p.1.
123. "Medi strike cost $67m", *The Age (Melbourne)*, 1 July 1976, p.3.
124. Donn 1979.
125. O'Lincoln 1993, p.65.

Medicare and the Accord

When Labor was re-elected in 1983, universal health insurance was restored under the new name Medicare.[126] This was done as part of the ALP-ACTU Prices and Incomes Accord, whose main purpose was to enforce wage restraint on an unruly working class that had yet to be tamed. The Accord curbed wage rises by offering unions low but guaranteed wage rises, along with a "social wage", in exchange for a commitment not to make above-award claims, which effectively was a promise never to strike. Medicare lent the otherwise vague "social wage" concept a concrete form, which was essential to successfully selling workers the rotten deal.[127] While Medicare has been beneficial for the Australian working class, signing up for the Accord turned the ACTU into an industrial police force and ushered in decades of declining wages and shrinking union membership rates.[128] Improved access to health care should not have come at such a high cost.

Union movement support for Whitlam's health scheme was key to reviving it, but not inevitable. After the dismissal, the ALP considered adopting alternative, even more moderate, policies. Union support for universal health insurance was an important factor in Labor committing to it again from 1980.[129] Although the scheme fell far short of the labour movement's earlier ambition for a national health service, it should be recognised as a positive that they campaigned to restore universal health insurance. This wasn't inevitable: the potential existed for Australian unions to go in the same direction as their US counterparts on health. Following the failure of an attempt at national health insurance in 1949, American unions had negotiated for employers to provide private health coverage as part of industrial agreements.[130] The Amalgamated Metal Workers and Shipwrights' Union (AMWSU) signed a similar agreement with oil industry executives in mid-1982 which committed the employers to pay for private health insurance in a new industrial award. If the

---

126. The scheme was the same as before, but it needed a new name because Fraser had established Medibank Private. Medicare began operating on 1 February 1984.
127. Boxall and Gillespie 2013, pp.122-26.
128. Bramble 2018, pp.4-14.
129. Boxall and Gillespie 2013, pp.116-20.
130. Boxall and Gillespie 2013, p.121.

AMWSU had secured the award it intended, and started a trend, it would have left workers worse off overall. However, in response to Hawke's campaign for the Accord, the AMWSU withdrew its claim until after the election.[131]

The universal health scheme was less contentious the second time round for a few reasons. While the Liberal Party remained ideologically hostile to it, most of the Senate was in favour: the Democrats (a breakaway from the Liberal Party) held the balance of power and they supported it. Labor argued to fiscal conservatives that Medicare was economically responsible, an argument bolstered by it being key to the Accord. The AMA had been substantially weakened by its opposition to Medibank, so it did not campaign against the scheme's revival.[132] More doctors were in favour of it the second time round, because many understood that Medicare would benefit them. Doctors had found bulk-billing profitable before it was axed: over 70 percent were bulk-billing at least some of their patients by October 1976, within a year of Medibank's introduction.[133] Hospital doctors in most states were not motivated to oppose Medicare: it would not affect their terms of employment as they had already worked on a contract basis since 1975 or earlier.

The exception was in NSW, where specialists yet again staged a revolt, refusing to accept an end to fee-for-service payments.[134] In response to NSW legislation to enable Medicare to function, which included a requirement for hospital specialists to abide by a schedule of fees, NSW specialists accused the NSW and federal Labor governments of conspiring to nationalise medicine. In mid-1984, numerous surgeons relinquished their appointments at public hospitals. Up to 40 percent resigned in their 17-month-long reactionary effort to halt progressive reforms. Although the NSW government repealed the most contentious part of its legislation, the specialists escalated their action. Patients with injuries that were not life-threatening suffered the consequences: for example, one young man had to wait six days for an operation on

---

131. Boxall and Gillespie 2013, p.125.
132. Boxall and Gillespie 2013, pp.126–31.
133. Boxall and Gillespie 2013, p.131.
134. Boxall and Gillespie 2013, pp.138–41; Gray 1991, pp.152–53; Crichton 1990, pp.122–26.

his broken jaw after a motorbike crash.[135] More surgeons threatened to resign by the end of February 1985, but a settlement was negotiated after federal and NSW Labor governments agreed to measures to encourage private health insurance.[136]

Howard fostering private insurance

John Howard's Liberal government further undermined the public system to promote the private health insurance industry. Howard had previously called Medicare "a total disaster", and said the Liberals would "pull it right apart".[137] However, by the mid-1990s the Liberal Party had worked out that opposing the scheme amounted to electoral suicide. So Howard promised that if elected his government would keep Medicare.[138] Howard's Liberals did not attempt to reintroduce the Fraser government's policies, but nonetheless attacked public health care. They froze the rates for Medicare rebates, and allowed bulk-billing to decline. Howard also insidiously undermined the concept of Medicare as a universal scheme, by repeatedly referring to it as a "safety net".[139] Talking about it as such could not, in itself, reduce Medicare to a residual system that served only the poorest citizens. However, this laid the ideological groundwork for future cutbacks.

More significantly, the Howard government introduced measures to subsidise private health insurance, to compete with and undermine the public system. Under the Hawke and Keating governments, private insurance had continued to operate, but public subsidies to the funds ceased after 1986.[140] Their membership had declined from a high of 68 percent of the population in 1982 to 30 percent by 1998.[141] Howard aimed to reinvigorate the private funds and increase their membership to 40 percent of the population. He used three main "carrot-and-stick" measures to achieve this. Firstly, the government introduced subsidies

---

135. Cooke 1985.
136. Gray 1991, p.153; Harris and Buckley 1985.
137. Quoted in Gray 2004, p.31.
138. Boxall and Gillespie 2013, pp.156–58.
139. Boxall and Gillespie 2013, p.162.
140. Gray 2004, p.32.
141. Swerissen and Duckett 2002, p.30.

for those who held private health insurance, and imposed an additional tax (the Medicare levy surcharge) of 1 percent on higher income-earners who did not. It substantially increased the subsidy from 1999, by granting a 30 percent rebate on private health insurance premiums. At an initial cost of $1.6 billion per year, which later increased, this was mainly a windfall for wealthier people who already had private insurance.[142] The third element, the "Lifetime Health Cover" policy, was the worst of all.[143] Introduced in July 2000, it allows insurers to charge policy-holders a 2 percent punitive fee for each year in which they did not purchase health insurance after their 30th birthday (up to a maximum of 70 percent). Its introduction was promoted by an extensive government advertising campaign using the tagline "run for cover". This policy and advertising campaign was explicitly designed to push higher-paid workers and more middle-class people into the private insurance sector. Studies indicated the ads succeeded by creating fear that Medicare was under threat and those without cover would face restricted access to hospitals.[144]

Disgracefully, all three measures have continued (with minor modifications) under successive ALP governments. This is consistent with their approach since the 1940s, when Curtin and Chifley established that the party is not opposed to handing over millions of taxpayer dollars to bolster the profits of the private health industry.

Victorian nurses' industrial action: 1985, 1986 and 2000

While the broad structures of health care have largely been decided at a federal level, fierce battles have also taken place to shape policies at the state level. Even as the Whitlam government was seeking to expand the public sector's role through Medibank, state governments were implementing cutbacks to their health services. From the 1970s onwards, health care workers have fought back through industrial action.

Nurses in that decade engaged in industrial struggle on a scale that was unheard of and almost inconceivable to prior generations. In 1970,

---

142. Gray 2004, p.36.
143. Gray 2004, pp.35–38; Boxall and Gillespie 2013, pp.171–73.
144. Gray 2004, p.38.

Canberra nurses went on strike for six weeks over pay, understaffing and long hours. Two thousand Sydney nurses staged a sit-down protest outside state parliament in 1976 when their wage rise was overturned. Although they did not follow through on their threat to strike, they implemented a series of work bans, including refusal to wear uniforms. Brisbane nurses successfully used clerical bans to make gains on a range of issues in 1978. In Melbourne, 4,000 protesting nurses stormed parliament in April 1975 over pay and staffing. Their placards included: "Dedication doesn't pay the rent".[145] Through work bans on non-nursing duties, they won a 12 percent pay rise.[146] Nurses, the great majority of whom were women, were beginning to challenge sexist expectations that they would submit to lousy wages and conditions because they cared. Amidst rising discontent, a clause in the constitution of the Royal Australian Nurses' Federation (RANF) Victorian branch that explicitly prohibited strike action was overturned at the end of 1983 by a membership ballot.[147]

In October 1985, Victorian nurses went on an indefinite strike that lasted five days. They raised the slogan: "Florence Nightingale is dead, so how come we're still getting her wages?"[148] At the time, unskilled shop assistants could earn more than a third-year nurse in the Victorian health system. Staff shortages and workloads were also major issues. Their industrial action began with a ban on wearing uniforms to work. It escalated when they implemented a work-to-rule from 7 October, to enforce the award nurse-patient ratio of one registered nurse to 10 patients during the day and one to 15 at night. Management at the Alfred Hospital were directed to scab, and did so, prompting nurses there to stage a 24-hour walk-off. Nurses then voted for a state-wide indefinite strike from 17 October; for most, it was their first time on strike. Their claims were for wage rises and better conditions, including improved nurse-patient ratios.[149] The existing ratio was absurdly outdated, as one nurse interviewed for a 2016 documentary explained. It dated back

---

145. Ross 2020, p.85; Stone 1980, pp.34–35.
146. Gardner and McCoppin 1987, p.20.
147. Gardner and McCoppin 1987, p.21.
148. Stone 1985.
149. Ross 1987.

to the 1930s, "before penicillin had been discovered, before plasma infusions took place, and they still weren't even complying with that!"[150] Nurses wanted a 1:5 nurse-patient ratio, which they had already won at Western General Hospital after work bans in 1982.[151] The result of the 1985 strike was mixed: some but not all nurses gained wage increases, and the government agreed to cooperate with the RANF on admissions and discharges, but made only a vague offer on ratios.[152] The major confrontation was deferred, but importantly, nurses had learnt how to strike.

The struggle blew up again in 1986 after the state industrial award gave many nurses a pay cut and made no progress on conditions. The award downgraded nurses with years of experience and additional qualifications to the lowest pay grade, even as nurses' underlying grievances went unmet. The insulting reclassifications and consequent wage cuts came amidst a severe shortage of staff. Ten thousand nurses left the profession in the year to October 1985, and a further 8,000 did not renew their practising certificates, leading to a shortfall of 14,000 nursing staff in 1986.[153] This put nurses under immense pressure: they were consistently caring for more patients than they could reasonably handle. But, having elected a new militant state secretary, Irene Bolger, in May 1986, they were more prepared to fight back.

The strike has been described in detail elsewhere, so only a short summary is needed here.[154] After fruitless negotiations with the state Labor government, nurses voted on 30 October to take indefinite strike action. Emergency departments were exempted, and a skeleton staff would remain at work elsewhere. Nurses organised to picket their hospitals, determined to prevent less urgent deliveries like laundry, while allowing essential supplies such as oxygen to go through.[155] The strike had popular support: 75–80 percent of people polled consistently

---

150. "Video: The context for the strike", in Australian Nursing and Midwifery Federation (ANMF) (Victorian Branch) 2016.
151. Gardner and McCoppin 1987, p.21.
152. Stone 1985.
153. Ross 2020, p.84.
154. Ross 2020, pp.83–98; ANMF 2016.
155. Ross 2020, p.95; Gardner and McCoppin 1987, p.29.

backed it throughout the 50 days.[156] Fellow unionists provided supplies and support for their picket lines.

After five weeks out, the government still refused to make a decent offer. The nurses therefore decided to escalate their action to include emergency departments. In Canada, a similar tactic had brought the government to the negotiating table in seven minutes. However, the Victorian government was not under the same pressure because 50 percent of hospital beds were in private hospitals, whose operations had continued largely unimpeded during the strike. Very few private hospital nurses walked out; those who did faced severe retribution. The public sector nurses pressed ahead with their strike for 11 more days. On 19 December, the government backed down completely, conceding to the nurses' demands. They returned to work victorious the next day, and the industrial award that made their gains law was handed down the following January.

The nurses' victory had a structural impact in terms of their employment and it influenced developments beyond Victoria. Through their 50-day strike, nurses won better pay and, importantly, recognition of their skills. The 1987 award set out occupational classifications for their profession which allowed for career progression and rewarded experience and additional qualifications.[157] The nurse-patient ratio, however, remained the same.[158] The fact that nurses had engaged in industrial militancy was important: they refused to allow management to push them around anymore, and many became lifelong militants from that experience.[159]

In the 1990s, nurses found themselves squeezed by the Kennett state government's aggressive neoliberal policies. Then, as a result of the Howard government's industrial relations attacks, award clauses on staffing levels (or ratios) were ruled "nonallowable matters", and therefore removed.[160] Despite that, Victorian nurses fought a successful struggle for substantially improved nurse-patient ratios in 2000.

---

156. Ross 2020, p.91.
157. Gardner and McCoppin 1987, p.29.
158. Industrial Relations Commission of Victoria 1987, p.17.
159. "Video: The aftermath" in ANMF (Victorian Branch) 2016.
160. Gordon, Buchanan and Bretherton 2012, p.121.

The impetus to make ratios central to their bargaining claims came from the rank and file.[161] They used persistent industrial action to win, particularly the tactic of escalating bed closures. They achieved a base ratio of one nurse to four patients on morning and afternoon shifts, and one to eight at night, with ward-appropriate variations. Again, nurses' industrial action had a structural impact, improving patient care as well as their working conditions, and set a useful precedent for other states.

Conclusion

Class struggle has shaped the modern health care system that developed from the 1940s, when significant federal government intervention began. The organised medical profession has played a particularly despicable role. Doctors, or an elite section of them, have ferociously defended their narrow sectional interests by fighting to block every major reform introduced. Reactionary collective action by practically the entire profession successfully prevented universal access to free medicine, which would have been especially beneficial for working-class patients. The Liberal Party and its political partners likewise formed an obstacle to reforms, repeatedly voting against or overturning legislative advances. The Liberals' main concern has consistently been to encourage a profitable private sector in health. Ideologically against governments providing anything without a user charge, they have sought to minimise access to cost-free care and promoted fee-for-service medical practice.

Once the Liberal Party understood that openly opposing Medicare made them unelectable, they worked to undermine it. Howard's promotion of private insurance has had the biggest detrimental impact. Tony Abbott's government tried to go a step further: its 2014 budget included the introduction of a $7 co-payment for bulk-billed GP consultations. Faced with mass (albeit unorganised) resistance, it eventually had to drop that attack completely. After such a humiliating backdown, the Liberals have not yet attempted to do anything similar, but they remain committed to private, for-profit services

---

161. Gordon, Buchanan and Bretherton 2012, pp.121–22.

being central to health care. The ALP has used this cynically in every election since 2014, portraying itself as the only party that will defend public health care.

The Labor Party trumpets its credentials on health, as the initiator of all major reforms and especially Medicare, which it portrays as a system guaranteeing health care as a right, rather than a quasi-universal health insurance scheme. Labor apologists depict the development of Australia's health care system as a tale of the heroic ALP battling its right-wing opponents and self-interested doctors to implement reforms beneficial to the working class. Although that narrative has a small grain of truth, it is an incomplete and misleading version of events. If Labor can claim credit for its reforms, it also largely bears responsibility for so much of the system being under private control and run for profit. Despite the fact that each of its initiatives prompted outcries of "socialism" from opponents, none of the measures the ALP proposed or introduced ever posed the least threat to capitalism. On the contrary, Labor's reforms from the 1940s onwards safeguarded private medical practice and subsidised profits. More recently, it has left Howard's regressive measures intact. This shows that to defend, let alone strengthen, the public elements of the health care system, electing a Labor government is not enough.

After decades of underfunding, and with no end in sight to the immense pressures sparked by the Covid pandemic, the health care system looks set to be the subject of further battles. Both Labor and Liberal governments have frozen and cut health spending before, and they are equally likely to cave in to future pressures to rein in spending on everything but the military. However, if fights waged by or on behalf of those who make profits from health care have largely shaped the system, working-class struggles have also had an impact. Where middle-class doctors have used their key role to obstruct reform, workers in health care can use their industrial power to win improvements. The Victorian nurses' determined industrial struggles and the gains they won in terms of pay, conditions, and patient care, are a case in point. Their victories are an important example today, as NSW nurses and midwives fight for a pay rise that keeps up with inflation after enduring two years of pandemic conditions.[162] A concerted working-class fightback has the potential to radically reshape health care for the better.

References

Australian Bureau of Statistics 2022, "Understanding the Different Approaches to Reporting Health Expenditure in Australia", 28 February. https://www.abs.gov.au/statistics/research/understanding-different-approaches-reporting-health-expenditure-australia

Australian Institute of Health and Welfare 2021, "Health Expenditure Australia 2019–20". https://www.aihw.gov.au/reports/health-welfare-expenditure/health-expenditure-australia-2019-20/

Australian Labor Party 1942, "Platform and Objective: As amended by Federal Conference held at Canberra, May, 1939", *Worker (Brisbane)*, 29 June. http://nla.gov.au/nla.news-article71446474

Australian Nursing and Midwifery Federation (Victorian Branch) 2016, "The 1986 50-day Victorian nurses and midwives strike" (online exhibit). https://stories.anmfvic.asn.au/86strike/

Australian Prudential Regulation Authority 2022, "Quarterly Private Health Insurance Statistics: March 2022", 25 May. https://www.apra.gov.au/sites/default/files/2022-05/Quarterly%20Private%20Health%20Insurance%20Statistics%20March%202022.pdf

Biggs, Amanda 2016, "Medicare: A quick guide", *Parliamentary Library Research Paper Series 2016–17*, 12 July. https://parlinfo.aph.gov.au/parlInfo/download/library/prspub/4687808/upload_binary/4687808.pdf

Biggs, Amanda and Lauren Cook 2018, "Health in Australia: A quick guide", *Parliamentary Library Research Paper Series 2018–19*, 31 August. https://parlinfo.aph.gov.au/parlInfo/download/library/prspub/6180529/upload_binary/6180529.pdf

Boxall, Anne-marie and James A Gillespie 2013, *Making Medicare: The Politics of Universal Health Care in Australia*, UNSW Press.

Bramble, Tom and Rick Kuhn 2011, *Labor's Conflict: Big business, workers and the politics of class*, Cambridge University Press.

Bramble, Tom 2018, "Our unions in crisis: How did it come to this?", *Marxist Left Review*, 15, Summer, pp.1–59. https://marxistleftreview.org/?issue-number=15

---

162. Rafferty 2022.

Cass, Moss 1964, *A National Health Scheme for Labour*, Fabian Society, Melbourne.

Communist Party of Australia 1948, "Who is Robbing You of Free Medicine?", Sydney.

Cooke, Jenny 1985, "Six-day wait to have jaw wired", *Sydney Morning Herald*, 1 February, p.5.

Crichton, Anne 1990, *Slowly Taking Control? Australian governments and health care provision 1788–1988*, Allen & Unwin.

Crisp, LF 1961, *Ben Chifley: A biography*, Longmans.

Donn, Clifford B 1979, "The ACTU, Trade Union Congresses, and Nation-Wide General Strikes", *Labour History*, 37, November, pp.78–85.

Gardner, Heather and Brigid McCoppin 1987, "The Politicisation of Australian Nurses: Victoria 1984–1986", *Politics*, 22 (1), pp.19–34.

Gillespie, James A 1991, *The Price of Health: Australian governments and medical politics 1910–1960*, Cambridge University Press.

Gordon, Suzanne, John Buchanan and Tanya Bretherton 2012, *Safety in Numbers: Nurse-to-Patient Ratios and the Future of Health Care*, Cornell University Press.

Gray, Gwendolyn 2004, *The Politics of Medicare: Who gets what, when and how*, UNSW Press.

Griffen-Foley, Bridget 1995, "'Four More Points than Moses': Dr. H.V. Evatt, the Press and the 1944 Referendum", *Labour History*, 68, May, pp.63–79.

Grove, Alex 2016, "The Pharmaceutical Benefits Scheme: A quick guide", *Parliamentary Library Research Paper Series 2015–16*, 7 April. https://parlinfo.aph.gov.au/parlInfo/download/library/prspub/4687808/upload_binary/4687808.pdf

Harris, Margaret and Amanda Buckley 1985, "Govt to encourage private health…", *Sydney Morning Herald*, 28 February, p.3.

Haynes, Mike 2009, "Capitalism, class, health and medicine", *International Socialism*, 123, Summer. http://isj.org.uk/capitalism-class-health-and-medicine/

Holcombe, April 2022, "NSW nurses and midwives lead the way with vote for state–wide strike", *Red Flag*, 11 February. https://redflag.org.au/article/nsw-nurses-and-midwives-lead-way-vote-state-wide-strike

Hunter, JG 1948, "Free Medicine" (Advertising), *Age (Melbourne)*, 1 June, p.3. http://nla.gov.au/nla.news-article206896988

Hunter, Thelma 1965, "Pharmaceutical benefits legislation, 1944–50", *Economic Record*, 41, September, pp.412–25.

Industrial Relations Commission of Victoria 1987, *Registered Nurses Award: no. 1 of 1987*, Victorian Government Printing Office on behalf of the Registrar of the Industrial Relations Commission.

O'Lincoln, Tom 1993, *Years of Rage: Social conflicts in the Fraser era*, Bookmarks Australia.

O'Lincoln, Tom 2011, *Australia's Pacific War: Challenging a national myth*, Interventions.

Rafferty, Chloe 2022, "Nurses' union raises pay claim under pressure from rank and file", *Red Flag*, 26 July. https://redflag.org.au/article/nurses-union-raises-pay-claim-under-pressure-rank-and-file

Ross, Liz 1987, "Sisters are doing it for themselves...and us", *Hecate*, 13 (1), 31 May (subsequently republished as a pamphlet, *Dedication doesn't pay the rent! The story of the 1986 Victorian nurses' strike*, Socialist Action 1987). https://labourhistorycanberra.org/2016/06/dedication-doesnt-pay-the-rent-the-1986-victorian-nurses-strike/#more-1712

Ross, Liz 2020, *Stuff the Accord! Pay Up! Workers' resistance to the ALP-ACTU Accord*, Interventions.

Sax, Sidney 1984, *A Strife of Interests: Politics and policies in Australian health services*, George Allen & Unwin.

Scotton, RB and CR Macdonald 1993, *The Making of Medibank*, School of Health Services Management, University of NSW.

Sheridan, Tom 1989, *Division of Labour: Industrial relations in the Chifley years, 1945–1949*, Oxford University Press.

Stone, Janey 1980, "The Politics of Health Care: Part two", *International Socialist*, 10, pp.20–37. https://www.reasoninrevolt.net.au/objects/pdf/d0513.pdf

Stone, Janey 1985, "No more Florence Nightingale", *Socialist Action*, 3, 1 November, p.5. https://www.reasoninrevolt.net.au/objects/pdf/d0130.pdf

Swerissen, Hal and Stephen Duckett 2002, "Health Policy and Financing", in Heather Gardner and Simon Barraclough (eds), *Health Policy in Australia: Second edition*, Oxford University Press.

Watts, Rob 1987, *The Foundations of the National Welfare State*, Allen & Unwin.

Whitlam, Gough 1985, *The Whitlam Government: 1972–1975*, Penguin Books.

Wilde, Sally 2005, "Serendipity, Doctors and the Australian Constitution", *Health and History*, 7 (1), pp.41–48.

RICK KUHN

Left populism versus revolutionary Marxism: Debating economic strategy in Australia

Rick Kuhn is the author of numerous writings, including the Deutscher Prize-winning book *Henryk Grossman and the recovery of Marxism* and contributions to *Class and struggle in Australia*. He is the editor and one of the translators of the four volumes of *Henryk Grossman Works*, for each of which he has written an introduction.

D URING THE SECOND HALF OF THE 1970S AND EARLY 1980S, there were important debates on the Australian left. Chastened by the Australian Labor Party's defeat in the 1975 elections, the dominant right wing of the party continued to moderate ALP policies, a process which had begun when it was in office. Left-wing union officials, the ALP left and the Communist Party of Australia countered with left reformist, populist policies, embodied in "alternative" economic programs and strategies. According to these analyses, transnational corporations and their allied conservative parties, rather than the capitalist system, were at the root of unemployment and attacks on pay. The solution was to elect a Labor government committed to more radical policies, particularly for the development of domestic manufacturing industry, and backed by union mobilisations. Revolutionary Marxists argued that class and social struggles were the only way to defend workers' interests, which were undermined by any strategy that involves taking responsibility for the health of Australian capitalism.

These debates are the focus of the discussion below. Although there is no significant left reformist current in Australia today, that is unlikely to remain the case. The idea that Australia is being underdeveloped by foreign capital and that "we" need to rebuild Australian manufacturing industry is still widespread. It is still pushed by some unions covering manufacturing workers and, in vague terms, was an element in Labor's campaigning before the 2022 election.[1] And the idea that the left should put up proposals that will make capitalism function better or shut up is very widespread. So the debates of the 1970s and 1980s are relevant today. They were not, however, unique and can be best understood in their historical context.

The following section very briefly traces the history of different left conceptions of Australian capitalism and responses to it. Then the background to and content of left populism after 1975 is examined. The third section summarises the revolutionary Marxist critiques of the alternative strategies. The degeneration of left populism into apologetics for the Hawke Labor government's Prices and Incomes Accord is the subject of the fourth section. In the concluding section changes that have taken place since are discussed.

Early economic controversies in the workers' movement

If the initial reasons for the invasion and colonisation of Australia were strategic and penal, rather than strictly economic, unfree and increasingly free labour was soon creating surplus value for local capitalists and their creditors in Britain. The most lucrative investments generating the most important exports were in primary industries, especially the production of wool. But there were also commercial, construction, manufacturing and local transport industries, if on a small scale, from early in the nineteenth century.

The development of manufacturing industry started to accelerate in the 1870s, expanding the size and influence of the non-mercantile, urban capitalist class, in comparison with pastoral, commercial and financial capitalists. There was enthusiasm within and beyond the labour movement in the following decade for ideas that focused on the control of land. The US political economist Henry George, in his 1879 book *Progress and Poverty*, identified rent derived from private ownership of land as the source of poverty and other social ills, and a "single tax" on it as the means to create prosperity and overcome

---

1. For example, see Murphy 2022; Albanese 2019; and Australian Labor Party 2022.

inequality. The fifth Australian Intercolonial Trade Union Congress in 1888 endorsed this panacea.[2] Like other variants of populism, George's ideas ignored or discounted the contradictory class interests of capitalists and workers and regarded the conflict between just a section of the capitalist class and "the people" as of greatest importance.

Within the labour movement, a pamphlet issued by the Australian Socialist League in 1890 refuted George's analysis, on the basis of a Marxist class analysis. It referred to Marx's analyses of private property and the exploitation of wage labour.[3] Most early Australian socialists from the 1880s, even those familiar with Marx, regarded their goal as state ownership under a parliamentary government dominated by workers' representatives, rather than a different kind of state, like the Paris Commune, which would wither away with the remnants of social class. Others believed that socialism could be achieved gradually by the establishment of cooperatives or were utopians, notably the followers of William Lane who went off to set up a workers' paradise in Paraguay in 1893. But, at least by the end of the nineteenth century, there were some who looked forward to the "abolition of the wages system" and a different means of collectively organising production to the existing form of state.[4]

Parliament, arbitration, protectionism and the "money power"

Trade union officials were decisive in the establishment of the colonial Labor parties and, through affiliated unions, had great influence in their affairs. Founded in the midst of the defeats of the great maritime and shearers' strikes of the early 1890s, the parties were shaped by this period of working-class weakness. During the "Great Depression" of that decade, the urban union movement came close to total collapse. For years the increasingly conservative Australian Workers' Union, which organised rural workers, dominated and in many places effectively was the party. Under these circumstances, the dominant currents in the colonial Labor organisations and, after 1901, in the federal,

---

2. Picard 1953, p.51.
3. Burgmann 1985, p.7. Melbourne anarchists were also critical of George's acceptance of capitalism; Scates 1984, pp.179–80.
4. Burgmann 1985, pp.14, 62, 110, 129.

national party saw parliamentary representation and government action within the framework of Australia's capitalist economy and capitalist state institutions, rather than class struggle, as the means to improve people's, particularly workers', lives. In particular, as a means to achieve class peace, they favoured arbitration of disputes between unions and bosses.[5] This has remained their orientation and they have therefore been dedicated to pursuing the "national interest", not international working-class solidarity. While substantial left currents in the party have had more favourable attitudes to at least some industrial struggles and international causes distasteful to Australian bosses, their orientation has also been essentially parliamentarist and nationalist.

In the 1890s, the Labor parties were not only divided between dominant groups content to ameliorate capitalism, who might call that socialism, and minorities who wanted to achieve socialism, understood as extensive state ownership, by means of reform. There were also major differences in and between the colonial Labor parties on the question of tariff protection.

The promotion of import-substitution industrialisation by means of protective tariffs had begun in Victoria in 1866, especially as a means of employing both capital and labour that would otherwise have been idle after the gold rushes.[6] An important goal of the federation of the Australian colonies in 1901 was the establishment of an internal free trade area, behind uniform tariffs. But governments only began to raise the level of duties, primarily for the purpose of protecting local industries, rather than raising revenue, with the Lyne Tariff of 1908. Tariff barriers were subsequently increased and remained high into the 1980s, supplemented by import quotas during some periods. The attenuation of international trade and the need to produce arms during the two World Wars intensified the process of industrialisation

---

5. The Labor Party was not alone in wanting class peace. The two parties of the Australian capitalist class, which merged to form the Liberal Party in 1909, were keen on arbitration too. The legislation setting up the Court of Conciliation and Arbitration, the predecessor of the Fair Work Commission, was drafted under Alfred Deakin's Protectionist government and passed in 1904 under George Reid's Free Trade government.
6. Wells 1989, pp.89–92.

as a means of expanding the scope for capital accumulation beyond primary production and commerce.

The leader of the capitalist Protectionist Party, Alfred Deakin, had come up with the formula of "new protection", according to which the benefits of protection for manufacturing industry would be shared with workers, through the operation of the Arbitration Court. On that basis, Labor voted for the Lyne Tariff in the parliament. But the new protection legislation of 1906 was overruled by the High Court less than two years later. The ALP, which had itself previously been internally divided over the issue of tariffs, replaced a referendum on the "fiscal question" with the restoration of new protection as a plank in its federal platform just two days after the High Court decision. After two referenda, initiated by Labor governments, failed to open the way to this goal, in 1913 the party's leader Prime Minister Andrew Fisher committed Labor to "effective protection".[7] The fiscal question was controversial within the Liberal Party for a while. But soon both Labor and the main conservative party agreed that protectionism was crucial for the development of Australian capitalism. That consensus lasted sixty years.

From the 1890s through to the 1930s, sections of the labour movement, especially inside the ALP, argued that the "money power", essentially banks and their stooges, was responsible for the suffering of ordinary people. Support for these ideas was associated with working-class defeats during three great social crises: the Depression of the 1890s, World War I and the Depression of the 1930s. The depressions highlighted the role of domestic and imperial financial institutions in the Australian economy. The left populist advocates of money power theory saw in Labor politicians champions of the people, able to counter plots by international financiers and their local allies, and to disempower them, when direct working-class action could not. *Kingdom of Shylock* by federal Labor parliamentarian Frank Anstey, for example, analysed World War I in terms of an international financial conspiracy, an argument continued in his *Money Power* and *Facts and Theories of Finance*.[8]

---

7. Kuhn 1987, pp.97–8.
8. Anstey 1917; Anstey 1921; Anstey 1930. For a detailed discussion see Love 1984 and Kuhn 1985, pp.101–51.

The right-wing NSW Labor leader Jack Lang drew on populist money power rhetoric in his campaign against the emergence of a radical left inside the party, organised in Socialisation Units. He had displayed little concern about the money power during the 1920s but emerged as the main antagonist of the "financial dictators" during the Depression. At a time when workers felt unable to defend their interests through struggle, his slogan "the socialisation of credit" was used to undermine the explicitly anti-capitalist Socialisation Units.[9]

Class peace through arbitration, protectionism, parliamentarism and the populism of money power ideas, all premised on Australian nationalism, were contested. During the 1890s and especially the first two decades of the twentieth century, there were radical socialists in various organisations outside the ALP, notably the Industrial Workers of the World, who rejected Labor's practical acceptance of capitalism. Eventually, these criticisms were integrated with a recognition of the need for a coherent political organisation in the outlook and practice of the Communist Party of Australia, which emerged, belatedly, from the heightened class struggles after World War I. For a few years from the mid-1920s, the CPA, while only a few hundred strong, embodied a consistently Marxist socialism whose goal was the self-emancipation of the working class. It continued the tradition of rejecting the populist notion that particular sections of the capitalist class were more deserving of support or hostility than others.

Hector Ross gently summed up the attitude of Communists and earlier revolutionaries that "the Arbitration Court enables armies of workers to be disciplined and driven back to work under vile conditions pending the decision of over-paid class-biased parasites".[10] The Marxist attitude to the debate between free traders and protectionists was expressed by Mick Considine: "A plague o' both your houses". Although he was never a member of the CPA, he was a veteran of pre-war Marxist groups. Between 1917 and 1922 he was the Labor and then the independent member for Barrier (Broken Hill) in the House of

---

9. Dixson 1977, p.164; Young 1961, pp.295–8, 333; Cooksey 1976, p.71.
10. Ross 1925, p.11. Also see Laidler 1924 [1920].

Representatives. On the floor of the house, in 1921, he summed up the case against protectionism:

> It is over the surplus value that is wrung from the working class in the place where they are exploited that the importers and the manufacturers quarrel, and attempt to use the workers and the political representatives of the workers to aid them in securing their respective share of the plunder for their particular sections.

Protection meant "that one section of workers will make an arrangement with manufacturers for which all other workers will be obliged to pay".[11] In the early 1930s, the Communist Party was particularly concerned to demonstrate that massive increases in tariffs introduced by the Scullin Labor government did not serve workers' interests.

The constraints imposed on Australian governments if they were to abide by the terms of their large international loans drew attention to the capitalist financial system during the Depression of the 1930s, as bank collapses had during the 1890s. Communists and socialists inside the ALP responded to the resulting appeal of money power ideas along the same lines as their critique of protectionism: the basis of capitalism was the extraction of surplus value and workers had an interest in overturning that process rather than siding with industrial capital against bank capital in their dispute over the distribution of the spoils of exploitation.[12]

Hostility to nationalist protectionism and money power populism drew on the internationalism of both the local socialist tradition and the Marxism of the Communist International. In the first issue of the CPA's journal, Esmonde Higgins had argued that "The alternative to the idea of the Empire lies, not in the petty-bourgeois 'cultivation of an Australian sentiment', but in cultivation of the sentiment of the international working class".[13]

---

11. Considine 1921, pp.7886, 7890, 7889.
12. *Workers Weekly* 1931; *Workers Weekly* 1933; Hade 1932, p.2. Hade was a once and future Communist; his article appeared in *Socialisation Call*, the organ of the Socialisation Units, on the left wing of the NSW Labor Party.
13. Higgins 1925.

Popular frontism

Under the influence of the Stalinised Communist International's popular front turn of the mid-1930s, the CPA abandoned internationalism, eventually pursuing an alliance with "progressive" capitalists, ostensibly in the Australian national interest. In the party's now populist analysis, there was still class struggle between capitalists and the workers they exploited. But the main enemy was the "financial oligarchy", "monopolists" or a few "rich families",[14] rather than the capitalist class as a whole. This approach was presented to a wider audience, particularly where Communists had won leadership posts in important unions, including the Miners' Federation, Seamen's Union, Waterside Workers' Federation, Federated Ironworkers' Association and the NSW branch of the Railways Union, during the 1930s. It also displaced money power theories on the left wing of the Labor Party. The forces of Australian Trotskyism, which attempted to maintain the tradition of revolutionary Marxist internationalism, were very slender indeed until the late 1960s.

The long economic boom after World War II saw further growth of local manufacturing, supported by tariff and quota protection, and a massive program of subsidised immigration. In the promotion of manufacturing industries, these policies encouraged and were complemented by an accelerated flow of capital from abroad. A greater proportion of this flow now took the form of direct investment, as opposed to private and especially government borrowing.[15] The main source shifted from Britain to the United States. The "defence" alliance between Australia and the USA, the world's greatest military as well as economic power, likewise came to overshadow relations with Britain.

Despite major setbacks during the late 1940s and early 1950s, Communists continued to be elected onto the leaderships of some powerful unions into the 1980s. In the context of the Cold War

---

14. For example Sharkey 1937; Rawling 1937; Communist Party of Australia (CPA) 1938; Fox 1940; Campbell 1963. See Kuhn 1985, pp.164–83 for a detailed account of the Communist Party's approach between 1934 and 1950.
15. Maddock 2015, p.279.

between Russia and the USA, the CPA, still loyal to Moscow, identified monopolists and rich families with US influence. Australia was losing its independence. The country's rulers had become devoted allies, "junior partners" of US imperialism, and the party's perspectives were pervaded by anti-American nationalism. The conservative government of Bob Menzies was not only selling out the Australian national interest to the US but was also jeopardising "the aims of Australian imperialism". Participation in the Vietnam War "lowers Australia's stature to that of a stooge for the US gendarmes".[16]

A section of the Communist Party's membership departed to join the Beijing-aligned Communist Party of Australia (Marxist-Leninist) in the split of 1964. Its members led the Victorian branches of the Builders' Labourers Federation and the Waterside Workers' Federation in the 1970s. The CPA(ML) was particularly strident in its own brand of Australian nationalism and explicitly sought to enrol the "national bourgeoisie" in the cause of Australian independence.[17] Unlike the Communist Party, its perspective was a revolutionary rather than reformist nationalism: US influence was so great that Australia had already lost its independence and needed a national revolution.[18] The sect's appeal rapidly declined after it shifted its emphasis to denouncing "Soviet social imperialism" as the breeze from Beijing changed following détente between China and the US in 1973.

The Communist preoccupation with monopolies and US influence after World War II overlapped with more statistically inclined studies of ownership and the influence of foreign capital in Australia during the late 1950s and early 1960s by the Sydney University economist and Labor Party supporter Ted Wheelwright.[19] Together with Brian Fitzpatrick, who had written influential left-wing histories of Australia, he published *The Highest Bidder*

---

16. Aarons 1963. Also see CPA 1958, pp.28–30, 50, 57; CPA 1964, pp.5, 16–18; Jones 1964, p.98; Robertson 1965a, p.74; Robertson 1965b, p.164.
17. CPA (Marxist–Leninist) 1976. Also see, for example, Hill 1973, p.134.
18. For a later expression of this perspective, with its combination of an emphasis on Australian ownership and revolution, see McQueen 1982, especially pp.85 and 229.
19. For example Wheelwright 1957; Wheelwright 1963. For these concerns in the parliamentary Labor Party see, for example, Peters 1968.

in 1965. It was a pivotal book in the history of Australian left populism. With its critique of the "subordinacy of our economy to foreign decision-makers", the book provided a manual of staple arguments which served left nationalists for two decades. Wheelwright and Fitzpatrick contended that Australia had become more vulnerable to restrictions of capital outflows from other countries. Multinational (later the term "transnational" was often preferred) corporations might also limit the flow of technology to Australia and exports by their Australian subsidiaries; avoid local taxation; damage the balance of trade through transfer pricing; and create local monopolies, which would be harder for workers to deal with. At the same time they squeezed Australian capital out from profitable investment opportunities. And their profits were repatriated. Foreign capital also influenced Australian politics and culture. Indeed, there was "little difference between the situation of Australia and that of poor, undeveloped countries". Public ownership was therefore necessary, although it might not extend to all large, Australian-owned enterprises.[20]

Fitzpatrick and Wheelwright regarded Australian capitalists as a decisive element among the forces which could implement their economic nationalist program. The book was couched as a plea to Australian bosses. The class structure portrayed in their analysis counterposed the Australian people (apart from a few allies of multinational corporations) to foreign capital, which "has been allowed to construct a gigantic pump for sucking up the cream of our industrial production".[21] Left populist rhetoric now identified multinational corporations, rather than monopolies, as the source of Australia's ills.

The very small numbers of Trotskyists in Australia in the 1960s were critical of the CPA's populism and nationalism. As a consequence they could recognise that Labor and conservative Australian governments pursued the interests of locally based capital, while conservative politicians were not simply puppets of the US. Their rejection of both nationalism and the idea that socialists should be concerned about

---
20. Fitzpatrick and Wheelwright 1965, pp.33, 15, 157–8.
21. Fitzpatrick and Wheelwright 1965, p.167.

Australian independence was distinctive on the left[22] and soon found a wider, though far from mass audience.

The rising level of social struggle, especially the movement against the Vietnam War and industrial action by increasingly militant workers, in the context of the booming economy, revived the far left. By the early 1970s, the most successful Trotskyist group was growing and ambiguously moving towards an understanding of the Australian ruling class as an imperialist actor in its own right. The Socialist Youth Alliance's newspaper declared that Australia was a "client of US imperialism" but, "Where Australian capitalism's own interests coincide with those of the United States it seizes the opportunity to have these interests defended by the greater imperialist power for the minor price of a token military and moral involvement in the struggle".[23] There were other Marxist critics of left nationalism. They demonstrated the consequences of Stalinism for the understanding of class in Australian history and the connection between nationalism and imperialism, and particularly the ALP's imperialist policies for Asia. The journal *Intervention*, associated with the "Left Tendency" in the CPA, carried material critical of nationalism, including a classic anti-nationalist "interview" with the cartoon koala Blinky Bill. One of the new Marxist left's notable products was the history of Australia's class structure by Bob Connell and Terry Irving.[24]

---

22. Australian Section of the Fourth International 1965, pp.2, 5, 3; Freney 1969; Dixon 1967, p.9. Ivan Dixon was a collective pseudonym used by people involved in the Socialist Perspective group, including Bob Gould and Roger Barnes. In 1966, their organisation, which was now the Australian Section of the Unified Secretariat of the Fourth International, had broken from the International group, which had previously been the Australian Section. On this phase of the history of Trotskyism in Australia see Greenland 1998, pp.227–37.
23. Direct Action 1971, p.10. On the other hand, a year later, in the journal of the organisation's successor it was argued that the Australian bourgeoisie was moribund, Dixon 1972; similarly, from a different Trotskyist current, Workers' Action (succeeded by the Socialist Labour League), Sandford 1971.
24. Berzins and Irving 1970; Rowley 1971; "T.T." 1977; Connell and Irving 1980. On the Left Tendency see O'Lincoln 1985, pp.153–56.

Left populism after Whitlam

Mainstream economists and elements of the Australian public service argued that government policy should promote the competitiveness of domestic industry rather than just protect it at the expense of other sectors.[25] The Whitlam government, from December 1972, took some steps in this direction. But, in the face of the deep recession of the 1970s, the shift to lower rates of protection slowed down. The ALP increased protection for the car industry. It also backed the wage indexation system introduced by the Arbitration Commission to restrain workers' pay, in the context of high inflation. The expenditure cuts in the government's final budget, introduced by Treasurer Bill Hayden in 1975, was justified in terms of monetarist economic theory, an ancestor of neoliberal doctrines.

The conservative government of Malcolm Fraser, placed in office by the constitutional coup of 1975 which dismissed the Whitlam government, went even further in supporting the profits of car makers and also textiles, clothing and footwear manufacturers, that were likewise already highly protected, by means of quotas and higher tariffs. Fraser's government trumpeted the virtues of free markets but its achievements in this area were limited. By 1982/83 average rates of assistance to manufacturing had actually increased, compared with 1976/77.[26] Yet the end of the long post-war boom and the onset of the deep recession of the mid 1970s had raised the costs of protectionist policies and made them even more burdensome for the capitalist class as a whole.

Although it engaged in robust denunciations of "union intimidation",[27] ultimately the industrial relations record of Fraser's government was no better in the eyes of Australia's bosses. The Fraser years saw some intense fights by workers and the oppressed with the federal and conservative state governments, and employers.[28] Titanic by the standards of the following four decades, the level of class struggle in this period was nevertheless significantly lower than during the late 1960s

---

25. For example, Rattigan 1986, p.25.
26. Emmery 1999, figure 1.
27. Fraser 1981. Also see Liberal Party Federal Secretariat 1980.
28. See O'Lincoln 1993. This first edition, unlike the otherwise essentially identical 2012 second edition, included footnotes.

and early 1970s. Many workers became warier about taking industrial action in the face of punitive government policies, especially during the recession of the mid-1970s, with unemployment higher than at any time since the 1930s. But between 1979 and 1981, during a mining boom which had lowered unemployment, there was a strike wave, peaking at an annual level of almost 800 strike days per thousand workers.[29]

The mainstream of the ALP, with the parliamentary party leading the way, responded to the defeat of 1975 by moderating its policies. In other words, by abandoning its enthusiasm for reforms and admitting that "the Whitlam government had tried to go too far, too fast". The 1977 ALP Conference approved an economic platform whose short-term policy section twice emphasised the importance of the money supply, the touchstone of monetarist thought.[30]

There was resistance. Between 1975 and 1978, major workplace confrontations took place over mass sackings at Chrysler in Adelaide, as well as at the Newcastle and Whyalla shipyards, and over management efforts to increase the pace of work more generally. But they ended in defeats. This led to a turn to politics in the class struggle, with industrial action not only over Medibank in 1976, but also against the export of uranium in 1977, to prevent the construction of the environmentally dangerous Newport power station in Melbourne and in support of the Queensland civil liberties movement in 1977 and 1978.

The turn to politics took other forms. Some combined class analysis and the illusion that Labor could reform Australia into socialism.[31] But the most widespread response to the economic crisis and Whitlam's dismissal in the labour movement was the populist, left reformist alternatives offered by the Communist Party and those in its orbit, the powerful Amalgamated Metal Workers and Shipwrights Union (AMWU)[32] and sections of the Labor left. In the left nationalist tradition, they blamed transnational corporations and their influence

---

29. Bramble 2008, pp.7, 70, 101, 110–13.
30. Australian Labor Party 1977, p. 13.
31. For example Connell 1978; Higgins 1978; Higgins 1979; Theophanous 1980, pp.380–2; Stilwell 1982; Hopkins and Curtain 1982.
32. The union participated in a series of amalgamations and is now part of the Australian Manufacturing Workers Union. For the sake of brevity, its various incarnations are referred to here as the AMWU.

on conservative governments, subordinate to the United States, for problems workers faced. The solution was to build the influence of left unions and elect a Labor government committed to a "progressive" approach to Australian economic development, formulated and implemented in association with the union movement. That approach would include the nationalisation of some corporations and would be in the interests not only of the working class but also small and medium-sized enterprises, especially in manufacturing.

The AMWU, in which the CPA was still influential, was at the forefront of the campaign around these ideas and issued a series of publications to publicise them. In 1976 the Victorian branch of the union issued a *People's Budget*. Pretty tame in its proposals, it espoused essentially orthodox Keynesian economics and called for a reflationary deficit, involving increased social welfare expenditure and public works, to overcome unemployment. The pamphlet argued that taxation of the wealthy and corporations should be increased, indirect taxes reduced; and the 35-hour week brought in. The politics involved can be summed up in the far from radical assertion that "Many economists argue that a deficit which fosters consumer spending would bring about an economic recovery strong enough to counteract the effects of the deficit".[33]

The arguments in the *People's Budget* did not offer a coherent analysis of the Australian economy's problems or practical solutions. Its framework was outmoded. By the mid-1970s all but the blindest observers of the world's economy accepted that the old Keynesian verities were about as useful as a professional economist at a lathe. The publication presented "alternative" policies as a way to restore capitalism's health. Nevertheless the *People's Budget* was an attempt to present a real critique of Fraser's cuts, more hard-hitting than that of the weak-kneed Labor opposition. The promise it held out for restoring the Australian economy within the framework of capitalism was to be a hallmark of subsequent alternative economic proposals.

In 1977 the AMWU's national office produced *Australia Uprooted*, a very professional, mass distribution pamphlet. Although the

---

33. See, for example O'Shaughnessy 1976, on the relationship between "economic" and "political" class struggle.

arguments were crude, it offered a much more comprehensive analysis of Australian capitalism than the *People's Budget*, reinvigorating the left populist tradition. The problem with the Australian economy, it argued, was the influence of the multinational corporations whose unregulated activities were also responsible for the international crisis of capitalism. Fraser's program was to restore profits at the expense of wages and public spending. He wanted to turn Australia into a quarry, allowing the multinationals to destroy Australian manufacturing industry. All of these things had to be fought. The AMWU officials put proposals for a "People's Economic Program" to the ACTU and ALP conferences of 1977, noting that "They are a departure from limited traditional alternatives precisely because experience of 1973-75 showed how vulnerable such limitations are".[34]

To achieve full employment, environmental protection and balanced economic development, corporations should be nationalised, so that the parliament could again effectively determine economic policy. "Democratic principles in work relations" should be introduced into the public sector. Interest rates, foreign investment and credit should be more tightly controlled; the taxation system should be made more progressive and government should provide assistance to small and medium-sized businesses. Industry should be restructured under government direction, by means such as the use of public funds to update equipment, tariffs and quotas. *Australia Uprooted* also affirmed that the People's Economic Program "needs to be developed in conjunction with the struggles and involvement of the people which will inevitably arise from the impact of the policies of the Fraser Government!"

The ALP did not adopt the People's Economic Program. But the mainstream left persisted with the approach and many justified it as a transitional strategy to achieve socialism, around which a mass movement could develop. A prominent proponent was Laurie Carmichael, in 1977 national president of the CPA and assistant national secretary of the AMWU.[35] Later versions of the alternative economic

---

34. Amalgamated Metal Workers' and Shipwrights' Union (AMWSU) 1977, p.18.
35. For Carmichael's views see Carmichael 1975; Carmichael 1977; and Carmichael 1980b. The CPA and the AMWU had very similar positions; see the programmatic CPA 1977b.

strategy filled in the details and added subtlety, but *Australia Uprooted* contained all the essentials of a left populism that had widespread currency into the 1980s: nationalisations, collaboration with some sections of business, conspiracy theory, nationalism, verbal endorsement of class struggle and especially strong, explicit support for the election of a Labor government.

The alternative economic strategy approach in Australia was, in part, inspired by the British academic Stuart Holland's concept of a "revolutionary reform".[36] It looked like a more radical version of the policy package advocated by Jeremy Corbyn when he led the British Labour Party between 2015 and 2020. In both, the assumption was that the key to progressive change was the election to office of a social democratic party with radical policies. Certainly they paid lip service to mass action, but their approach was in practice counterposed to an orientation of bringing about change through workers' own struggles against bosses and governments.

Communists still acknowledged that workers' fights to defend jobs, wages and conditions were important. But the CPA retreated from previous efforts to ride the wave of radicalisation among students and workers. Towards the end of its shift to the left, the party's journal *Australian Left Review* had observed of one of Whitlam's most left-wing ministers: "[Jim] Cairns is arguing that workers and socialists should help solve capitalism's crises then raise the struggle for a socialist solution when the system has recovered – clearly a futile exercise".[37] That ceased to be the party's perspective, as it reaffirmed its earlier left populist outlook.

The views expressed in *Australia Uprooted* reflected the interests of a section of the trade union bureaucracy which shared ways of thinking and overlapped in membership with the Labor left and CPA. Ultimately, they and other officials owe their positions to capitalism, a system where wage labour is a commodity. Unions are organisations whose main function is wholesaling that commodity, negotiating its

---

36. For example, Carmichael 1977, p.47; Connell 1980, p.290; Stilwell 1982.
37. *Australian Left Review* 1975, p.4. Also see the revolutionary rhetoric in an official party document in 1974, CPA 1977a, p.45. For the CPA's trajectory in this period see O'Lincoln 1985, pp.139–65.

price and conditions of sale. They are essential for the defence and improvement of wages and conditions, but their purpose is struggle within the system rather than against it. Union officials are, primarily, managers. Their jobs usually provide them with better pay and working conditions than those of the rank and file. To keep control over their organisations and to hold onto their jobs they have to balance between their members and employers, trying to maintain credibility with both. With the members who elect them, that they can defend and even improve pay and conditions. With the employers who are the other party in negotiations, that they are in control and can enforce agreements by avoiding, containing or repressing rank-and-file dissent. So both outbreaks of independent rank-and-file action and employers' attacks are a threat to union officials.[38]

A particular stage in the balancing act of left union officials, those more open to pressure from their members, and their political supporters, was the context for *Australia Uprooted* and the alternative economic strategies of the late 1970s and early 1980s. Nationalism, common to the mainstream left's economic thought before and since, expressed their practical acceptance of capitalism. Verbal endorsement of the class struggle reflected a recognition that, despite the decline in militancy after 1975, there were still large numbers of well-organised workers in Australia capable of taking concerted industrial action, independently of the officials if necessary.

After the publication of *Australia Uprooted*, a variety of discussions and publications, mainly by people in the Labor left or Communist Party, developed the idea of alternative economic strategies by means of which a Labor government, under pressure from below, could legislate socialism into existence. In a workshop paper Roger Jowett, a research officer of the Australian Railways Union (later general secretary of its successor) summed up the approach. On the job struggles by workers, he argued, had to be an important part of a Labor strategy. But Jowett articulated union officials' accommodation to the wage indexation system, when he asserted that the ability of wages struggles to "mobilise, unite and educate workers" was questionable: after all,

---

38. For a more detailed account of the nature of the union bureaucracy see Cliff and Gluckstein 1986, chapters 2 and 3.

wages had not even been mentioned at the last ACTU Congress. Instead workers had to take the offensive with their own plans and to engage in the "progressive conquest of power",[39] which entailed making capitalism operate as efficiently as possible.

Australia Ripped Off, produced in late 1978 as a sequel to *Australia Uprooted*, offered a convincing analysis of the nature of income and wealth distribution in Australia, including a brief exposition of the labour theory of value. Having failed to get the ACTU and ALP to adopt the AMWU's modest proposals, it laid somewhat greater stress on mass action, including organisation on the job over technology, redundancies and shorter hours. But not, despite the pamphlet's convincing account of income and wealth inequality in Australia, pay. Its explanations of the problems faced by workers was populist: multinationals and the Fraser government were responsible. "The rules of this economic game are set by the largest corporations and the few thousand Australians who control them." And the message that workers would be saved by a Labor government was conveyed with sledge-hammer subtlety by quotations from then ALP leader (and later top-hatted conservative governor general) Bill Hayden strewn throughout. This was repeated in the pamphlet's 1982, pre-election successor, *Australia on the Rack*.[40]

As economic recovery and the mining boom of the late 1970s and early 1980s improved the bargaining power of the unions, the rank and file put pressure on the AMWU leaders for action to improve their living standards. The union officials preferred a decentralised hours campaign, which did not contravene the indexation guidelines, to a combined assault on hours and wages. Carmichael made clear the role of the hours campaign as a safety valve to save wage indexation:

> Diversions will inevitably be encountered and it must be assumed that there will be deliberately sponsored diversions. Probably wage demands will be more complex to handle as we progress through the campaign. Only most careful but insistent efforts will ensure that the shorter hours issue remains as the highest priority![41]

---

39. Jowett 1978.
40. AMWSU 1978, pp.11, 20, 46; AMWSU 1982.
41. Carmichael 1980a, p.16.

The resources boom also gave populist arguments about the sway of transnational mining corporations an added veneer of credibility. In 1982, Wheelwright and Greg Crough argued that because the Australian bourgeoisie could not protect its own interests against transnational corporations, the ALP and unions had to build up local industry and, in the process, build socialism.[42]

At its 1979 Congress the CPA essentially adopted the alternative economic strategy, affirming that parliamentary "left governments" would be central to the transition to socialism. Struggles over wages were important, but were defensive and workers needed to fight around alternative plans for their industries.[43] As late as 1981 the CPA could still affirm that "'Social contracts', deals between employers and unions regulated by Government and which restrict workers' rights to fight for a better deal must be resisted".[44]

But this soon changed.

The real alternative

Elements within the new Marxist left oriented to the Communist Party. Terry O'Shaughnessy, for example, discussed the politics of the transition away from the strategy of import substitution industrialisation in Australia and pointed out that, contrary to the dominant CPA/AMWU argument, Fraser was "not presiding over the wholesale dismantling of manufacturing".[45] But after the left inside the CPA was defeated in 1976, its prominent protagonists generally faded from the fray or moved to the right with the party.[46]

Other organisations in the Trotskyist tradition were more enduring vehicles for internationalist class analysis than the dead-end of the Communist Party. They continued to provide alternative Marxist accounts of the Australian economy and critiques of left populism into the 1980s and beyond. Their emphasis on class struggle against

---

42. Their most sustained popular argument is in Crough and Wheelwright 1982. Also see Crough 1975; Catley and McFarlane 1981.
43. CPA 1979, pp.46, 49.
44. CPA 1981, p.15. Also see Carmichael 1980b, p.243; *Australian Left Review* 1981.
45. O'Shaughnessy 1978, pp.52, 54. Also see Game and Pringle 1978, for a critique of Carmichael.
46. O'Lincoln 1985, p.156.

oppression and exploitation, on internationalism, meaning hostility to the "Australian national interest", and on revolution distinguished them from other currents on the left.

In 1979, citing the scope of Australia's manufacturing industry, high living standards and imperialist policies, as well as the support of the Australian bourgeoisie for investment from abroad, Jon West of the Socialist Workers Party (SWP, descended from the Socialist Youth Alliance and a predecessor of both Socialist Alliance and Socialist Alternative) contested the notion that Australia was a neo-colony. Australian-based enterprises, he pointed out, are just as likely to sack workers and move operations off-shore as foreign owned corporations. Protectionism is not only an unreliable way of saving jobs, especially in the face of economic crises and technological change, it is also imposed at the expense of workers in other countries, fuels inflation and is a false "substitute for a class struggle approach" to defending pay, conditions and jobs. Crucially, "The Australian bourgeoisie retains firm control of the apparatuses of the Australian state and utilises these apparatuses for its own advancement and defence". So "the labour movement needs to break away from seeing its interests as linked to those of the capitalist class", whether embodied in free trade or protectionist policies. Australia was "a medium sized imperialist power".[47]

Tom O'Lincoln, of the International Socialists (IS, a predecessor of Socialist Alternative), argued in 1980 that Australia was "an independent spearhead and springboard for the great powers". This conclusion was justified with reference to the history of Australia's relationships with Britain and then the USA. Drawing on a mainstream newspaper article about Menzies and the Vietnam War, he pointed out that:

> The pattern of Australia as more hawkish than the great powers is perhaps clearest in the case of Vietnam. Left nationalists are fond of attacking US imperialism for dragging this country into the war. But the truth is that Australia did a fair bit of dragging itself.

---

47. West 1979b, pp.62, 67. West 1979a, pp.28–9, 41. Also see Kieg 1977; Lorimer 1977; Socialist Workers Party 1977, pp.65, 161.

Subsequent research demonstrated not only that the Australian government was keen to draw the United States deeper into the conflict but also contrived to have Australia invited to participate, to this end, by the South Vietnamese government.[48]

O'Lincoln attempted to distinguish his analysis from that of the larger and more orthodoxly Trotskyist SWP. Australian nationalism should be opposed because the country was not oppressed. The argument that it was had some plausibility because of the substantial presence of US corporations in Australia and the obsequious behaviour of Liberal politicians in the presence of their US counterparts. But Australia was not "an imperialist power in its own right", because of its alliances with Britain and then the USA.[49] In essence, his position was, nevertheless, the same as West's. Earlier, O'Lincoln himself had, if briefly, identified Australia as straightforwardly imperialist. The IS's successor organisations did likewise, sometimes at greater length and with greater attention to capital exports from Australia, and O'Lincoln's own 2014 *The Neighbour from Hell* was subtitled *Two Centuries of Australian Imperialism*.[50] Other states, ranging from Britain, France and Germany to Canada, the Netherlands and Belgium were and are similarly small imperialist states in alliance with the USA.

Like West, a couple of years later, I attacked the left nationalist contention that transnational corporations and the Fraser government were determined to deindustrialise Australia, in *International Socialist* (a predecessor of *Marxist Left Review*) and the *Journal of Australia Political Economy*.[51] The left reformist proposals, I accepted, addressed real problems faced by workers: employment insecurity, low pay, cuts in the social system and attacks by the government. But they were false solutions. During the 1970s declines in manufacturing were less due to changes in levels of protection than the end of the long post-World War II boom and technological changes with increasing economies of scale, which undermined the competitiveness

---

48. O'Lincoln 1980, p.44. Sexton 2002 (first edition 1981); Pemberton 1987.
49. O'Lincoln 1980, p.43.
50. O'Lincoln 1978 [1977], p.13, identified "the ugly face of imperialism" in Australian military ventures. Later: *Battler* 1981; Emerson 1988; O'Lincoln 1991, O'Lincoln 2014.
51. This and the following three paragraphs summarise the arguments in Kuhn 1981–2 and Kuhn 1982.

and relative efficiency of some Australian manufacturing industries. Import controls are also an unreliable means of securing local jobs because they can prompt other countries to retaliate in kind, reducing markets for Australian exports. Declining shares of manufacturing in national economic activity were also characteristic of developed countries. And, it is worth adding today, Australia is a developed country, on the fundamental criterion of the level of accumulated capital per worker across the economy. Furthermore, it was not Fraser but the *Labor* governments of the 1980s and 1990s which took the first systematic steps to reduce protection and adopt an approach to Australian capitalist development that departed from the strategy of import substitution industrialisation.

Protectionism is not simply a matter of redistributing income from protected to unprotected sectors. It is a class question too. It also transfers income from consumers, including workers, who pay higher prices for imported products, particularly to bosses in protected industries. It was, moreover, primarily transnational corporations manufacturing in Australia which benefited from the tariffs and quotas on car imports. The extent to which pay is good or bad in protected industries, as elsewhere, is mainly determined by workers' ability to extract higher wages from employers through industrial struggle.

The logic of the left nationalist approach was apparent in the middle of 1980 when General Motors Holden decided to close its Pagewood plant in Sydney, where about 1,500 highly protected jobs were at stake. Officials from both the right-wing Vehicle Builders' and the left-wing Metal Workers' unions were united in arguing that the fight was over the level of redundancy pay and in heading off a militant struggle. But there were shop stewards who wanted the workers to occupy the factory over demands for nationalisation and no redundancies. The unions' tacit acknowledgement that concern about employers' profitability should be shared by workers – the identification with the employer's interests inherent in supporting protectionism – undermined struggles against redundancies on the ground that an enterprise was not profitable.

Like traditional reformist socialism, which still had adherents and did not regard some sections of the capitalist class as potential allies, the alternative economic strategies all hinged on fundamental change coming through parliament. Both approaches made a series of utopian assumptions, each less likely than the previous one, in comparison with the strategy of workers' revolution. These were that a powerful left wing can win control of the Labor Party; the party can win control of parliament; a Labor government can succeed in implementing its policies in full, without being sabotaged by the Labor right, the unelected parts of the state (governor general, armed forces, public service and courts) or the responses of capitalists to the resulting erosion of their ability to make profits. The repertoire of such responses, used to discipline the far from radical governments of Ben Chifley in the late 1940s and Whitlam, it can be added, includes media and organisational mobilisations, and investment strikes.

Both the SWP and IS were convinced that a revolutionary socialist strategy was more plausible than the "alternative strategies" they criticised. They also agreed that a successful workers' revolution depended on the existence of a mass, socialist party, which was based in the working class. Under the leadership of such a party, the working class could smash the Australian capitalist state.[52] Despite their differences on a series of questions, notably their analyses of Stalinist and third world nationalist states, and the nature of the trade union bureaucracy, they were both attempting to promote the emergence of a revolutionary party.

Later, in *Militancy Uprooted*, I developed these criticisms and noted that one of their advocates, Bruce Hartnett, an ACTU official and ALP member, had identified where their weakness lay: "A socialist strategy for Australia...must include, firstly, an alternative economic programme which is realistic, credible and achievable".[53] But such an alternative economic program to achieve sustained full employment and rising living standards was unachievable under capitalism. The capitalist imperative of accumulation, replacing living with dead labour, necessarily leads to recurrent crises. It is workers and not machines who create new wealth. In the medium to long term, employers spend more and more on equipment compared to outlays on

---

52. For example, Socialist Workers Party 1977, p.169; Kuhn 1982, p.93.
53. Hartnett 1980, p.252; Kuhn 1986, p.10.

wages and there is consequently a tendency for the rate of profit to fall. Australia is, moreover, inextricably involved in the international organisation of production and exchange. Attempts to withdraw from the world economy can only lead to lower living standards. The alternative economic strategies did not come to terms with Australia's necessary economic relationships with the rest of the world. Instead, they attributed most of Australia's problems to conspiracies by transnational corporations rather than the reality of international accumulation, production and exchange.

Australian workers' living standards, I argued, are heavily and, given the small size of the population, unavoidably dependent on international trade. The importation of a wide range of commodities, from raw materials and machine tools to much of our clothing, not only sustains local industry but also our personal comfort. Attempts to solve unemployment by eliminating these imports can only result in an inferior quality of life, and would still fail to eliminate the cause of unemployment in the dependence of production on the rate of profit. Additional measures of protection would both raise the cost of protected goods and risk retaliation against the country's mainly primary exports, leading to further declines in living standards.

Investments from abroad have long expanded the scope of Australian industry and employment. To survive without infusions of overseas capital while industry and employment are maintained would require an increase in the social rate of savings. That is, the amount available for workers to consume would have to be cut. This would especially be the case as capital equipment, produced by protected local industries, would be more expensive than imported capital goods. Any strategy, no matter how much nationalisation it involves, which fails to confront and challenge this reality could not be realistic or credible, let alone achievable.

The most positive element in the alternative economic strategies was their insistence that struggles outside parliament, including industrial action on the shop floor and mobilisations in the streets, were important. At least the reformist left still endorsed the progressive nature of class struggle, even, at a pinch, struggles over "economic" issues. But other *key* features of the strategies worked in the opposite direction. Theories about multinational corporate conspiracies were associated with the idea that there was scope for collaboration with Australian bosses. The nationalist defence of the manufacturing industry established a further common interest with sections of the bourgeoisie.[54] The strategies' reliance on a left parliamentary government, whatever qualifications were made, offered a substitute for working-class action. For union officials the *development* of the strategy could be an alternative to leading struggles around economic questions. But in the absence of such struggles workers were not self-confident enough to fight for more wide-ranging demands embodied in alternative programs, no matter how "open-ended". Eventually the contradiction between endorsement of the class struggle and the other components of the alternative economic strategies could not be sustained. The effects of the recession from 1982 and the class interests of the union bureaucratic elements of the left determined the way in which this contradiction was resolved.

Alternative economic strategy turns into incomes policy

Under the governments of Bob Hawke (1983–90) and Paul Keating (1990–96) the resolution took the form of the Prices and Incomes Accord with the unions.[55] It was the direct descendent of the alternative economic programs. In the rhetoric of left reformists – the ALP left, Communist Party and left union officials – the Accord was not only about workers' conditions, the paid and social wage; it was a path to socialism.[56] In effect between 1983 and 1996, the Accord centralised Australian wage setting, while promising to maintain real wages "over time". It co-opted union officials into the process of industry restructuring, while committing "to a diversified manufacturing sector",

---

54. Carmichael 1980b, p.246 advocated mobilisation "under the leadership of the working class" of "small- and medium-scale business" (which would hardly be attracted by workplace struggles over pay and conditions), among others, in "a counter-strategy to the transnationals".
55. See Kuhn 1993, pp.26–48; Bramble 2008, 124–58; Bramble and Kuhn 2010, pp.104–11; Humphrys 2019, pp.109–66.
56. See, for example, Labor left Senator Arthur Gietzelt 1982, in an ALP organ; CPA 1984; CPA 1985.

no reduction in industry protection "for the foreseeable future" and improvements in the social wage.[57]

The new government's neoliberal fervour put Fraser to shame. One of its first steps was to move away from government efforts to set the exchange rate between the Australian and US dollars, and reduce controls over the financial sector. To facilitate competition, Hawke's government relaxed rules on the ownership of print and electronic media, expediting the expansion of Rupert Murdoch's empire and his domination of the Australian daily press. Labor terminated the "two airline policy" (one privately, one publicly owned) and ended the state-owned monopoly of Telecom (now Telstra) over the telephone/telecommunications network.

In terms of the social wage, Labor expanded "user pays" principles for public services, including, in 1989, the reintroduction of university fees, abolished under Whitlam; and the increasing substitution of compulsory superannuation, funded out of wages, for the state-financed pension. Various government-owned enterprises were turned into corporations, which opened the way to their privatisation. Although the Hawke government had already sold the Williamstown Dockyard in 1987, privatisation of public assets took off in the early 1990s. Out the door went 49.9 percent of Telstra, the Commonwealth Bank, AUSSAT (now Optus), Qantas, the Snowy Mountains Engineering Corporation and the Commonwealth Serum Laboratories (now CSL). State governments got in on the act too. John Howard's conservative Liberal-National government only continued the sell-off. Labor presided over the legislative demolition of industry-wide bargaining over wages and conditions and the introduction of the system of enterprise level negotiations that persists today.

The alternative strategies had been presented as "open-ended". It turned out that this meant they were subject to rightward revision, to accommodate the left nationalists' abandonment of their strategy's most positive feature: a willingness to support, at least verbally, workers' struggles to defend their wages and conditions. With the

---

57. Australian Labor Party and the Australian Council of Trade Unions 1983.

Accord all that remained of the reformist left's principles was reliance on the state and nationalism. Increased state ownership, as a short-term demand, had been ditched. Although the Accord had committed the government to "a diversified manufacturing sector",[58] the Hawke government's policies reflected the orthodox economic prescription that Australia needed more specialised, competitive manufacturing industries. This approach had something to offer Australian capitalism: a degree of rationalisation so that local industry could compete more effectively with overseas competitors. Left nationalists eventually came to accept the (capitalist economic) wisdom of this approach. For a while they maintained their hostility to the multinationals, adapting it to a modified apologetic purpose by contrasting the Labor government's virtuous policies to the evil intentions of foreign corporations.[59]

John Halfpenny, secretary of the AMWU in Victoria and a former Communist, summarised the embrace of the new consensus. Trade unions, he wrote, "want sustainable growth, stable jobs and a wealth creating economy. We want more jobs, and not just any old jobs. We want more wealth so that there is a bigger cake to be distributed in a fair and equitable manner". And, when making a bid for an ALP seat in the Senate, he made clear that this actually meant attacking hard-won conditions of work:

> "Changes in work practices, including the avoidance of demarcation disputes, are vital to assist the development of industry", he said.

> "Unions will encourage and co-operate in the elimination of inappropriate work practices, having regard to the particular circumstances in each plant and workplace."

---

58. Australian Labor Party and the Australian Council of Trade Unions 1983, p.132.
59. See National Metal Trades Union Campaign Committee, Australia on the Brink, March 1985. This publication was a direct descendent of *Australia Uprooted*, but the transformation in the politics of the "left" Metal Workers' union leaders had gone so far that a joint publication on economic policy was now possible with all the metal trades unions, including the right wing Federated Ironworkers' Association.

"…Many workers could be retrained and relocated in the interests of efficiency and quality of production", he said.[60]

There was little discernible difference between this attitude of encouraging workers to identify their interests with those of their bosses and Liberal leader John Howard's comment in his reply to Labor's 1986 budget: "We want workers and employers to get together and agree to get rid of restrictive work practices".[61]

Under the Accord, key advocates of an alternative economic strategy for Australia went over to the emerging, mainstream policy consensus about the way forward for Australian capitalism.[62] *Australia Reconstructed*, the 1987 report of the ACTU/Trade Development Council Mission to Europe, reflected this change among left-wing trade union officials. The left populist diagnosis of the country's problems was nowhere to be seen. Still less mention of class struggle or working-class consciousness. The new strategy focused on the need for local industry to be internationally competitive and saw a positive role for market forces. One of the report's very many recommendations was: "There is an urgent need in the community to develop in Australia a Production Consciousness and culture, both in industry and the community".[63]

The mission was made up of senior trade union officials, from the left and right of the movement, along with Ted Wilshire, the Executive Director of the Trade Development Council's secretariat, and Terry Counihan, also from the TDC secretariat. None of the participants dissented. That the report's title echoed those of the AMWU's publications on economic strategy in the 1970s was no coincidence. Wilshire had been on the team which produced them and made his way via Labor Minister for Trade Lionel Bowen's office into the public service.[64]

---

60. Halfpenny 1986, p.90; Voumard 1986.
61. Howard 1986, p.501.
62. Kuhn 1988, p.110.
63. ACTU/TDC 1987, p.154.
64. Jones 1997, p.17. *Australian Financial Review*, 3 December 1985, pp.1, 4 for Ted Wiltshire's role in educating union officials on the costs of industrial unrest to Australia's export performance.

It is not difficult to establish whose interests the class collaboration embodied in the Accord served.⁶⁵ Critics on the left early pointed out what the main consequences would be.⁶⁶ For the Australian working class, the benefits of the Accord were free retraining opportunities that just those workers made redundant under plans that restructured the steel, car, heavy engineering and textile, clothing and footwear industries could take up; and some limited improvements in the social wage and welfare payments. The limited improvements workers and the poor gained were far outweighed by the costs imposed on them.

The benefits for the capitalist class were far weightier. Without precedent in Australian history, there was no improvement in real wages during the economic recovery of the 1980s. The feat was repeated during the 1990s. Work practices which limited the pace of work and maintained the number of jobs in enterprises were sacrificed to achieve pay rises which just kept up with inflation. The *Australian Financial Review* noticed that at BHP's steelworks, "One continuing problem has been the difficulties of the union management in convincing its rank and file that some entrenched methods of work should be ditched for something as general as industry rationalisation".⁶⁷ The profits share of national income rose, the wages share fell. While the living standards of the bulk of the working class stagnated, income redistribution upwards, to the capitalist class, outbalanced what went down to the poorest, through expansion in health, education and welfare spending. Centralised wage fixing and productivity bargaining led to a severe erosion of workplace union organisation and accelerated declining union density. The reluctance of union officials to spread industrial action to support workers in dispute was decisive in a series of landmark defeats for the movement and victories for employers, at the South East Queensland Electricity Board, Mudginberri abattoir, Dollar Sweets, all in 1985, and the massive Robe River iron ore operation, a bastion of union strength, in 1987.

---

65. For an overview, see Bramble and Kuhn 2010, pp.205–11.
66. McPhillips 1985; Ross, O'Lincoln and Willett 1986; Minns 1988. For accounts of the course and consequences of the Accord see Kuhn 1993; Bramble 2008, pp.125–80; and Humphrys 2019.
67. *Australian Financial Review*, 10 September 1986.

While officials from other unions were complicit, supportive of government action or silent, the militant Builders' Labourers Federation was destroyed in 1986 and a strike by domestic airline pilots broken by the air force in 1989. Both unions had pursued improved pay outside the Accord's provisions.[68]

Most senior union officials also did well out of the Accord. By embracing it, they sold the union movement's birthright – the struggle to defend and improve workers' lot – for a mess of pottage. Those at the top of the union movement supped on a very generous share of the pottage – not just the hefty fees enjoyed by some senior union officials appointed to part-time government offices and industry superannuation funds, but also the enhanced status and public recognition that went along with these posts, photo-ops with ministers, and their role as very junior partners in the management of Australian capitalism, which came in handy when union elections came around.

In left debates over the nature of Australian capitalism and strategy, the arguments of revolutionaries in tiny organisations were overshadowed by those of the much more influential reformist left. Among my first publications, from over forty years ago, and some later ones were contributions to those debates.[69] My broad assessment and criticisms of the developments during the 1970s and 1980s, outlined above, draws heavily on what I wrote then and like my political orientation are little changed. My commitment to both was reinforced by the outcomes of the Accord. If I have, in this sense, been conservative in my views that is not the case for left reformists. For my concluding prediction in *Militancy Uprooted* was wrong.

Lack of discord

In 1986, I argued that disillusionment with the Accord and the Hawke government would probably grow over the next few years and that the left would be reconstituted as a stronger force, more independent of the Labor right. But there was a danger that it could continue to be populist and reformist. In fact, there was no sustained revival of class struggle or the reformist left, even during the long period of

---

68. For overviews of these disputes, see Bramble 2008, pp.135–6, 140–4, 156–7.
69. Kuhn 1981–2; Kuhn 1982; Kuhn 1986; Kuhn 1987; Kuhn 1988.

economic growth after the 1990–92 recession. But the nationalist left's preoccupation with domestic manufacturing industry, earlier shared across the political spectrum to the right, has remained a widespread, common-sense notion.

The reformist left had entered a period of prolonged decline well before upticks in social conflict: against the industrial relations policies of the newly elected conservative government of John Howard in 1996 and again in 2005–6; the attempt to break the Maritime Union by Patricks Stevedores and the government in 1998; the 2000 S11 protests against the World Economic Forum in Melbourne; and movements against the invasions of Afghanistan in 2001 and, featuring the largest demonstrations in Australian history, Iraq in 2002–3. In 1991, after years of stagnation, the CPA had already liquidated itself into the New Left Party, which promptly disappeared, and the SEARCH Foundation, whose front web page now appropriately has a link to "Obituaries".[70] The distinction between left- and right-wing union officials has almost evaporated. Most former left reformists remained true to the Labor Party. Some saw hope in the Greens, which grew and achieved a consistent presence in most Australian parliaments, though unlike Labor, it did not even have a declining organic relationship with the working class. But the big shift in the labour movement was away from any vision of radical social change let alone a "socialism" that is more than a slightly more humane version of capitalism, under which workers' lives improve as the size of the cake increases, not because they win a bigger slice.

The Labor Party and the Labor left continued an uneven shift to the right. Eventually the left of the ALP caught up with the right. Organised left reformism in Australia collapsed. So today there is little to differentiate the Labor left and Labor right except as rival ladders occupied by union officials, politicians, their families, friends and staffers, along with the mates of ambitious university students and graduates, seeking jobs with trade unions, in politicians' offices, on local councils or, at the pinnacle, seats in the parliamentary pastry shops that front the capitalist bakery.

---

70. https://www.search.org.au/.

Left reformist ideas may be in eclipse today but can become influential again, particularly if there is a sustained revival in the level of class struggle. Taking responsibility for the course of Australian capitalism's development has been a defining characteristic of both mainstream and left reformists. By accepting the logic of capitalist profit-making, it is counterposed to workers' interests. The still minuscule far left, mainly embodied in Socialist Alternative today, has fared better than left reformist currents over recent decades. The far left has continued to advocate the combination of the fight for improvements now, to expand workers' share of the cake they produce, with a longer term perspective not of being governmental assistants to capitalist confectioners but of workers' revolutionary takeover of the whole bloody bakery. So, at present, the contrast between the Labor-Liberal consensus about the management of Australian capitalism and the revolutionary alternative is stark and uncomplicated by social democrats with socialist rhetoric who are, ultimately, defenders of capitalism.

References

Aarons, Laurie 1963, "Monopoly & Australia's Foreign Policy (from Report to the March Central Committee meeting)", *Communist Review*, May, pp.156–61.

ACTU/TDC 1987, *Australia Reconstructed: ACTU/TDC Mission to Western Europe*, Canberra.

Albanese, Anthony 2019, "Jobs And The Future Of Work: Vision Statement 1: Address to the Committee for Economic Development of Australia (CEDA), Perth", speech on Tuesday 29 October. https://anthonyalbanese.com.au/media-centre/speech-jobs-and-the-future-of-work-tuesday-29-october-2019

Amalgamated Metal Workers' and Shipwrights' Union (AMWSU) 1977, *Australia Uprooted*, Sydney.

AMWSU 1978, *Australia Ripped Off*, Sydney.

AMWSU 1982, *Australia on the Rack*, Sydney.

Anstey, Frank 1917, *The Kingdom of Shylock*, Labor Call Print, Melbourne.

Anstey, Frank 1921, *Money Power*, Fraser and Jenkinson, Melbourne.

Anstey, Frank 1930, *Facts and Theories of Finance*, Fraser and Jenkinson, Melbourne.

Australian Labor Party 1977, *Platform, Constitution and Rules, as Approved by the 32nd National Conference, Perth 1977.*

Australian Labor Party 2022, "A Future Made in Australia: A plan for good, secure jobs". https://www.alp.org.au/policies/a-future-made-in-australia

Australian Labor Party and the Australian Council of Trade Unions 1983, *Statement of Accord.* https://parlinfo.aph.gov.au/parlInfo/search/display/display.w3p;query=Id%3A%22library%2Fpartypol%2F992745%22

Australian Left Review 1975, "Viewpoint", *Australian Left Review*, 47, July, pp.3–6.

Australian Left Review 1981, "Comment: Resources Boom", *Australian Left Review*, 76, June, pp.2–5.

Australian Section of the Fourth International 1965, "Australia in Imperialist World Strategy and the Tasks of the Revolutionary Marxists (Resolution of conference of the Australian Section of the Fourth International, 11, 12 September, 1965)", *International: Organ of the Australian Section of the Fourth International*, 46, September.

Battler 1981, "Aussie Imperialism Is No Better", *The Battler*, 27 June, p.7.

Berzins, Baiba and Terry Irving 1970, "History and the New Left", in Richard Gordon (ed.), *The Australian new left: critical essays and strategy*, Heinemann, pp.66–94.

Bramble, Tom 2008, *Trade Unionism in Australia: A History from Flood to Ebb Tide*, Cambridge University Press.

Bramble, Tom and Rick Kuhn 2010, *Labor's Conflict: Big business, workers and the politics of class*, Cambridge University Press.

Burgmann, Verity 1985, *"In Our Time": Socialism and the Rise of Labor 1885–1905*, George Allen and Unwin.

Campbell, EW 1963, *The 60 Rich Families Who Own Australia*, Current Book Distributors.

Carmichael, Laurie 1975, "Multinationals and the Crisis", *Australian Left Review*, 48, September, pp.11–16.

Carmichael, Laurie 1977, "A People's Programme", *Intervention*, 9 October, pp.42–53.

Carmichael, Laurie 1980a, "The Campaign for a Shorter Working Week", *Australian Left Review*, 73, March, pp.8–16.

Carmichael, Laurie 1980b, "A Transitional Programme to Socialism", in Greg Crough, Ted Wheelwright and Ted Wiltshire (eds), *Australia and World Capitalism*, Penguin, pp.240–50.

Catley, Bob and Bruce McFarlane 1981, *Australian Capitalism in Boom and Depression*, Alternative Publishing Co-operative.

Cliff, Tony and Donny Gluckstein 1986, *Marxism and Trade Union Struggle: The General Strike of 1926* Bookmarks. https://www.marxists.org/archive/cliff/works/1986/tradeunion/index.htm

Communist Party of Australia (CPA) 1938, *Unite for peace freedom democracy*, Modern Publishers.

CPA 1958, *Report of L.L. Sharkey; Resolution: A Land of Plenty Free from War*, Current Book Distributors.

CPA 1964, *Resolution: 20th Congress, Communist Party of Australia*, D.B. Young, Forest Lodge.

CPA 1977a, [1974], "1974 Congress" in *CPA Documents of the seventies: 1970, 1972, 1974 and 1976 Congress Documents plus A New Course for Australia*, Red Pen Publications.

CPA 1977b, "A New Course for Australia" in *CPA Documents of the seventies: 1970, 1972, 1974 and 1976 Congress Documents plus A New Course for Australia*, Red Pen Publications.

CPA 1979, *Towards Socialism in Australia: Program of the Communist Party of Australia*, Sydney.

CPA 1981, *The Workers' Movement*, Sydney.

CPA 1984, *Socialist Perspective on Issues for the '80s*, Sydney.

CPA 1985, *Australian Socialism: A Proposal for Renewal*, Sydney.

Communist Party of Australia (Marxist-Leninist) 1976, "People's Mass Movement For Independence Grows – Certain To Get Marxist-Leninist Leadership", *The Australian Communist*, 75. https://www.marxists.org/history/erol/australia/ac-75.htm

Connell, RW 1978, *Socialism and Labor*, Labor Praxis Publications.

Connell, RW 1980, "The Transition to Socialism", in Greg Crough, Ted Wheelwright and Ted Wiltshire (eds), *Australia and World Capitalism*, Penguin, pp.289–302.

Connell, RW and TH Irving 1980, *Class Structure in Australian History: Documents, Narrative, and Argument*, Longman Cheshire.

Considine, Michael 1921, *Commonwealth Parliamentary Debates*, 95, 28 April.

Cooksey, Robert 1976, *Lang and Socialism*, Australian National University Press.

Crough, Greg, 1975, "Transnational Corporations and Australian Manufacturing", *Australian Left Review*, 75, September, pp.6–13.

Crough, Greg and Ted Wheelwright 1982, *Australia: A Client State*, Penguin.

Dixon, Ivan 1967, *Socialist Perspective*, 3, May, p.9.

Dixon, Ivan 1972, "A Ruling Class in Decay: The Australian Bourgeoisie and Imperialism", *Socialist Review*, 2 (2), May 1972, p.19.

Dixson, Miriam 1977, *Greater than Lenin? Lang and Labor 1916–1932*, Melbourne Politics Monograph.

Direct Action 1971, "Mass Action and the Anti-war Movement: A Strategy for Socialists", *Direct Action*, May, pp.10–11.

Emerson, Richard 1988, "The New Aussie Imperialists", *Socialist Action*, January, pp.7–9.

Emmery, Michael 1999, "Australian Manufacturing: A Brief History of Industry Policy and Trade Liberalisation", Parliamentary Library Research, Paper 7, 1999–2000. https://www.aph.gov.au/About_Parliament/Parliamentary_Departments/Parliamentary_Library/pubs/rp/rp9900/2000RP07

Fitzpatrick, Brian and EL Wheelwright 1965, *The Highest Bidder*, Lansdowne.

Fox, Len 1940, *Monopoly*, Research Department, Left Book Club.

Fraser, Malcolm 1981, "Speech to the Melbourne Chamber of Commerce", 26 March. https://pmtranscripts.pmc.gov.au/release/transcript-5553

Freney, Dennis 1969, "The Crisis of Australian Imperialism", *International: Organ of the Australian Section of the Fourth International*, 9 (72), September–November, pp.1–4.

Game, Anne and Rosemary Pringle 1978, "Reply to Carmichael", *Intervention*, 10/11 August, pp.107–12.

Gietzelt, Arthur 1982, "Paths to a socialist Australia", *Labor Forum*, 4 (4), December.

Greenland, Hall 1998, *Red Hot: The Life and Times of Nick Origlass*, Wellington Lane Press.

Hade, Matt 1932, *Socialisation Call*, 1 (1), April.

Halfpenny, John 1986, "Union View", in Bureau of Industry Economics, *Revitalising Australian Industry*, Australian Government Publishing Service.

Hartnett, Bruce 1980, "Towards a Counter-Strategy for Labour", in Greg Crough, Ted Wheelwright and Ted Wiltshire (eds) *Australia and World Capitalism*, Penguin, pp.251–6.

Higgins, Esmonde 1925, "The British Empire", *The Communist*, 1, January.

Higgins, Winton 1978, "The Left Social Democratic Challenge", *Intervention*, 10/11, August, pp.87–96.

Higgins, Winton 1979, "Working Class Mobilization and Socialism in Sweden", *Intervention*, 13 October, pp.5–18.

Hill, EF 1973, *Australia's Revolution: On the Struggle for a Marxist-Leninist Communist Party*, Melbourne.

Hopkins, Andrew and Richard Curtain 1982, "The Labour Movement and the Protection versus Restructuring Debate: A Proposal", *Journal of Australian Political Economy*, 12/13, June, pp.74–92.

Howard, John 1986, Commonwealth Parliamentary Debates 150, 21 August, p.501.

Humphrys, Elizabeth 2019, *How Labour Built Neoliberalism: Australia's Accord, the Labour Movement and the Neoliberal Project*, Brill.

Jones, Claude 1964, "Australia and Asia", *Communist Review*, April.

Jones, Evan 1997, "The Background to Australia Reconstructed", *Journal of Australian Political Economy*, 39, June, pp.17–38.

Jowett, Roger 1978, "Labour and the Economy: Towards a Counter Strategy", in *TNC Reportback No. 3: Labour and the Economy*, TransNational Co-operative, Sydney.

Kieg, Nita 1977, "Australian Nationalism: A Reactionary Ideology", *Socialist Worker*, 2, May–June, pp.4–6.

Kuhn, Rick 1981–2, "Whose Boom: Left Nationalism and the Resources Boom" *International Socialist*, 12, Summer, pp.18–30. https://www.reasoninrevolt.net.au/objects/pdf/d0515.pdf

Kuhn, Rick 1982 "Alternative strategies: Left Nationalism and Revolutionary Marxism", *Journal of Australian Political Economy* 12/13, June, pp.93–109, reissued http://dspace.anu.edu.au/handle/1885/47995

Kuhn, Rick 1985, "Paradise on the Instalment Plan: The Economic Thought of the Australian Labour Movement between the Depression and the Long Boom", PhD, Department of Government, University of Sydney. http://hdl.handle.net/2123/1271

Kuhn, Rick 1986, "Militancy Uprooted: Labour Movement Economics 1974–1986", *Socialist Action*.

Kuhn, Rick 1987, "Industry Policy and the Working Class", *Politics*, 22 (2), November, pp.97–102.

Kuhn, Rick 1988, "From One Industry Strategy to the Next", *Politics*, 23 (2), November, pp.110–16.

Kuhn, Rick 1993, "The Limits of Social Democratic Economic Policy in Australia", *Capital & Class*, 51, pp.17–52.

Laidler, Percy 1924 [1920], *Arbitration*, Ruskin Press.

Liberal Party Federal Secretariat, Research Department 1980, "1980 Election Year: Reference Notes". https://parlinfo.aph.gov.au/parlInfo/search/display/display.w3p;query=Id%3A%22library%2Fpartypol%2F1104178%22"

Lorimer, Doug 1977, "Why Socialists Oppose Australian Nationalism", *Socialist Worker*, 3, August–September, pp.7–14.

Love, Peter 1984, *Labour and the Money Power*, Melbourne University Press.

Maddock, Rodney 2015, "Capital Markets", in Simon Ville and Glenn Withers, *The Cambridge Economic History of Australia*, Cambridge University Press.

McQueen, Humphrey 1982, *Gone Tomorrow: Australia in the 1980s*, Angus & Roberson.

McPhillips, Jack 1985, *The Accord and its Consequences: Trade Union Experiences*, New Age.

Minns, John 1988, *The Hawke Government: Class Struggle and the Left*, International Socialists, Melbourne.

Murphy, Steve 2022, "Editorial", *AMWU News*, Autumn, p.3.

O'Lincoln, Tom 1978 [1977], "Imperialism: A World-Wide System", in Tom O'Lincoln, *You Can Say That Again*, Redback Press, pp.13–4.

O'Lincoln, Tom 1980 "An Imperialist Colony", *International Socialist*, 10, August, pp.39–45. https://www.reasoninrevolt.net.au/objects/pdf/d0513.pdf

O'Lincoln, Tom 1985, *Into the Mainstream: The Decline of Australian Communism*, Stained Wattle Press.

O'Lincoln, Tom 1991, "The New Australian Militarism", *Socialist Review*, 4, Winter, pp.27–47. https://marxistleftreview.org/articles/the-new-australian-militarism/

O'Lincoln, Tom 1993, *Years of Rage: Social Conflicts in the Fraser Era*, Bookmarks, Australia.

O'Lincoln, Tom 2014, *The Neighbour from Hell: Two Centuries of Australian Imperialism*, Interventions.

O'Shaughnessy, Terry 1976, "Economic Notes", *Australian Left Review*, 53, pp.26–31.

O'Shaughnessy, Terry 1978, "Some Recent Conflicts in the Ruling Class", *Intervention*, 10/11 August, pp.40–58.

Peters, Edward William 1968, *A Financial Invasion: The Takeover of Australia*, published by the author, Fitzroy.

Picard, F 1953, "Henry George and the Labour split of 1891", *Historical Studies*, 6, November 1953, pp.45–63.

Rattigan, Alf 1986, *Industry Assistance: The Inside Story*, Melbourne University Press.

Rawling, JN 1937, *Who owns Australia?*, second edition, Modern Publishers.

Robertson Mavis, 1965a, "The Conscription Lottery", *Communist Review*, April, pp.73–5.

Robertson Alec, 1965b, "War Against Democracy", *Communist Review*, July, pp.163–6.

Ross, Hector 1925, "The Last Phase of Arbitration: Hamstringing the Australian Workers", *The Communist*, 10, November/December, pp.10–12.

Ross, Liz, Tom O'Lincoln and Graham Willett 1986, *Labor's Accord: Why It's a Fraud*, Socialist Action, Melbourne.

Rowley, Kelvin 1971, "Dr Cairns on Tariffs: Planning, Imperialism and Socialism", *Farrago*, 29 July.

Sandford, Phil 1971, paper presented to the National Anti-war Conference, Sydney, February (National Library of Australia, Jill Jolliffe Papers, MS 4969).

Scates, Bruce 1984, "'Wobblers': Single Taxers in the Labour Movement, Melbourne 1889–1899", *Historical Studies*, 21 (83), pp.174–96.

Sexton, Michael 2002 [1981], *War for the Asking: How Australia Invited Itself into Vietnam*, New Holland.

Sharkey, Lance 1937, "The federal elections", *Communist Review*, December, pp.6–7.

Socialist Workers Party 1977, *Towards a Socialist Australia: How the Labor Movement Can Fight Back. Documents of the Socialist Workers Party*, Pathfinder Press.

Stilwell, Frank 1982, "Towards an Alternative Economic Strategy", *Journal of Australian Political Economy*, 12/13, June, pp.40–59.

"T.T." 1977, "The Blinky Bill Interview: Nationalism on the Brink", *Intervention*, 8 March, pp.36–44.

Theophanous, Andrew 1980, *Australian Democracy in Crisis*, Oxford University Press.

Voumard, Sonya 1986, "Root out Wasteful Practices: Unionist", *The Age*, 25 August, p.5.

Wells, Andrew, 1989, *Constructing Capitalism: An economic history of eastern Australia, 1788-1901*, Allen & Unwin.

West, Jon 1979a, "Nationalism and the Labor Movement", in Jon West, Dave Holmes and Gordon Adler 1979, *Socialism or nationalism? Which road for the Australian labor movement?*, Pathfinder Press, pp.11–41.

West, Jon 1979b, "Is Australia a Neo-Colony?", in Jon West, Dave Holmes and Gordon Adler 1979, *Socialism or nationalism? Which road for the Australian labor movement?*, Pathfinder Press, pp.43–70.

Wheelwright, EL 1957, *Ownership and Control of Australian Companies*, Law Book Company.

Wheelwright, EL 1963, "Overseas investment in Australia", in A Hunter (ed.), *The Economics of Australian Industry*, Melbourne University Press.

Workers Weekly 1931, "Lang's Repudiation of Interest Is of No Concern to the Working Class", 10 April, p.2.

Workers Weekly 1933, "'Nationalising Banks' – Lang's New Effort to Sidetrack Workers from Class Struggle", 3 February, p.2.

Young, Irwin Edward 1961, "Conflict within the NSW Labor Party 1919–1932", MA Thesis, Department of Government, University of Sydney.

VASHTI FOX

Stalinism's failure to fight fascism

Vashti Fox became involved in revolutionary politics in the anti-capitalist movement. She was a founder of Students for Palestine and has been a leading activist in anti-fascist campaigns.

RUSSIAN REVOLUTIONARY NOVELIST VICTOR SERGE described the period of Stalinist and fascist counter-revolution as "the midnight of the century".[1] And so it was. The experience of the black jackboot of fascist power and the silent snowy prisons of the Soviet gulags should not be forgotten. Fascist regimes were responsible for some of the most unimaginable barbarisms. Fascism rounded up millions; shaved their heads, starved them, beat them, poisoned them, humiliated them, raped them, marched them into death camps and made them watch their children, wives, husbands, brothers, sisters, aunts, uncles, friends and lovers die. Fascism was a social force that broke bones, bodies and hearts. Stalinism was responsible for other horrors. The Soviet regime murdered the brightest lights of the revolutionary working-class movement. It had, in the words of Serge, "lowered [Lenin's companions and friends] into graves [and] shot them in the back of their necks".[2] Soviet Russia starved its population and cowed them into submission. It shaped a society where fear whispered its way into every skull. Where repression was manifest in every government knock on every door. Where famine and want reigned.

1. Serge 2015.
2. Serge 1938.

When these regimes clashed militarily, as they did in the Second World War, the conflict almost brought the planet to the brink of destruction. One lasting myth of the left, in the Western world at least, is that the USSR and the global Stalinist movement played the key role in defeating fascism. As with many myths, this narrative holds a half-truth. In military terms the Red Army did play a very important part in the broader Allied fight against the fascist states of the Axis powers. Between 1943 and 1945 the USSR deployed superior numbers across key fronts in the war which resulted in the ultimate defeat of the Axis militaries. In doing so, they helped conclude the war on the European stage. For many, these facts are enough to prove that Stalinism defeated fascism.

This article will argue however that there were many points *prior* to 1943 where fascism could have been defeated and wasn't. Indeed, far from being the key force to challenge fascism in the twentieth century, Stalinist politics both enabled and, on occasion, collaborated with fascist movements, parties and states. Furthermore, in country after country throughout the 1930s and 1940s the Communist Parties undermined revolutionary working-class anti-fascism – the only kind of politics that was capable of smashing the far right for good.

Fascism

Any serious discussion of this topic must start by defining the nature of the interwar fascist movements. This article draws on the writings of several Marxists whose work remains vital in understanding classical fascism, the most important of whom are Leon Trotsky, Antonio Gramsci, Clara Zetkin and Erich Fromm.[3] These revolutionary activists, all writing as the fascist menace bore down upon them, argued that fascism emerged from within the contradictions of capitalism, not from outside it, as if from some alien force. Specifically, they argued that the fascist movements were a response to the deep capitalist crises of the interwar period. Fascism emerged at a moment of social and economic breakdown. The previous decades in Italy, Germany, France and Spain had seen revolutionary working-class upheaval.

---

3. Trotsky 2005, Gramsci 1921, Zetkin 2017 and Fromm 1942. A useful collection of Marxist writing on fascism is Beetham 2019.

The Russian Revolution loomed large, as an inspiration to the left and a mortal enemy for the right. Thwarted ruling class imperial ambition and extreme economic distress created a situation of intense social crisis. Trotsky describes the atmosphere in Germany as one "brought to white heat by war, defeat, reparations, inflation, occupation of the Ruhr, crisis, need and despair".[4]

For Trotsky, the crisis was not merely economic. There were important socio-political factors involved. He emphasised both the inability of the ruling class to stabilise society through their existing institutions *and* the inability of the working class to overthrow capitalism. Gramsci expressed this as a crisis of ruling class hegemony, which opened a space for fascist ideology to take hold among various social classes. This analysis holds true for all the fascist movements that emerged in the interwar years.

Fascism was different from other conservative or reactionary movements in that it was a mass phenomenon. This mass base was organised into extra parliamentary forces, such as the "squadristi" in Italy and the Brownshirts in Germany. There grassroots organisations gave fascism greater social roots and capacity for terror, and allowed them relative autonomy from the state. Although in Italy the fascist organisations often worked hand in glove with the police and army, Gramsci states: "Fascism is a movement which the bourgeoisie thought should be a simple 'instrument' of reaction in its hands, but once called up and unleashed is worse than the devil, no longer allowing itself to be controlled".[5] Another Italian Marxist, Ignazio Silone, put it this way:

> The entire institutions of the established constitutional state (the army, police, judiciary, educational institutions) find themselves naturally driven to take part in the struggle for the fascist reorganisation of the state. But the character of fascist reorganisation is such that its basic features cannot be supplied by any of the institutions of the established constitutional state. Otherwise fascism would be superfluous, and superfluous also

---

4. Trotsky 1933.
5. Gramsci, cited in Beetham 2019, Introduction, p.9.

> the subversion of the whole existing party system and the civil war that is long, hard, bloody and of uncertain outcome.[6]

In other words, there was a contradiction inherent to the mass fascist movements of the interwar years. They were an expression of capitalist society but not reducible to the simple interests of the capitalist class. They would ultimately reinforce the worst elements of capitalism, including racism and anti-Semitism, while appealing to a certain hostility to capitalism.

This meant that fascist ideology was contradictory and incoherent. Fascists claimed to represent the "little person" – the marginalised and oppressed against the elites and the state – and drew on an eclectic range of populist ideas to give themselves broad appeal. Yet their goal was to uphold key institutions of capital. This explains why, despite its radical veneer, fascism was fundamentally counter-revolutionary, animated by a violent hostility to working-class organisation and democratic rights. Indeed, they were frantic in their desire to "[raze] to their foundations all the institutions of proletarian democracy", political parties, trade unions and other more informal associations.[7]

Where and when fascist movements came to state power the ambiguities of their positions were resolved. The state they ran prioritised imperialism and the interests of big capital, not the mass base of the fascist movement. So, for instance, the autonomy of the mass movement was crushed after the fascists came to power in Italy when, in 1925, Mussolini turned on his fascist squads and dissolved them. In Germany the situation was less clear, but certainly in 1934 Hitler turned on and murdered many of the leaders and key activists in the fascist mass organisations during "the night of the long knives". It was also when the fascists came to state power that they were capable of unleashing the most unimaginable horror: the imperial violence of the Axis powers during the war and the industrial barbarism of the Holocaust.

Fascism, in the interwar years, found its most fanatical supporters among sections of the middle class. Across Europe, fascism particularly

---

6. Silone 1934, cited in Beetham, pp.239–40.
7. Trotsky 1971, p.159.

appealed to and organised the urban small traders and state officials, managers and clerks as well as the impoverished rural petty bourgeoisie, an urban underclass, demobilised soldiers, university students and sections of the unemployed, especially those from middle-class backgrounds. A survey conducted by Fromm in 1929 of the German population and their social and political attitudes revealed starkly that while the bulk of the working class were resigned to fascism, the political psychology of the lower middle class predisposed them, in situations of social breakdown, to take up the ideology of Nazism with gusto. He describes the following features of their social psychology as predisposing them to support for Nazism:

> ...their love of the strong, hatred of the weak, their pettiness, hostility, thriftiness with feelings as well as with money, and essentially their asceticism. Their outlook on life was narrow, they suspected and hated the stranger and they were curious and envious of their acquaintances, rationalising their envy as moral indignation; their whole life was based on the principle of scarcity – economically as well as psychologically.[8]

The tactics of fascist organisations, including their violence and street mobilisations, were a reflection of this class's limited social power. "Not every exasperated petty bourgeois could have become Hitler, but a particle of Hitler is lodged in every exasperated petty bourgeois", wrote Trotsky in 1933.

It is important to note that none of the Marxist theorists I have referred to denied that there was ever any working-class support for fascism. In seeing the interwar fascisms as emerging from a particular political climate, they acknowledge the political factors that may have led some workers into supporting fascism. Importantly here they include the failures of the working-class upsurges and revolutions in both Italy and Germany, as well as the complicity of the social democratic parties in capitalist rule. This allowed some space (small though it was) for the fury of a minority of workers to be turned

---

8. Fromm 1942, p.182.

towards extreme nationalism and anti-Semitism. Fromm and Gramsci break down the sociological composition of workers who might have been drawn to fascism: unemployed workers, recently demobilised soldiers and some sections of the white-collar workforce. In other words, sections of the class who had been both dislodged from a stable working-class environment and those who had not been traditionally well organised by working-class organisations were more likely to join or support fascist organisations. Fundamentally however, these Marxists maintain that the core activists, the most fervent supporters of fascism, are drawn from the middle classes.

Germany and Spain

For those who wish to extol the virtues of the Red Army in World War II, it is politically expedient to stay quiet about the pre-war fascist movements. It is as though history begins only once the Soviet Union enters the war in 1941 and ends after the death of Hitler. But for those who are serious about combating the threat of fascism, it is vital to consider how they came to power in the first place.[9] It is here that the question of the anti-fascist politics of the Stalinised Communist Parties comes into play, particularly in Germany and Spain. In both countries the Communist Parties played a disastrous role in directing the anti-fascist movements. This is not to impugn the many sincere and dedicated communist militants who fought bravely, but it is to insist that the politics of anti-fascism matters.

Of course, the fascists first came to power in Italy in 1922, preceding the rise of Stalin by some years. Here the problems were a capitulation by reformists and an ultra-left refusal to defend democracy on the part of the communists. By mid-1921 the reformist socialists were beginning to cave in in the face of fascist violence, before eventually signing a pact with the fascists in the hope that they could avoid conflict. So they pulled back from supporting the Arditi del Popolo (ADP) – the armed anti-fascist fighting force – and ordered their members to put their trust in the laws of the state and

---

9. It is also useful here to consider places where mass fascist movements were pushed back for a period, for example the initial struggles against the far right in France that led to the election of the Popular Front government in 1936; see Bloodworth 2020.

the parliamentary process. This argument effectively led Italian workers to the slaughterhouse.

Tragically, the Italian Communist Party (PCI), led by Amadeo Bordiga, also argued for communists to withdraw from the ADP. This conservative policy was coated with revolutionary rhetoric and bombast about the need to establish exclusively "communist" squads. This approach was challenged inside the party by rank-and-file communists and by the Comintern (which was not as yet Stalinised), both of whom could see the disastrous consequences of such an approach. Despite this, the communist militants withdrew from the coordinated militias and vowed instead to fight in their own cells run by the PCI. This sectarian approach failed to fight fascism and offered no strategy to win over more reformist workers to a revolutionary worldview by uniting with them in struggle.[10]

This disastrous defeat was a product of terrible mistakes, but they were the mistakes of an inexperienced revolutionary organisation still finding its footing. By the time the fascists were challenging for power in Germany and Spain, however, the local Communist Parties had been thoroughly Stalinised.

The Stalinist bureaucracy in charge of the USSR from the late 1920s was a barbaric, dictatorial state that came to power by crushing the revolutionary movement that had triumphed in 1917. The new Russian ruling class not only liquidated all political opposition but organised a social system that was violently and brutally exploitative of its working class. It was a system that ruled through terror on a vast scale.

Having consolidated its power domestically by 1928, the Stalinist bureaucracy sought next to expand its power and control across the world system. It was a key player in world imperialism through to the collapse of the Eastern Bloc in the 1990s.

Throughout this period, the USSR consciously traded off the reputation of the Russian Revolution, and so embodied the hopes and dreams of the global working class even as it trashed them in reality. This methodology, of using the language of Marxism in the service of pragmatic and entirely pro-capitalist purposes, was then spread

---

10. See Behan 2003.

throughout the international communist movement by the Comintern. Communism came to mean a highly centralised, state-run economy with none of the basic freedoms necessary for working-class democracy. It meant submitting to party diktats, and unquestioningly following every twist and turn of the line coming from Moscow.

Nevertheless, Communist Parties across the world organised workers and this brought with it many contradictions. In order to maintain and expand their memberships the CPs found ways to connect to the daily concerns of workers, playing an important part in union and industrial struggles, and were opposed by some bosses and some governments. This reality, the history of the Russian Revolution, as well as the illusion that Stalin was a genuine fighter against fascism, could give the parties the appearance of genuine radicalism. In many countries the CPs managed to draw into their ranks some of the best fighters and most determined working-class militants. This contradiction is one of the biggest tragedies of the twentieth century; that so many working-class fighters had their energy, passion, devotion and determination squandered in the interests of this monstrous state.

So, despite their rhetoric, the Communist Parties were ultimately organised to advance the national interests of the USSR, and that in turn meant orienting to the stabilisation of the global capitalist order. These dynamics became particularly clear throughout the course of World War II.

From 1928 Stalin developed a new political strategy designed to justify an internal offensive against his domestic opposition and a purging of the Communist Parties overseas. This perspective, known as the "third period", declared that capitalism would soon be convulsed by intense crisis. Imperialist war was imminent and revolution was on the agenda. Social democratic parties suddenly became the primary enemy, often with barely a distinction made between the leadership of these parties and their rank-and-file working-class membership. The reformist parties were declared to be "social fascists" and were, more often than not, the primary target of the communists' rage.

When some communists resisted this shift, they were purged. Anyone who opposed these unprecedented arguments was labelled a traitor to the cause and was driven out of the movement. This left Communist Party leaderships with a self-selecting group of supine bureaucrats who would obey the line from Russia without question.

On the surface, and particularly after 1929, the third period line could seem to have merit. The Great Depression *was* immiserating workers across the world, and it *was* the reformist leaders who were responsible for betraying the working class on the most dramatic scale. Nevertheless, the third period line was not a mistaken response to these developments, but an artificial and counter-revolutionary policy developed in the service of the Soviet bureaucracy. It led the international communist movement to adopt an ultra-sectarian approach which would ultimately result in the defeat of the German working class by the Nazis.

To put this into context, the German working class had some of the most militant and radical political traditions in the world. A revolutionary upsurge following World War I saw soviets emerge across the country, as workers began arming themselves against proto-fascist militias and the German bourgeoisie. This rebellion was successfully contained by the Social Democratic Party (SPD) and by the late 1920s, a fascist movement, organised primarily in the Nazi party, was gaining ground. Nevertheless, hundreds of thousands of militants remained in the left wing of the SPD or in the Communist Party of Germany (KPD), and were impelled into anti-fascist action. For example, the KPD had 300,000 members by 1932. Historian Dave Renton also argues that the

> organisation could, in addition, call on the support of red unions, organisations of school and university association, fellow travellers involved in red sports clubs and in KPD-dominated anti-Nazi networks such as *Anti-faschistiche Aktion* or *Kampfbund gegen den Faschismus* (the latter claimed 100,000 members in summer 1932).[11]

In other words, this was an organisation that could have had a decisive effect on the dynamics of the struggle.

---

11. Renton 2020, p.103.

Between 1929, the beginning of the economic collapse, and Hitler's coming to power in 1933, thousands of communist workers across Germany fought the Nazis in their workplaces and on the streets. These battles cost hundreds of KPD members their lives, but the general strategy of the party was disastrous. The main enemy, according to the party leadership and the Comintern, were the "social fascists" of the SPD. Indeed, the KPD newspaper regularly declared that fascism was already in power, under governments led by the SPD and then the Centre Party. In several instances this led to unholy alliances between the Nazis and the KPD as they united against the SPD. So for instance, when, in 1931 the Nazis campaigned for a referendum to dismiss the Social Democratic regional government in Prussia, the KPD backed it, claiming that their participation turned this reactionary fascist attack on social democracy into a "Red Referendum".

It was patently obvious to any thinking German worker that the "Red Referendum" argument was utterly hollow. The KPD never seized the initiative during the campaign. Nor did the party succeed, as they claimed, in "exposing" the hypocrisy of the Nazis, thus winning influence among the misled fascist following. The opposite was true; all indications suggest that the KPD rank and file were confused and disillusioned by the decision to work with the Nazis. Moreover, there is evidence that the communists, far from using the referendum as part of some new ideological initiative against the Nazis, actually sought to limit competition with them in an attempt to ensure the success of the referendum.[12]

This appalling sectarian approach not only mistook the enemy, it also undermined the capacity for unified working-class anti-fascist activity. This would prove disastrous in the face of a fascist force that saw little difference between reformist and revolutionary workers. German revolutionary Clara Zetkin had rightly argued that

> proletarian struggle and self-defense against fascism requires a proletarian united front. Fascism does not ask if the worker in the factory has a soul painted in the white and blue colors of Bavaria;

---

12. Daycock 1980, p.253.

or is inspired by the black, red, and gold colors of the bourgeois republic; or by the red banner with a hammer and sickle. All that matters to fascism is that they encounter a class-conscious proletarian, and then they club him to the ground. That is why workers must come together for struggle without distinctions of party or trade-union affiliation.[13]

By 1932 the Nazis were growing steadily as broader bourgeois forces were in disarray and their supporters going over to the Nazis. In 1933 Hitler was installed in power by the arch-conservative German Chancellor von Hindenburg. Hitler moved quickly to outlaw all opposition parties, purge the state of any dissenting voices and begin a reign of terror over the population.

In the afternoon that Hitler's victory was declared the KPD Central Committee issued a leaflet demanding "Strikes; Mass Strikes; General Strikes". Unfortunately, this was a totally empty cry. Nothing had been done to build this mass action beforehand. Confusion reigned. For far too long the party had been declaring the SPD the main fascist threat. And while many in the rank and file of the KPD (and SPD) could see the truth of the situation, it was too late. Their resistance was simply too sporadic and disorganised. The KPD's failure to play a decisive role in developing united, serious and radical working-class anti-fascist resistance led to disaster. Nearly every third KPD member went to prison under Nazi rule, and thousands were murdered.[14] Put more poetically and more devastatingly is this description from Georg Glaser, a Communist and artist who was in Berlin after Hitler came to power:

> Dead men were found in the surrounding forests, and no one dared to know anything about them. People disappeared without a sound, and their best friends did not have the courage to ask where they had gone. Only very rarely did a scream, a gruesome rumour...make itself heard; they were paid less notice than everyday traffic accidents. The New Age came silently and

---

13. From Zetkin's report to the Executive Committee of the Comintern, 20 June 1923, in Zetkin 2017.
14. Wilde 2013.

invisibly. The only thing one could feel was the emptiness that each of its footsteps left behind, like the emptiness of a bookshelf from which all the books have suddenly disappeared.[15]

The Spanish Revolution

After the ascension of Mussolini and then Hitler to power, fascist movements across the world gained great confidence. While the consolidation of fascism in Italy and Germany represented a serious blow to the workers' movements, there were still parts of the world where workers remained powerful. Spain was the scene for the last major pre-war battle against fascism. While the German experience could be written off as a mistake, the Spanish Revolution revealed most starkly the political impact of a consolidated Stalinist rule in Russia.

Just one year after the Nazis came to power, the Russian ruling class changed tack. As with the previous turn, there was nothing in the objective situation that necessitated such a dramatic change; rather it was prompted by the requirements of the Stalinist ruling class.[16] By 1934 Stalin had definitely defeated his rival Nikolai Bukharin and set out to smash any further real or potential opposition. Inside the USSR, brutal purges of the state bureaucracy were accompanied by high-profile show trials of former leading Bolsheviks. The most prominent former Bolshevik who came under fire was Leon Trotsky, who had been driven out of the country in 1928 and was organising anti-Stalinist opposition. Internal political considerations were only part of the picture, however. The inter-imperial power plays were Stalin's prime consideration. Hitler's policies had made it clear that Germany was preparing for war and that the USSR would be a target. Although Stalin had no in principle objection to an alliance with Nazi Germany, he had to look elsewhere for diplomatic and military support. His only alternatives were Britain and France.

These intersecting dynamics provoked a new political turn designed to reorient the Comintern parties. This turn, announced at

---
15. Cited in Renton 2020, p.104.
16. Gluckstein 1994.

the Seventh Comintern Congress, denounced the "ultra-leftism" of the earlier phase. Alliances with social democratic parties and even openly capitalist forces were now mandated. This had big implications for their approach to fighting fascism, which a speech by Georgi Dimitrov set out:

> German fascism is acting as the spearhead of international counter-revolution, as the chief instigator of imperialist war, as the initiator of a crusade against the Soviet Union, the great fatherland of the working people of the whole world.[17]

Dimitrov acknowledged the failure of the Communist Party in Germany to halt the march of the Nazis. Unity became the new catchcry and would come in a variety of forms. Unity firstly meant alliances between the USSR and other capitalist nation states prepared to develop pacts of collective security. This would be achieved under the auspices of the imperialist alliance, the League of Nations.[18] Thus fighting fascism was now primarily understood in the framework of international diplomacy and imperial alignments. Secondly, this unity referred to the need for communists to develop relationships with the previously maligned "social fascists" (the Social Democrats), with peasants and middle classes, and eventually even with right-wing parties. This supposedly anti-fascist policy became known as the "popular front".[19] In Spain this policy was revealed to be thoroughly counter-revolutionary.

Spain had been the site of intense class struggles for much of the early twentieth century. Its political institutions were particularly weak. It was ruled by a constitutional monarchy based narrowly on the Castilian ruling class in Madrid, backed up by the Catholic Church, which resisted both Republicanism and the universal right to vote. This conservative ruling elite faced opposition both from workers' and peasants' revolts and from restless bourgeois and semi-aristocratic forces based in the surrounding provinces, which had long raised

---

17. Dimitrov 1935.
18. Gollan 1975, p.43.
19. Carr 1982.

separatist slogans. After years of revolutions and counter-revolutions, failed risings and mass strikes, a centre-left government was elected in 1936. At first the Communist Party played a relatively minor part, supporting the bourgeois Republicans and their allies in the social-democratic Socialist Party (PSOE).

Faced with this unprecedented governmental alliance, the right wing took a stand and backed General Franco in an attempted military coup. This attempt to overthrow the Spanish Republic prompted an immediate, instinctive rising across much of Spain. Workers and peasants led the revolt, and organised some of the most beautiful, creative, determined and at times violent displays of revolutionary action, that managed to hold off Franco's far-right forces. Alongside the physical fighting, the rising initiated a process of social revolution, as workers utilised their bravery and social weight, and seized weapons to fight the fascists. But this revolutionary initiative was not universally welcomed by all Republican forces. After all, it threatened to not only hold back the fascists but to totally disrupt all capitalist power relations.

Between July 1936 and May of 1937, in what would become known as the Republican zone, there developed something like dual power. On one side there was the nominally anti-fascist bourgeois Republican government which had little real power. On the other side, mainly in the industrial state of Catalonia, there were vast networks of workers and peasants who controlled the economy, justice, transport and education sectors. One eyewitness to the events, Franz Borkenau, offered the following description:

> The amount of expropriation in the few days since 19th July is almost incredible. The largest hotels, with one or two exceptions, have all been requisitioned by working class organisations… So were most of the larger stores. Many of the banks are closed, the others bear inscriptions declaring them under the control of the Generalitat [the Catalonian provincial government]. Practically all the factory owners, we were told, had either fled or been killed, and their factories taken over by the workers. Everywhere large posters at the front of impressive buildings proclaimed the fact of

expropriation, explaining either that the management is now in the hands of the CNT [the anarcho-syndicalist union federation], or that a particular organisation has appropriated this building for its organising work.[20]

This was the power that could defeat fascism – militarily, socially and politically.

The fascist and military forces, now united under General Franco, were determined to oust any oppositional power and they began to seek and obtained military backing from Italy and Germany. Spain's civil war thus took on global proportions.

The other imperialist powers – France and Britain – attempted to wash their hands of Spain by signing a "non-intervention pact". Their ruling classes had no interest in helping the Spanish working class defeat fascism, when such a struggle threatened capitalism as a whole. The same was true of the USSR. Stalin's primary goal was to get France and Britain to agree to an alliance with the USSR against Germany. A successful workers' revolution in Spain would disrupt these negotiations, while also casting doubt on Russia's claim to be an outpost of workers' power. The Comintern therefore did everything possible to end the revolution in Spain, demanding that the Spanish communists subordinate the working-class movement to the Republican "shadow bourgeoisie".[21] The Spanish CP took up this argument with gusto.

> "It is absolutely false", declared Jésus Hernández, editor of *Mundo Obrero* (August 6, 1936), "that the present workers' movement has for its object the establishment of a proletarian dictatorship after the war has terminated. It cannot be said we have a social motive for our participation in the war. We communists are the first to repudiate this supposition. We are motivated exclusively by a desire to defend the democratic republic".[22]

---

20. Borkenau 1932, p.71.
21. These were the liberal capitalist forces that had not gone over to Franco.
22. Quoted in Morrow 1938, chapter 5.

In other words, the battle in Spain was not to be one between socialism and fascism but rather between "capitalist democracy" and fascism. This line was adopted by Communist Parties across the world. They argued that workers needed to greatly limit their expectations and demands in order to avoid pushing the capitalist class into the arms of the Nazis. In an echo of the Menshevik argument in Russia, communists now insisted that all that could be won during this period was capitalist democracy. What this argument meant in practice was the smashing of revolutionary working-class democracy in the interests of bourgeois rule. In a number of cases, including Spain, this led directly to a fascist or proto-fascist victory.

As the civil war dragged on, the Soviet Union poured advisors and agents into Spain. Their main goal was to direct a counter-revolutionary offensive against the anarchists and independent communists who were involved in leading the working-class agitation. They used their control over guns and funds sent by the USSR to reverse a number of gains. For instance, they abolished both democracy and women's participation in the militias in order to turn them into a more traditional army. But it was in May of 1937 that tensions came to a head in Barcelona. Workers, seeing that the vestiges of their revolutionary power were at stake, began to move. They set up barricades to defend the parts of the city under workers' control. It was here that the Spanish Stalinists, with weapons provided by the Soviet Union, began their most decisive counter-revolutionary battle. Trotskyist historian Felix Morrow describes the Spanish CP members as:

> ex-members of the Fascist CEDA, Cuban gangsters, brothel-racketeers, passport forgers, sadists. Spawned by the petty-bourgeois composition of the Communist party, nurtured by its counter-revolutionary programme, these organized bands of the Spanish GPU exhibited toward the workers the ferocity of Hitler's bloodhounds, for like them, they were trained to exterminate revolution.[23]

---

23. Morrow 1938, chapter 8.

Hundreds of independent communists, anarchists and working-class militants were tortured and murdered by the Spanish Stalinists. Part of this intervention into Spain was also devoted to extinguishing any forces or individuals sympathetic to Trotskyism. Thus Alexander Orlov, the Comintern agent appointed by Stalin, ordered the arrest of Andres Nin, the leader of the independent Communists of the POUM (Workers' Party of Marxist Unification). Nin was tortured for several days. Jésus Hernández, the Communist minister of education in the Popular Front government, later admitted:

> Nin was not giving in. He was resisting until he fainted. His inquisitors were getting impatient. They decided to abandon the dry method. Then the blood flowed, the skin peeled off, muscles torn, physical suffering pushed to the limits of human endurance. Nin resisted the cruel pain of the most refined tortures. In a few days his face was a shapeless mass of flesh.[24]

Andres Nin was executed on 20 June 1937. This was the reality of the Stalinists' "anti-fascism" in Spain. Enforcing their popular front with the imperialist bourgeoisie of France and Britain necessitated the extinguishing of the revolutionary hopes raised by the Spanish Civil War, drowned in blood not by fascists but by the Stalinists.

Now, the Spanish Civil War was turned from a revolutionary war against fascism into a conventional military struggle. On one side were the degraded remnants of bourgeois democracy, led by the reactionary Communist Party of Spain. Confronting them were the fascist and Catholic forces of Spain, backed by the fascist states of Italy and Germany. The Spanish Republican forces were totally outgunned. Fearful of pushing Britain and France away, the USSR invested just enough to keep the fighting going, but not enough to decisively win the battle. In the end, the Republican and Stalinist forces were defeated, and it was clear that world war was on the horizon.

This was not the final horror and indignity that Spanish anti-fascists were to face. Those who were able to fled fascist terror and crossed

---

24. Quoted in Simkin 2020.

the Pyrenees hoping for protection in Republican France, where a Communist- and Socialist-backed Popular Front government was in office. Their hopes were smashed upon arrival as the anti-fascist refugees were herded into concentration camps. María Luisa Fernández, who, at the age of two, was held at one of these camps along with her mother and father, recalled:

> When we crossed the French border, families were separated. My father was sent to Argelès-sur-Mer where there was no protection from the elements except wire fences to stop them escaping. My mother and I were herded into cattle trucks for a whole month, along with the elderly and injured, until we were dumped in a field in Magnac-Laval. There we were given just straw to sleep on whilst we were "guarded" by the *gendarme* [French police].[25]

It is estimated that around ten thousand Spanish refugees died in these Popular Front-sponsored camps.

World War II

The following years saw more dizzying twists and turns in Stalinist anti-fascist policy. From 1936 to 1939, the Comintern shifted their rhetorical focus; German and Italian fascism were the main threat to world peace. There were now fascist nations (the enemy) and sympathetic, supposedly democratic peace-loving nations (the Allied powers). Only once fascism was broken could the class struggle be picked up again. This rhetorical emphasis meant limiting the anti-fascist struggles, developing cross-class alliances, squashing class struggle and in many instances subsuming domestic anti-fascist struggles into Russia's military requirements.

In 1939, having failed to pressure France or Britain into a collective security agreement, Stalin signed a non-aggression pact with Nazi Germany. As American socialist Joel Geier argues:

> This collaboration was grotesquely conveyed when swastika flags

---

25. Quoted in Mead 2022. For more on the betrayals of the French Popular Front, see Bloodworth 2020.

> graced Moscow streets to welcome the Nazi negotiators for the Hitler-Stalin Pact – and Russian foreign minister Vyacheslav Molotov proclaimed at the Pact's signing: "Fascism is a matter of taste", while Stalin toasted Hitler: "I know how much the German nation loves its Fuehrer".[26]

The agreement sent shockwaves through the international communist movement. It caused confusion and heartbreak. In Australia, the Communist Party's paper *Workers' Weekly* of 23 August 1939 demanded: "No compromise with the fascist warmakers!" Yet on the very same day,

> the news arrived of Stalin's non-aggression pact with the Nazis – the CP leaders hailed the compromise they'd always opposed as "one of the greatest victories of the Soviet Union's long struggle to save the world from a second imperialist war".[27]

The Hitler-Stalin pact was justified as a "tactic" designed to save the Soviet state from fascist aggression. Rather than being a dirty deal with the mass-murdering Hitler, this was the Soviet power "boxing clever". In turn, Britain, France and the US, the forces that only yesterday had been "peace loving democracies", now became "imperialist robber barons".

This appalling pact continues to be justified by some left commentators today. In 2019 *Counterpunch* published a full-throated defence of the agreement by historian Jacques Pauwels, in which he declared that without the Hitler-Stalin pact, "Today, on the continent, the second language would not be English, but German, and in Paris the fashionistas would promenade up and down the Champs Elysees in Lederhosen".[28]

Defenders of the notion that Stalin was an anti-fascist maintain that the "non-aggression pact" was a peace pact. Nothing could be further from the truth. A useful response to Pauwel's piece by Louis Proyect

---

26. Geier 2022, p.224.
27. Sparrow 2007, pp.242–43.
28. Pauwels 2019.

and Paweł Szelegieniec appeared in *Counterpunch* shortly after. They argued that:

> The Ribbentrop-Molotov Non-Aggression Pact [was a] pact that divided Eastern Europe between Nazi Germany and Stalinist USSR. The secret agreements not only decided how Poland had to be divided, but also Romania, in which the Bessarabia region was united with the Soviet state, and likewise the Baltic states. Concerning Poland, the secret Nazi-Soviet agreement defined the borders between the two states in a fashion similar to the "scramble for Africa" of the 19th and early 20th century left that continent divvied up.[29]

Around the signing of the pact there were several top-secret conferences between the Gestapo and Stalin's secret police, the NKVD. One of their main joint goals was to combat the Polish underground that was now fighting simultaneously against both the Russian state and the Nazis. The NKVD agreed to combat all anti-Nazi Polish propaganda in the Soviet-controlled areas of the former Polish Republic. This involved dissolving the Communist Party of Poland in 1938, which understandably led to significant demoralisation and confusion among Polish communists. Indeed Proyect and Szelegieniec describe an incident where after the 1939 invasion the Nazis started to purge the communists.

> The rhetoric of an alliance "against Anglo-French imperialism" enticed Polish Communists to accept an invitation to meet and greet the Nazis. When some Communists, without a clear class understanding of the situation, agreed to come to such a meeting with the Nazi party activists, they were arrested and then shot dead.[30]

As part of these negotiations, Stalin also agreed to transfer German communists who had escaped Hitler back to the Third Reich.

---

29. Proyect and Szelegieniec 2019.
30. Proyect and Szelegieniec 2019.

This decision reveals the reality of the Stalinist regime. It wasn't socialist, it wasn't even anti-fascist.

Research from the now open files of the USSR has revealed that between 1935 and 1941 around one thousand people were deported from the USSR to Germany. Three hundred of these deportees were communists, Jews and anti-fascists. Some of these were people who had been anti-fascist activists in Germany, who had fought the rise of Hitler until they had no other choice but to flee. They made their way to the USSR hoping for some safety, but the Stalinists could only see them as pawns in their global imperial game. Historian Bini Adamczak writes powerfully of these deportations:

> As inconceivable, almost as inconceivable, as the deportations themselves, the expulsion of communists by communists, a gift to the Nazis from the hands of the Nazis' mortal enemies. So inconceivable that not even the Gestapo can believe it, and takes a large proportion of the anti-fascists, people who had often been jailed on the charge of *fascist espionage*, to be agents of the GPU, the Soviet Secret Service. Even more so, because the Germans expressly oppose many of the deportees' repatriation and refuse to accept them numerous times, at least until 1939. The German Embassy and the Foreign Ministry want Germans, not anti-Germans, not *enemies of Germany*. They want *Volksdeutsche*, the people with German roots, not Jews, the expatriates, anti-fascists. And yet they get them, to the Gestapo's great delight. Eighty anti-fascists before the 1939 Hitler-Stalin Pact, more than 200 (out of 350 deportees) afterward. Only now do the Germans press for deportations, stressing the *mutual friendly relations between the German Reich and the USSR*. There is no evidence of other pressure or of any "reciprocation" to follow. The Nazis give the numbers, the Soviets supply the names. The anti-fascists are sacrificed not according to some overarching principle of political calculus nor as currency in an exchange but rather as a kind of gift.[31]

---

31. Adamczak 2021, pp.7–8.

After the pact, the Comintern declared that the coming war was transformed. It was no longer a supportable anti-fascist war of defence against Hitler and Mussolini. Now it was reframed as an imperialist war which Communist Parties across the world would vehemently oppose.[32] This supposedly anti-war stance was in reality effectively a pro-German stance. From 1939 until 1941 much of the Comintern's anti-fascist rhetoric was replaced with condemnations of the imperial designs of the Anglo-French alliance. Australian playwright and former member of the CPA, Oriel Gray, describes this transformation thus:

> After the signing of the German Soviet pact, all references to Hitler and fascism vanished from the pages of the *Tribune* [the CPA paper]… Attacks on the reactionary governments of Britain and France intensified… We all became ardent pacifists – and we would fight anyone to prove it.[33]

This was not to be the last of the dramatic about-turns. Hitler invaded the USSR just a year and a half later. Now the Soviet Union entered the war with gusto, and the Comintern changed its line again. It threw its support behind the Allies, so that Communist Party anti-fascism became almost indistinguishable from the broader Allied war effort. Indeed, the levels of enthusiasm for the war met, and in some instances even exceeded, those in the rest of society. In Australia, the war had "changed form" according to CPA leader Ralph Gibson; "anti-fascist unity" meant Australian workers should now throw themselves into the war effort.[34] The communist general secretary of the Federated Ironworkers Association, Ernie Thornton, in June 1942 declared:

> [W]e decided that we have a new attitude to the war and a new attitude towards production. So on our management committee we decided to campaign for increased production and this

---

32. Gollan, p.84.
33. Gray 1985, p.50.
34. Gibson 1966, p.91.

campaign was not without result. We campaigned to avoid strikes, with the result that it has been surprisingly successful.[35]

Party events would now play *God Save the King* before the *Internationale*. To be a communist was to be anti-fascist and to be anti-fascist during the war was to be a patriotic Australian. This anti-fascism was very far from the anti-capitalist, class-war anti-fascism encouraged by the Comintern in the early 1920s. It instead laid the basis for a deepening and consolidation of nationalism across the international communist movement; a nationalism that was to play a decisive and disastrous role in many places.

Partisan resistance

World War II was a contradictory beast. For the Allied powers, the war was a straight-up imperial battle. They wanted the war fought through formal national military structures which they could politically and socially contain. In several countries, however, the war was more than a simple imperial conflict. Countries that were occupied by the fascist forces, such as Poland, Greece, Italy, France, Belgium, Norway, Czechoslovakia, Albania and the Netherlands saw the proliferation of significant partisan and local resistance movements. This contradiction is well expressed by the British socialist Donny Gluckstein:

> The Allies fought for imperialism – their imperialism against a rival imperialism. The masses fought against imperialism (of the Axis variety). They frequently discovered that this brought them into conflict with Allied imperialism too. The notion of wars running along parallel lines (but simultaneously intersecting) may not sit well with Euclidean geometry, but it rips apart the circle... the common view that Winston Churchill, Joseph Stalin, Franklin D Roosevelt and the ordinary people were "all in it together".[36]

These partisan movements were mixed socially and politically but, in many countries, the workers and peasants played a decisive

---

35. Quoted in Short 1992, p.58.
36. Gluckstein 2013.

role in the defeat of fascist forces. The active mobilisation of the population, from the factory floor to the streets of their suburbs to their villages, often transformed these struggles. Many felt they were fighting not just for their country, as their rulers would want it, but for a post-war society they could have some say over. For large numbers, a socialist society was their goal. In this sense, anti-fascism became a dynamic part of the struggle for a better world: a world not just better than fascism, but a world better than what capitalist democracy could offer.

Tragically, the CPs were incapable of supporting and expanding this kind of anti-fascism. Although communist networks organised many tens of thousands of bold, brave and self-sacrificing militants, the politics of Stalinism ensured disastrous defeats for the working-class movements and the left. It is beyond the capacity of this article to detail the specific dynamics of each partisan movement but the Italian example is emblematic.[37]

Italy

By the outbreak of World War II, Italy had been under fascist rule for almost two decades. Mussolini's deeply repressive state had successfully crushed much working-class resistance. The Communist Party (PCI) had gone underground, and while they continued to organise where they could, their efforts were patchy and largely unsuccessful. This changed in 1943, when Italy's military fortunes began to flag and workers in the north of the country, increasingly frustrated by the privations of war, began to stir. By mid-March over 200,000 workers were on strike and the PCI emerged from the underground. This was an extremely significant event and, despite widespread repression, signalled a fundamental shift in the dynamics of the war.

Later that year the Allies invaded the south of the country and cut a deal with the former friends of Mussolini, the Italian king and military Field Marshal Pietro Badoglio. This move signified an internal

---

37. For more on the Greek partisan movements see the relevant chapter in Bramble and Armstrong 2021, or Eudes 1972. For accounts of other partisan movements see Gluckstein 2012.

collapse of Italian ruling class coherence and strength. As Dante Puzzo so eloquently puts it, "Italy was like a body whose skeletal frame had suddenly liquefied", collapsing under its own weight.[38] In response to this Allied offensive, Nazi Germany invaded the north of Italy and marched southward to try and shore up Mussolini's rule. The bulk of the country was effectively occupied by German forces. It quickly became clear that any serious anti-fascist struggle could not rely on the Italian elites for aid, given they had so recently backed Mussolini. If the Nazis and their local collaborators were to be defeated, resistance would have to be mounted by ordinary people themselves. This resulted in some of the most magnificent and determined moments of resistance of the twentieth century.

In some form or another up to 700,000 Italians were involved in the resistance. Partisan bands were organised in small rural villages and urban industrial centres. In the countryside they fought the German military and engaged in sabotage; they "blew up bridges, ripped up railways, attacked ammunition dumps, sabotaged power lines and communications and ambushed German soldiers, seizing their weapons".[39] In the cities partisans engaged in lightning raids on both the occupying and collaborationist forces. They also, importantly, took strike action. This was a particularly important anti-fascist action in the war industries. Historian of the Italian resistance Tom Behan offers this description of events in Genoa in late 1943:

> A major strike wave was preceded by a tram drivers' strike at the end of November, an action that was obviously noticed in all areas of the city, but the more generalised movement was soon nicknamed "the olive oil strike", since one of the main demands was an increase in the ration. Perhaps due to the relative success obtained in Turin and Milan, workers in Genoa went a stage further and marched out of their factories, to be immediately joined by a significant number of local people. The authorities responded by shooting three workers on the third day. The Resistance answered by declaring public

---
38. Puzzo 1992, quoted in Behan 2009, p.74.
39. Bramble and Armstrong 2021, p.333.

mourning across the city. In the areas where the workers lived everything was closed down and there were pickets outside the major theatres and cinemas. When work was due to resume on the Monday morning, a political strike was called against the executions. The movement had now extended beyond factory workers and involved bakers, street cleaners and hospital workers.[40]

The bravery of such action cannot be underestimated. To strike in the face of, not only the displeasure of your boss, but also the violent fury of the Wehrmacht, required an unmatched degree of determination. These anti-fascist workers saw their friends, lovers, family and comrades murdered. They knew the price of failure was torture or death and yet they persisted. This type of incredible social mobilisation resulted in the defeat of six of the 25 German divisions in northern Italy.

There is no debate among historians that it was the partisans that liberated Naples, Florence and Milan. In 1945 a general strike was called by the Resistance in the North and, even before the Allied forces arrived, workers seized factories and fought hand-to-hand battles against the fascists. Mussolini, when discovered, was hung in a public square by the partisans. In the South, whole villages and towns were overtaken by locals who began running them along democratic lines as production was collectivised.

Behan makes the important point that what fired many Italians' determination was not a desire for tepid parliamentary democracy. They dreamed of and fought for a fundamentally different kind of post-war society where their lives, needs and desires were not mere playthings for those at the top of society. What's more, they certainly did not want a post-war agreement that saw the return of the very same fascists and collaborators that they had fought so hard to defeat. This desire was contradicted however by the politics of the PCI which was, despite the insurgent spirit of much of the partisan resistance, committed to the popular front. Stalin's man in

---

40. Behan 2009, p.82.

Italy, Palmiro Togliatti (who had previously overseen the execution of dissident communists in Spain) was explicit that the goal of the PCI was to engender national cross-class unity; socialism was not on the agenda. He declared that "the insurrection we want does not have the goal of imposing social or political changes in a socialist or communist sense".[41]

The PCI was numerically dominant in the broader Resistance coalition known as the National Liberation Committee (CLN), particularly among industrial workers. Inside the PCI there was a significant left wing – separated from the day-to-day directives of the Stalinist leadership, but unable to cohere itself, partly because it lacked an understanding of Stalinism both in the USSR and globally. With the backing of the Comintern, Togliatti and the other bureaucrats were able to assert themselves.

For these figures, the partisan movement was simply a means to an end. It was a movement that could, if victorious, consolidate PCI involvement in a parliamentary deal which could then enable the USSR to maintain a stronger position in post-war geopolitics.

Indeed, as Italian workers and peasants were fighting and dying in October of 1944, Stalin was in the process of negotiating an imperial carve-up of the world. Historian Joseph Siracusa describes his meeting with Churchill in Moscow, when these two ageing leaders divided Europe into spheres of influence and control. Churchill made the following proposal to Stalin:

> Let us settle about our affairs in the Balkans... Your armies are in Rumania and Bulgaria. We have interests, missions, and agents there. Don't let us get at cross purposes in small ways. So far as Britain and Russia are concerned, how would it do for you to have ninety percent predominance in Rumania, for us to have ninety percent of the say in Greece, and go fifty-fifty about Yugoslavia?[42]

Churchill's memoirs reveal the staggering cynicism with which the fate

---
41. Quoted in Vassiley 2022.
42. Quoted in Siracusa 1981.

of millions of people's lives was decided. While his suggestion to Stalin was being translated,

> I wrote out on a half-sheet of paper: Rumania: Russia 90% – the others 10%, Greece: Great Britain (in accord with USA) 90% – Russia 10%, Yugoslavia: 50-50%, Hungary: 50-50%, Bulgaria: Russia 75% – the others 25%.[43]

Stalin happily signed off on these proposals, and left the meeting determined to impose the agreement on the relevant Communist leaders. This and other deals between Stalin, Churchill and Roosevelt had profound implications for the anti-fascist partisan struggles. In Italy, the decision propelled what became known as the Salerno turn; a compromise between anti-fascist parties, the monarchy and the prime minister. This allowed the former fascist, Pietro Badoglio, to set up a government of national unity and ensured the postponement of radical social transformation. David Broder explains how the mass action of workers and peasants liberated much of the country but that the PCI traded off these achievements in return for positions in the post-war settlement:

> The party had thus used mass mobilization to secure itself a place in institutional life, but without antagonizing other democratic forces. Indeed, the PCI press of 1943–45 (and later party mythology) cast even the most evidently class-war aspects of the resistance – mass strikes, land occupations, draft resistance – in "patriotic" terms, a mass working-class contribution to a progressive national movement more than an assertion of workers' anticapitalist class interests.[44]

In doing so, the opportunities to overturn both the fascist regime *and* capitalist injustice were squandered. Indeed, many former fascist officials retained their places in the state. Togliatti, who had been appointed justice minister in the post-war settlement, issued an

---
43. Quoted in Siracusa 1981.
44. Broder 2016.

amnesty to known fascists. Some partisans themselves became the target of political trials pursued by ex-fascist judges and police.

The Italian experience was not an outlier. Indeed, in country after country Stalinism was responsible for containing the revolutionary dynamics of anti-fascist struggle during the war. As well, the deals they made allowed fascists and Nazis to retain their roles in society even as workers and the left were suppressed.[45]

Conclusion

Fascism was not purely a military or wartime phenomenon. Rather, fascism in the 1930s was a mass counter-revolutionary middle-class movement that could have been defeated by significant united working-class action. In many instances the political will was there from workers, but what was lacking was a strategy, ultimately committed to working-class revolution and fundamental social transformation.

By the 1930s the leaders of the Stalinised Communist Parties were almost entirely concerned with meeting the geopolitical needs of the capitalist USSR. This informed every aspect of their politics and had disastrous consequences for the working class. Indeed, as this article has argued, it facilitated fascist counter-revolution.

Unfortunately, however, the ideas of the Comintern did not disappear with the collapse of the Eastern Bloc. The politics of the popular front have left a legacy. In the United Kingdom prominent journalist and former socialist Paul Mason has for the last few years been campaigning to resurrect the popular front for today's conditions. Indeed, his latest book, *How to Stop Fascism: History, Ideology, Resistance*, devotes a whole chapter to extolling the virtues of the popular front governments in France and Spain.[46] Mason argues these were the gold standard of how to develop a mass popular, anti-fascist culture. He goes further than offering his own dubious take on the history though, by suggesting that in the absence of a strong working-class movement, the radical left needs to pursue alliances with liberal capitalists and their institutions. In doing so, workers will need to forgo their own demands.

---

45. For more detail see Bramble and Armstrong 2021.
46. Mason 2021.

Such arguments are disastrous. History has demonstrated that, even when confronted with a mortal threat, liberal institutions of capitalism are unwilling and incapable of resisting any fascist threat. To orient an anti-fascist movement, regardless of its size, in this direction is merely to disarm it.

Although we are not confronted today with the same conditions as we faced in the 1930s or 1940s, the history offered above is vital. We face unprecedented capitalist crises on multiple fronts, which are feeding the growth of the far right in a number of countries. At the same time, we are witnessing something of a revival of interest in Stalinism in the English-speaking world. This current presents itself as radical and uncompromising, an alternative to years of failed social-democratic experiments. We must ensure that a left is built that rejects this bankrupt tradition and its legacy of gulags and gas chambers.

References

Adamczak, Bini 2021, "The Nazi-Soviet Pact: A Betrayal of Communists by Communists", in *Yesterday's Tomorrow: On the Loneliness of Communist Specters and the Reconstruction of the Future*, MIT Press. https://thereader.mitpress.mit.edu/the-nazi-soviet-pact-a-betrayal-of-communists-by-communists/

Beetham, David (ed.) 2019, *Marxists in the face of fascism: Writings by Marxists on fascism from the inter-war period*, Haymarket.

Behan, Tom 2003, *The Resistible Rise of Benito Mussolini*, Bookmarks.

Behan, Tom 2009, *The Italian Resistance: Fascists, Guerrillas and the Allies*, Bookmarks.

Bloodworth, Sandra 2020, "From revolutionary possibility to fascist defeat: The French Popular Front of 1936–38", *Marxist Left Review*, 19, Summer. https://marxistleftreview.org/articles/from-revolutionary-possibility-to-fascist-defeat-the-french-popular-front-of-1936-38/

Borkenau, Franz 1932, *The Spanish Cockpit*, Pluto Press.

Bramble Tom, and Mick Armstrong 2021, *The Fight for Workers' Power. Revolution and counter-revolution in the 20th century*, Interventions.

Broder, David 2016, "The Lost Partisans", *Jacobin*, 25 April. https://www.jacobinmag.com/2016/04/italy-liberation-mussolini-fascism-pci/

Carr, EH 1982, *Twilight of the Comintern: 1930–35*, Pantheon Books.

Daycock, Davis William 1980, "The KPD and the NSDAP: A study of the relationship between political extremes in Weimar Germany 1930–1933", PhD thesis, University of London. http://etheses.lse.ac.uk/4102/3/Daycock_KPD-NSDAP-Weimar-Germany.pdf

Dimitrov, Georgi 1935, "The Fascist Offensive and the Tasks of the Communist International in the Struggle of the Working Class against Fascism", speech at the Seventh World Congress of the Communist International, 2 August. https://www.marxists.org/reference/archive/dimitrov/works/1935/08_02.htm#s2

Eudes, Dominique 1972, *The Kapetanios: Partisans and Civil War in Greece 1943–1949* (trans. John Howe), NLB.

Fromm, Erich 1942, *The fear of freedom*, Routledge & Kegan Paul. https://pescanik.net/wp-content/uploads/2016/11/erich-fromm-the-fear-of-freedom-escape-from-freedom.pdf

Geier, Joel 2022, "Trotskyism confronts World War II: The origins of the International Socialists", *Marxist Left Review*, 23, Summer. https://marxistleftreview.org/articles/trotskyism-confronts-world-war-ii-the-origins-of-the-international-socialists/

Gibson, Ralph 1966, *My Years in the Communist Party*, International Bookshop, Melbourne.

Gluckstein, Donny 1994, *The Tragedy of Bukharin*, Pluto Press.

Gluckstein, Donny 2012, *A People's History of the Second World War Book: Resistance Versus Empire*, Pluto Press.

Gluckstein, Donny 2013, "Socialism and the Second World War: A response to Leandros Bolaris", *International Socialism*, 140, Autumn. http://isj.org.uk/socialism-and-the-second-world-war-a-response-to-leandros-bolaris/

Gollan, Robin 1975. *Revolutionaries and Reformists: Communism and the Australian Labour Movement 1920–1955*, Australian National University Press.

Gramsci, Antonio 1921, "The two fascisms", *Ordino Nuovo*, 25 August. https://www.marxists.org/archive/gramsci/1921/08/two_fascisms.htm

Gray, Oriel 1985, *Exit Left: Memoirs of a Scarlet Woman*, Penguin.

Mason, Paul 2021, *How to Stop Fascism: History, Ideology, Resistance*, Penguin.

Mead, Nick 2022, "Fleeing Franco: Spain's Civil War Refugees", *Metropolitan*, 27 March. https://www.barcelona-metropolitan.com/features/history/fleeing-franco-spain-civil-war-refugees/

Morrow, Felix 1938, *Revolution & Counter-Revolution in Spain*. https://www.marxists.org/archive/morrow-felix/1938/revolution-spain/

Pauwels, Jacques 2019, "The Hitler-Stalin Pact of August 23, 1939: Myth and Reality", 26 August, *Counterpunch*. https://www.counterpunch.org/2019/08/26/the-hitler-stalin-pact-of-august-23-1939-myth-and-reality/

Proyect, Louis and Paweł Szelegieniec 2019, "The Hitler-Stalin Pact, Reconsidered". *Counterpunch*, 30 August. https://www.counterpunch.org/2019/08/30/the-hitler-stalin-pact-reconsidered/

Puzzo, Dante 1992, *The Partisans and the War in Italy*, Peter Lang Publishing, Inc.

Renton, David 2020, *Fascism. History and Theory*, Pluto Press.

Serge, Victor 1938, *The Hangman's Year*. https://www.marxists.org/archive/serge/1938/01/hangman.htm

Serge, Victor 2015, *Midnight of the Century*, New York Review of Books.

Short, Susanna 1992, *Laurie Short: A Political Life*, Allen and Unwin.

Simkin, John 2020 [1997], "Andres Nin", *Spartacus Educational*. https://spartacus-educational.com/SPnin.htm

Siracusa, Joseph M 1981, "The Night Stalin and Churchill Divided Europe: The View from Washington", *The Review of Politics*, 43 (3), pp.381–409. http://www.jstor.org/stable/1406941

Sparrow, Jeff 2007, *Communism: A Love Story*, Melbourne University Press.

Trotsky, Leon 1933, *What is national socialism?*, 10 June. https://www.marxists.org/archive/trotsky/germany/1933/330610.htm#:~:text=In%20the%20atmosphere%20brought%20to,their%20university%20sons%20without%20posts

Trotsky, Leon 1971, *The Struggle Against Fascism in Germany*, Pathfinder.

Trotsky, Leon 2005, *Fascism: What it is and how to fight it*, Aakar Books.

Vassiley, Alexis 2022, "Italian Resistance to Fascism", *Red Flag*, 3 February. https://redflag.org.au/article/italian-resistance-fascism

Wilde, Florian 2013, "Divided They Fell: The German Left and the Rise of Hitler", *International Socialism*, 137, Winter. http://isj.org.uk/divided-they-fell-the-german-left-and-the-rise-of-hitler/

Zetkin, Clara 2017, John Riddell and Mike Taber (eds), *Fighting Fascism: How to Struggle and How to Win*, Haymarket. (One article from this book, "The Struggle Against Fascism", is available at https://www.marxists.org/archive/zetkin/1923/06/struggle-against-fascism.html)

DUNCAN HART

Draper, Lenin and the dictatorship of the proletariat

Duncan Hart is a socialist activist in Brisbane.

> The question of the dictatorship of the proletariat is the fundamental question of the modern working-class movement in all capitalist countries without exception... Whoever has failed to understand that dictatorship is essential to the victory of any revolutionary class has no understanding of the history of revolutions, or else does not want to know anything in this field.
>
> – Lenin, "A Contribution to the History of the Question of the Dictatorship", 20 October 1920[1]

THE CONCEPT OF THE "DICTATORSHIP OF THE PROLETARIAT" is not common in the day-to-day lexicon of Marxists. The word "dictatorship", combined with popular associations of socialism with Stalin, Mao and other dictators, has led modern socialists to sensibly emphasise that the society they stand for would extend, and not curtail, democracy. Nonetheless, the dictatorship of the proletariat remains of central concern for revolutionary socialists as the form of a post-revolutionary workers' state. In fact, attachment to the concept marks out genuine Marxists from both reformists, who oppose the

---

1. Lenin 1965b.

overthrow of the capitalist state in a workers' revolution, and Stalinists, who identify their own models as multi-class "people's democracies".[2]

Of modern Marxist examinations of the concept, Hal Draper's treatment stands out. Draper dedicated an entire volume of his five-volume *Karl Marx's Theory of Revolution* (KMTR) to a detailed enquiry into the context of the usage of the word "dictatorship" in Marx's day, as well as an examination of the context and significance of every time he and Frederick Engels used the phrase "dictatorship of the proletariat". Draper's conclusion following this exhaustive review was simple – Marx and Engels used the phrase "dictatorship of the proletariat" to mean nothing more or less than a workers' state that *must* be established following a working-class revolution.[3]

The term had no particularly "dictatorial" or "suppressive" meaning according to Draper, and was mostly used as a way to counter popular support among revolutionary socialists in their time for an "educational dictatorship" of the consciously revolutionary minority. These socialists, most significantly adherents of the French socialist Blanqui, believed in a transitional period to communism where a dictatorship of the elect would remake society on behalf of the masses, who required a period of education and re-socialisation before being fit to rule themselves.[4] Marx and Engels encouraged socialists to instead support a dictatorship of an entire class – the working class – as part of "the self-conscious, independent movement of the immense majority, in the interest of the immense majority" as the only way to lay the basis for the dissolution of classes altogether.[5]

As well as this better-known work of Draper's, he produced a detour from KMTR in the form of a survey of the phrase "dictatorship of the proletariat". *The "Dictatorship of the Proletariat" from Marx to Lenin* both summarised Draper's findings from KMTR Volume 3 and discussed the subsequent evolution of the phrase by Marxists during

---

2. Tony Cliff meticulously broke down the nature of the "people's democracies" established by the USSR in Eastern Europe following World War II, but no so-called socialist states identified themselves as a "dictatorship of the proletariat" following Khrushchev's dropping of the term in 1961. See Cliff 1950.
3. Draper 2011, p.1.
4. Draper 2011, p.212.
5. Marx and Engels 1999, p.20.

the Second International, among the Russian social democrats and Lenin in particular. Draper also devotes a chapter to the "International Debate on Dictatorship", which discusses the views of Rosa Luxemburg, the left-wing of the Independent Social-Democratic Party of Germany (USPD), Kautsky and leading Bolsheviks besides Lenin on the subject. In this work Draper concludes that, with the exception of Luxemburg and the left wing of the USPD in Germany, Marx's successors tended to transform the meaning of the "dictatorship of the proletariat" away from being a synonym of a workers' state to refer "to *specific governmental forms and policies* – 'dictatorial' ones".[6] This process started under the Second International (formed in 1889), and according to Draper, by 1900, five years since the death of Engels, *"there was not one person using the word 'dictatorship' in any combination who showed awareness of the term's recent past*, who even suspected that Marx had used 'dictatorship' with a meaning no longer current" [emphasis in original].[7] In Draper's account, this "dictatorial" understanding of proletarian dictatorship was subsequently taken up by Lenin and the Third International, justifying authoritarian practices in the Russian Revolution which helped pave the way for Stalin's counter-revolutionary regime.

This article is primarily concerned to defend Lenin and the early Third International's conception of the "dictatorship of the proletariat" against Draper's critique. Contrary to Draper's perspective, Lenin and the early Comintern substantially built upon Marx and Engels' own concepts, imbuing them with new life and clarity out of the experience of the international revolutionary wave of 1917–23. The article will focus on three substantive topics in reply to Draper's work: the nature of dictatorship and the "dictatorship of the proletariat" as Marx understood it, Lenin's theoretical contribution to an understanding of the issue flowing from his experience of the 1905 and 1917 revolutions, and the debate around the concept in the international socialist movement in the post-1917 period.

---

6. Draper 1987, p.44.
7. Draper 1987, p.45.

Marx and "dictatorship"

In both Volume 3 of KMTR and his summary of Marx and Engels' view on the "dictatorship of the proletariat" in *From Marx to Lenin*, Draper outlines that the concept was a synonym for the workers' state. For Draper this did not imply any particular "dictatorial" elements of that state, rather, a workers' state would entail a massive expansion of democracy.[8] This conclusion however is at odds with the evidence Draper presents and flies in the face of Marx and Engels' understanding of the state in class society.

As Draper points out, the word "dictatorship" around the middle of the nineteenth century meant something quite different from its modern usage as supreme power in the hands of an individual or small clique. This was the time when Marx first used the phrase "dictatorship of the proletariat", in the aftermath of the European revolutions and civil wars of 1848.[9] The context for the usage of the word was its Roman origins, and its revival during the French Revolution of 1789–95, which borrowed freely from the classical period for its symbols and significance. The ancient Roman institution of dictatorship which operated from 501 until 44 BCE, says Draper, is more comparable in the modern world with a period of martial law or emergency powers, than the concept of autocracy.[10] This is because the dictatorship was a provision of the Roman Republic's constitution intended to defend the legal framework of the state, not to usurp it. It involved a single man, the dictator, assuming emergency powers at the behest of the Roman authorities for a limited period, usually just six months. The Roman dictator wielded greater powers than any other Roman magistrate, but his power was nonetheless limited.

However, while referencing the ancient institution, the usage of "dictatorship" in the French Revolution was not entirely in keeping with its classical meaning. The term was often used as a term of abuse, possibly in reference to the manner that Julius Caesar ultimately transformed the office into an autocracy, as echoed by the titles of

---

8. Draper 1987, p.30.
9. Marx first used the phrase in *The Class Struggles in France*, written in 1850, which assessed one theatre of the revolutionary struggle of 1848.
10. Draper 2011, p.11.

many subsequent kings and emperors (Caesar, Tsar, Kaiser, Kaysar). "Dictatorship" in this period, though not losing entirely the meaning of an *individual* wielding supreme power, was also used to refer to the forceful rule of any group over another. The term dictatorship was applied, usually by the republican right (Girondins) to refer to the rule of the National Convention (ie the elected parliament), the "multitude", the Paris local government (the commune), and the Jacobins. Jean-Paul Marat was the only leading figure in the French Revolution who actually advocated for any kind of dictatorship, in the sense of the granting of emergency powers to an individual or small group, as a temporary measure to crush counter-revolutionary conspiracy.[11] Thus by the period of the 1848 revolutions and Marx's day, while the concept of dictatorship was not cognate with its modern connotation, it was a little more rubbery than a straight-up description of the ancient Roman institution. Generally, it was used to refer to any kind of forceful authority, particularly one which acted beyond the existing laws.

Draper tracks in KMTR Volume 3, chapters 3 and 4, the essential usage of "dictatorship" in this way in the mid-nineteenth century. That it was not necessarily associated with the rule of a single person is shown by the conservative fear of the time of the *dictatorship of the people*, referring to moves to introduce universal suffrage in numerous countries at the time. The speech of the reactionary Spanish politician, Juan Donoso Cortés, delivered on 4 January 1849, sums it up quite well:

> It is a question of choosing from the dictatorship from below or the dictatorship from above: I choose the dictatorship from above, since it comes from a purer and loftier realm. It is a question of choosing, finally, between the dictatorship of the dagger and the dictatorship of the sabre: I choose the sabre, because it is nobler.[12]

It was with this contemporary usage in mind that Marx and Engels advocated for a revolutionary dictatorship, as partisans of the radical left during the revolution in Germany. At this time, Marx and Engels saw themselves as the radical left wing of "the Democracy", a coalition of

---

11. Draper 2011, pp.19–22.
12. Draper 2011, p.71.

proletarians, peasants and small-craftsmen, which would push for the most radical revolutionary reforms possible within the bounds of the "bourgeois revolution" which they believed was all that was possible at the time. In this vein, they criticised Camphausen, the prime minister of Prussia, whose appointment arose from the revolutionary movement of March 1848, with shrinking away from "dictatorial measures". This was not something Marx pulled out of thin air, but reflected the manner in which liberal politicians such as Camphausen counterposed a concern with legality and acting within the existing order to "dictatorship", which is to say, wielding power outside of the constraints of the existing legal framework. This was not a case of a minority seizing power, but of the first democratically elected parliament in Germany (the Frankfurt Assembly), carrying out a program of democratisation irrespective of the letter of the existing law. Draper quotes Marx in his articles from the *Neue Rheinische Zeitung*, making it abundantly clear that "dictatorship" meant the democratically elected parliament acting outside of the bounds of the law, in a revolutionary way:

> The [National] Assembly in Frankfurt is doing parliamentary school exercises and lets the governments [of the German states] do the acting. Granted that this learned council succeeds after the mature deliberation in working out the best agenda and the best constitution: what is the use of the best agenda and the best constitution if the governments meanwhile have placed bayonets on the agenda?[13]

Instead of wasting time on febrile debates the National Assembly had to take "dictatorial" action:

> It only needed to dictatorially oppose the reactionary encroachments of the outlived governments and it would have won over the power of public opinion against which all bayonets and rifle butts would have shattered.[14]

---
13. Draper 2011, p.62.
14. Draper 2011.

Not only was it a case that *this revolution* required a dictatorship, ie a revolutionary power unafraid to act in a revolutionary way, but Marx went on to say that:

> Every provisional state set up after a revolution requires a dictatorship, and an energetic dictatorship at that. From the beginning we taxed Camphausen with not acting dictatorially, with not immediately smashing and eliminating the remnants of the old institutions. So while Herr Camphausen lulled himself with constitutional dreams, the defeated party strengthened its positions in the bureaucracy and the army – indeed here and there even ventured on open struggle.[15]

Every provisional state set up after a revolution requires a dictatorship, says Marx. Why? Because only a dictatorial state that is not "lulled with constitutional dreams" will not shy away from "smashing and eliminating the remnants of the old institutions". The tragedy in the case of Germany in 1848 was that the bourgeoisie "leading" the revolution were more afraid of the incipient workers' movement and shrank from these necessary measures, allowing the aristocratic states to regain the initiative and crush the movement.

Dictatorship, for Marx and Engels, then, was clearly not just a word synonymous with "rule", and nor does the evidence that Draper presents on its general usage at the time illustrate that. While we can agree with Draper that the dictatorship of the proletariat in Marx and Engels' view was synonymous with a workers' state, Marx and Engels understood the state to exist *for the purposes of forceful suppression of the oppressed classes*. This was famously drawn out by the pair in the *Critique of the Gotha Program*, written in 1875 as a critique of the proposed program of the newly formed German Social Democratic Party (SPD). Says Engels:

> [S]ince the state is merely a transitional institution of which use is made in the struggle, in the revolution, to keep down one's

---

15. Draper 2011, pp.63–64.

enemies by force, it is utter nonsense to speak of a free people's state; so long as the proletariat still *makes use* of the state, it makes use of it, not for the purpose of freedom, but of keeping down its enemies and, as soon as there can be any question of freedom, the state as such ceases to exist.[16]

In this same critique Marx declared that "between capitalist and communist society there lies the period of the revolutionary transformation of the one into the other…in which the state can be nothing but *the revolutionary dictatorship of the proletariat*". [emphasis in original][17]

Summing up Marx and Engels' views, a revolutionary state needed to be a "dictatorship" of the working class directed against its oppressors, and which was not afraid to behave in a revolutionary way, to "smash and eliminate" the old institutions.

Lenin and the theorisation of revolutionary dictatorship

Draper's review of Lenin's thought on the dictatorship of the proletariat and revolutionary dictatorship generally is remarkably hostile. Draper credits Lenin with "[inventing] a unique definition of dictatorship, which as far as I know, came out of his own head", whereas the evidence he presents shows that Lenin was very aware of Marx and Engels' writings on the subject.[18] As Draper shows, Lenin began to develop his understanding of dictatorship during and following the 1905 revolution in the Russian empire. At this time Lenin held to the view that a successful revolution should result in the establishment of the "democratic dictatorship" of the workers and peasants, and not a dictatorship of the proletariat. This related to the view, held almost universally by Russian Marxists until 1917, that Russia's largely feudal society restrained the possibilities of revolutionary outcomes to the setting up of a bourgeois republic rather than the establishment of socialism. Lenin's discussion of dictatorship in this period relates to his view of the democratic dictatorship and "dictatorship" generally, rather

---

16. Engels 1947, p.55.
17. Marx 1947, p.39.
18. Draper 1987, p.80.

than the dictatorship of the proletariat specifically. Nonetheless, there are useful points to draw out.

In his 1906 pamphlet *The Victory of the Cadets and the Tasks of the Workers' Party*, produced originally as a document for a conference of the Bolsheviks, Lenin outlined in some detail a definition of revolutionary dictatorship. This pamphlet was significant in that Lenin reproduced much of the section on dictatorship in 1920 for an article entitled "A Contribution to the History of the Question of the Dictatorship", where he said that the question of revolutionary dictatorship was "essential to the victory of any revolutionary class".

Lenin argued that there were three constituent elements of the "dictatorship of the revolutionary elements of the people" which had burst forth in the "revolutionary whirlwind" of 1905. These were:

> (1) *the seizure by the people of political liberty* – its exercise without any rights and laws, and without any limitations (freedom of assembly, even if only in the universities, freedom of the press, freedom of association, the holding of congresses, etc.); (2) the creation of new organs of *revolutionary authority* – Soviets of Workers', Soldiers', Railwaymen's and Peasants' Deputies... [thirdly]; *the use by the people of force against those who used force against the people*. [emphases in original][19]

Draper highlights Lenin's condensed definition of dictatorship in the following paragraph: "Authority, unlimited, outside the law, and based on force in the most direct sense of the word – is dictatorship". He rails against this view of Lenin's, labelling it a "theoretical disaster, first class". Draper concedes that this situation might describe the brief period of "pitched battle" before workers can establish their own state, but that

> victory in the battle means that workers' state *begins* to operate. It must, to be sure, defend itself, suppress counterrevolution, recast the old state institutions, etc... Without any laws whatever? Without rules? Without standards? On the contrary, its

---

19. Lenin 1965a.

operation means that it establishes its own new, class-oriented laws... according to Lenin's definition, as soon as it does so, the "dictatorship" *ceases*; according to everyone else, the new workers' state *begins*.[20]

Did Lenin really mean that dictatorship meant that a workers' state would have no laws whatsoever? It seems bizarre that Draper would advance this critique, since he was aware of Marx and Engels' similar arguments in favour of drastic action against counter-revolutionaries. This is clearly what Lenin himself had in mind, rather than an adolescent scream against all rules. In order to make his point, Lenin draws a simple analogy:

> Let us suppose that Avramov is injuring and torturing Spiridonova. On Spiridonova's side, let us say, are tens and hundreds of unarmed people. On Avramov's side there is a handful of Cossacks. What would the people do if Spiridonova were being tortured, not in a dungeon, but in public? They would resort to force against Avramov and his body-guard...they would forcibly disarm Avramov and his Cossacks, and in all probability would kill on the spot some of these brutes in human form; and they would clap the rest into some gaol to prevent them from committing any more outrages and to bring them to judgement before the people.[21]

This analogy provides a small example of "the dictatorship *of the people*, because the people, the mass of the population, unorganised, 'casually' assembled at the given spot, itself appears on the scene, exercises justice and metes out justice, exercises power and creates a new, revolutionary law".[22] Lenin is for "new, revolutionary law" created by the insurgent people. What he labels "dictatorship" is the way this new law and new authority overthrows the existing law and existing authority of the "military and police dictatorship". This is made clear

---

20. Draper 1987, p.91.
21. Lenin 1965a.
22. Lenin 1965a.

when he discusses the theoretical opposition to the people's "dictatorial" behaviour by a liberal, who is likely to

> be opposed to rescuing Spiridonova from Avramov by force, thinking it to be against the "law". They would no doubt ask: Is there a "law" that permits the killing of Avramov? Have not some philistine ideologists built up a theory of non-resistance to evil?[23]

Draper himself seems to be quite close to this view, asking "why a lynch mob is not also a 'dictatorship of the people'?"[24] He could have asked the same of the murderous pogroms instigated by reactionary mobs and government agents in Russia at this time. Lenin himself makes it very clear what the difference in content is, in a lengthy but fruitful passage:

> The [organs of the tsarist state] were the instruments of the rule of the minority over the people, over the masses of workers and peasants. The [soviet] was an instrument of the rule of the people, of the workers and peasants, over the minority, over a handful of police bullies, over a handful of privileged nobles and government officials. Such is the difference between dictatorship *over* the people and dictatorship *of* the revolutionary people: mark this well... As the dictatorship of a minority, the old regime was able to maintain itself solely with the aid of police devices, solely by preventing the masses of the people from taking part in the government and from supervising the government. The old authority persistently distrusted the masses, feared the light, maintained itself by deception. As the dictatorship of the overwhelming majority, the new authority maintained itself and could maintain itself solely because it enjoyed the confidence of the vast masses, solely because it, in the freest, widest and most resolute manner, enlisted all the masses in the task of government. It concealed nothing, it had no secrets, no regulations, no formalities.[25]

---

23. Lenin 1965a.
24. Draper 1987, p.92.
25. Lenin 1965a.

This underappreciated work illuminates many of the themes Lenin would return to with greater clarity in *State and Revolution*. The dictatorship of the majority relied not on "the force of bayonets...not the power of the 'police force', nor the power of money" but upon the "confidence of the vast masses". Nonetheless it was a "dictatorship" because it rested upon force against the old authorities. Force was necessary, even for the vast majority, because "the new authority does not drop from the skies, but grows up, arises parallel with, and in opposition to, the old authority, in struggle against it. Unless force is used against tyrants armed with the weapons and instruments of power, the people cannot be liberated from tyrants".[26] The significance of understanding "dictatorship" as authority recognising no laws and based on force was that it was a *revolutionary authority* directed against the existing laws and for the use of force by the oppressed classes against the oppressors.

Draper advances one final argument against the "authoritarianism" of Lenin, alleging that Lenin was for a Blanquist-style, minority dictatorship. This is based on a reading of the section of *The Victory of the Cadets and the Tasks of the Workers' Party* where Lenin says that the revolutionary dictatorship is administered by the "revolutionary people" and not the whole people. Lenin says this is so because "among the whole people...there are some who are physically cowed and terrified; there are some who are morally degraded by the 'resist not evil' theory, for example, or simply degraded not by theory, but by prejudice, habit, routine". Nonetheless, the revolutionary people "do not shun the whole people, [but] explain to all the people the motive of their actions in all their details, and...willingly enlist the *whole* people not only in 'administering' the state, but in governing it too".[27]

Draper describes this as "the transmogrification of the class dictatorship into a party dictatorship...exactly what the traditional 'revolutionary dictatorship' had meant before Marx".[28] But where does Lenin say that this is a minority dictatorship or a dictatorship of the "elect"? As we have seen, he said multiple times in the same publication that he was describing the "dictatorship of the overwhelming majority".

---

26. Lenin 1965a.
27. Lenin 1965.
28. Draper 1987, p.92.

In his later works, such as *State and Revolution*, he talks about the workers' state in the same manner. Draper is here misunderstanding the fact of uneven and contradictory consciousness among the workers which means that not all workers will agree with the establishment of the proletarian dictatorship, even after the revolution. Nonetheless, it is glaringly apparent from Lenin's statements during 1917 that a workers' revolution could only be made once a majority of workers had been won to the necessity of it.[29] This was repeated by Lenin in the first theses passed at the inaugural congress of the Communist International in March 1919, which declared that "winning a communist majority in the soviets is the principal task in all countries".[30]

Draper struggles to paint Lenin as "dictatorial" even to the extent of disagreeing with Marx. Lenin's 1905 work, *Two Tactics of Social Democracy in the Democratic Revolution*, references Franz Mehring's 1902 book on Marx which cites quotes on "dictatorship" from the *Neue Rheinische Zeitung* in 1848. Lenin says that only "from the vulgar bourgeois standpoint are the terms dictatorship and democracy mutually exclusive". Quoting Marx's views, reviewed above, Lenin boils down "dictatorship" to: "destroy[ing] the remnants of the old institutions... lastly, it follows from these words that Marx castigated bourgeois democrats for entertaining 'constitutional illusions' in a period of revolution and open civil war".[31] Responding to this, Draper says: "But what is 'dictatorial' about *that*, given a democratically based revolution?"[32] What indeed! Draper seems to have fallen prey to his own terminological trap and wants to paint Lenin quoting Marx almost verbatim as devilish heresy.

Lenin was clearly well aware of Marx's writings on "dictatorship" and did his best to apply them to the revolutionary situation Russia was living through. His writings, far from contradicting the founders of Marxism, further flesh out the meaning of "revolutionary dictatorship" in light of the experience provided by the 1905 revolution. This emphasised that dictatorship implied the use of force by the

---

29. Lenin 1964.
30. Riddell 1987, p.163.
31. Lenin 1977, p.132.
32. Draper 1987, p.89.

revolutionary class against its oppressors and was revolutionary in that it ignored the existing laws and erected its own authority in their stead.

The Comintern and the international debate on "dictatorship"

Draper's book deals with Comintern debates on this issue in quite an unsatisfactory way. Though he repeatedly says that the concept of the dictatorship of the proletariat was a centrepiece of the early Comintern, he barely references what early Comintern publications said on the question. Instead he focuses most on the debate between Kautsky and the Bolsheviks on the issue. Nonetheless, this is a welcome topic of discussion that has not received the attention it deserves. But Draper fails to substantially grasp the issues at stake.

A reading of Kautsky's first two books to critique the Russian Revolution and the Bolsheviks is a fruitful endeavour for Marxists, providing further useful context to Lenin's *State and Revolution* and *The Proletarian Revolution and the Renegade Kautsky*. Kautsky wrote *The Dictatorship of the Proletariat* in August 1918 and followed it up with *Terrorism and Communism* in June 1919. Draper correctly identifies major weaknesses of Kautsky's critique as being his identification of parliamentary democracy in a capitalist society as pure, or abstract democracy, and his inability to perceive the Russian Revolution in its international context. Unfortunately, Draper does not grasp the significance of Kautsky's critique of "dictatorship", which he attacks as the essential element of Bolshevism.

In his earliest anti-Bolshevik work, Kautsky attempted to draw a sharp demarcation between the dictatorship of the proletariat as a "political condition" and "a form of government", arguing that Marx only supported the former, and not the latter. There are two problems with this half-truth from Kautsky. Marx did not conceive of the dictatorship of the proletariat as a form of government because he believed it to be the necessary form of a *workers' state*. Kautsky does not want to use the phrase "workers' state", which would open up the question of smashing the *capitalist* state. This is an example of how Kautsky blurs the lines between different forms of state, as Draper usefully points out.[33]

---

33. Draper 1987, pp.129, 132.

But Draper misses the significance of Kautsky's rejection of "dictatorial" methods. "Dictatorship [says Kautsky]...means disarming the opposition, by taking from them the franchise, and liberty of the press and combination."[34] Kautsky rejects dictatorship as the road for socialists either in the situation where "capitalists and their supporters are an insignificant handful" or where they represent a great mass "in a parliament elected on the basis of universal suffrage".[35] In contrast, he argued for socialists to fight on the terrain of democracy, which meant not just rule by the majority, but importantly, "protection of minorities", ie the bourgeoisie.[36] Kautsky renounced the idea of violent revolution, arguing that civil war, which was another consequence of dictatorship, was a barrier to the creation of socialism.[37] Instead he argued that socialism would come about by workers' parties attaining a majority in conditions of universal suffrage in a parliamentary democracy.[38]

Draper seems to misunderstand Lenin's critique of this central element of Kautsky's argument. All Draper says of Lenin's *The Proletarian Revolution and the Renegade Kautsky* is that Lenin "implicitly repudiates" Kautsky's support for "majority revolution" by saying that "a dictatorship is needed in order to suppress the bourgeois resistance". All quotations are Draper's words, not Lenin's.[39] As we have seen, Kautsky did not support "majority revolution" at all.

Draper is also wrong to argue that Lenin opposed majority revolution, even implicitly. This can be easily disproved due to Lenin being so forthright and clear in his argumentation. Against Kautsky's argument that "the majority" should not have to use "dictatorship" against the capitalists, Lenin lays it out clearly:

> To assume in a revolution that is at all profound and serious the issue is decided simply by the relation of the majority and the minority...is the *deception of the masses*, concealing from them a well-established historical truth. This historical truth is that in

---

34. Kautsky 1919, p.45.
35. Kautsky 1919, pp.75–76.
36. Kautsky 1919, p.34.
37. Kautsky 1919, p.58.
38. Kautsky 1919, p.98.
39. Draper 1987, p.134.

> every profound revolution, the *prolonged, stubborn, desperate* resistance of the exploiters, who for a number of years enjoy important practical advantages over the exploited, is the rule. Never, except in the sentimental fantasies of the sentimental simpleton Kautsky, will the exploiters submit to the decision of the exploited majority without making use of their advantages in a last desperate battle, or a series of battles.[40]

Polish revolutionary Karl Radek in *Proletarian Dictatorship and Terrorism* (1920) similarly challenged a formalistic obsession with majorities. Radek does not disavow the concept of "majority revolution", but says that pegging the workers' revolution to the "mathematically established" support of the majority of the population is folly, because the capitalists will "suppress the workers' press, dissolve the workers' organisations and attempt to provoke the proletariat into premature outbreaks". In these circumstances "it will scarcely be possible to ascertain, by any kind of elections, which side has the majority".[41]

This might offend the sensibilities of those who would prefer a pure and orderly revolution, but it is backed up by historical experience. The Finnish Social Democratic Party had just lost its majority in the parliament to the bourgeois parties in fresh elections in November 1917 when it led a (failed) revolutionary general strike. Only a soulless pedant would say that the Finnish workers, because their party had only achieved 45 percent of the popular vote, should have laid down in the snow and accepted the repression being prepared against them without rising in revolt in January 1918. In July 1936, when the Spanish workers defeated the fascist military coup across the majority of Spain, there was no way to test if the workers' organisations had clear majority support. Indeed, the Popular Front, which was made up primarily of bourgeois liberals, had only won 47 percent of the vote in January, as against 46.5 percent for avowed reactionaries. Yet revolutionaries, including Draper himself, have always insisted that workers should have gone even further in the social revolution already taking place to defeat fascism. In Chile, Salvador Allende's party only won a maximum

---
40. Lenin 1942, p.35.
41. Radek 1921, p.56.

of 42 percent of the popular vote during his presidency, but efforts by workers to defend his government and their own organisations from being violently overthrown by the military were far from "Blanquism".

What Draper seems unable to grasp is the central theoretical disagreement at the heart of Kautksy's polemic, which rejected "dictatorship" – as in the *revolutionary seizure of power* by the workers regardless of whether they were the majority of the population or not. Lenin was at pains in *The Proletarian Revolution* to stress that the question of "dictatorship" was about the necessity of *establishing a workers' state*, with all that entails. The form of the workers' state and how suppressive it would be forced to be in each country was a "specifically national question". This included whether or not the bourgeoisie would be actively disenfranchised, as had occurred in Russia. The only "necessary condition of dictatorship" was "the *forcible suppression* of the exploiters as a class, and consequently, the *infringement* of 'pure democracy', ie of equality and freedom for that class".[42]

This actively contradicts the assertion that Draper makes throughout his book that Lenin and the Communist International saw in the dictatorship of the proletariat a particular form of government, rather than a universal description of the workers' state. Lenin even spends a couple of pages highlighting that "the dictatorship of the bourgeoisie" may also take different forms, such as republics or monarchies, without changing the capitalist nature of those states.[43] In *The Immediate Tasks of the Soviet Government* (April 1918), Lenin highlighted the obverse in relation to the dictatorship of the proletariat:

> If we are not anarchists, we must admit that the state, *that is, coercion*, is necessary for the transition from capitalism to socialism. The form of coercion is determined by the degree of development of the given revolutionary class, and also by special circumstances, such as, for example, the legacy of a long and reactionary war and the form of resistance put up by the bourgeoisie and the petty bourgeoisie.[44]

---

42. Lenin 1942, pp.37–38.
43. Lenin 1942, pp.20–21.
44. Lenin 1972, p.34.

Again, the state, ie the proletarian dictatorship, is *necessary for the transition period*, echoing Marx, because the fundamental basis of the state, ie the division of society into classes, has not disappeared. The circumstances facing the new workers' state and the strength of the workers does not determine whether the state is a "dictatorship" or not, but solely the "form of coercion".

Lenin used the term "proletarian democracy" interchangeably with "proletarian dictatorship" in *The Proletarian Revolution*. This was part of proving the hollowness of Kautsky's craven obsequiousness to the capitalist state, which he described as "democratic" compared to the Bolshevik "dictatorship". Lenin points out that "proletarian democracy is a million times more democratic than any bourgeois democracy" because it provides genuine equality rather than hypocritical formal equality:

> Freedom of the press ceases to be hypocrisy, because the printing presses and stocks of paper are taken away from the bourgeoisie. The same thing applies to the best buildings, the palaces, the mansions and manor houses. The Soviet Government [has taken these buildings] and in this way it has made the right of assembly – without which democracy is a fraud – a million times more "democratic".[45]

The right to elect and to recall soviet representatives at any time, and the abolition of the existing state with its networks of privilege and bureaucracy made the Soviet state the first since the Paris Commune to engage the workers in the task of government. Bukharin in *The Program of the World Revolution* (May 1918) described well the difference between the workers' state and the "parliamentary republic [where] every citizen hands his vote once in every four or five years, and there his part in the matter ends".

> The bourgeois State is based on the deception of the masses, keeping them half-awake, by the method of depriving them of

---

45. Lenin 1942, p.30.

any active part in the everyday work of the state, by summoning them once every few years "to vote", and by deceiving them with their own vote. It is an entirely different thing in a Soviet republic. The Soviet republic, embodying the dictatorship of the masses, cannot even for a minute tear itself away from these masses. Such a republic is the stronger in proportion to the greater activity and energy manifested by the masses... It is not a matter of mere chance, therefore, that the Soviet Government in issuing its decrees addresses the masses with the demand that the workers and poorest peasants themselves should carry these decrees into execution.[46]

Lenin also uses the example of foreign policy, from which the Soviet government "[tore] the veil of mystery". The period of debate on the Brest Litovsk treaty, which at different points was opposed by the majority of soviets in Russia until eventually being ratified at a Soviet Congress, is ignored by Kautsky. Lenin's condemnation rings true up to the modern day:

> In the present era of predatory wars and secret treaties for the "division of spheres of influences" (ie for the partition of the world among the capitalist bandits), the subject is of cardinal importance, for it is a matter...of life and death for millions of people.[47]

Lenin could also have referenced the right of self-determination that the workers' revolution had recognised for the oppressed majority nationalities of the Russian empire.

Dictatorship versus democracy

The view that the dictatorship of the proletariat as represented by Soviet power in Russia was more democratic than bourgeois democracy was not an isolated view of Lenin's but echoed by all of the leading Bolsheviks, such as Trotsky, Radek, Bukharin and Zinoviev.

46. Bukharin 1920, p.30.
47. Lenin 1942, p.29.

Nonetheless, there was an important point to be made about the dictatorship of the proletariat in *contrast to democracy itself*.

Draper argues that soon after the October Revolution, Lenin and the Bolsheviks began championing a "specially organised dictatorial regime, dictatorial in the sense that had become increasingly dominant, and increasingly counterposed to abstract democracy…thus facilitating the societal counterrevolution represented by Stalin".[48] Draper dates the "theoretical disaster" of abstractly counterposing "democracy" to "dictatorship" to a speech by Lenin in January 1918, though he associates any discussion by the Bolsheviks with the "dictatorship of the proletariat" *at all* with the dissolution of the Constituent Assembly around the same time, in keeping with Kautsky's erroneous argument from 1918.[49] In fact, as Lenin explained in his *Theses on the Constituent Assembly* (December 1917), and again in *The Proletarian Revolution*, the Bolsheviks since April 1917 had consistently highlighted that the soviets were a higher form of proletarian democracy than that of a bourgeois republic and represented an incipient state power of the working class.[50]

So why did Lenin and a number of leading Bolsheviks, while identifying the dictatorship of the proletariat as a higher form of democracy than capitalism, still argue against "democracy"? In *The Proletarian Revolution*, Lenin describes how bourgeois democracies are a mask for the dictatorship of the capitalists.

> The learned Mr Kautsky has "forgotten" – no doubt accidentally – …that the ruling party in a bourgeois democracy extends the protection of minorities only to the other *bourgeois* party, while on all *serious, profound and fundamental issues*, the working class get martial law and pogroms, instead of the "protection of minorities".

Lenin draws out examples of this from the lynching of Black people and Wobblies in the United States, the suppression of the Irish

---

48. Draper 1987, pp.104–5.
49. Draper 1987, p.102.
50. Lenin 1942, p.46.

independence struggle by the United Kingdom, and persecution of Jews in France, all crimes committed by so-called "democracies".[51] Since 1918 we could add to that list countless US and European military interventions in favour of dictators, the persecution of communists in the US and Australia in the mid-twentieth century and more recently the armed suppression of the Black Lives Matter revolt in the USA. All these examples can only scratch the surface of this fundamental truth – that all states are ultimately "dictatorships" of the ruling class.

The "point" of bourgeois democracy, Lenin discusses later in *The Proletarian Revolution*, is that "while exercising the dictatorship of the bourgeoisie...[it] cannot tell the truth and is compelled to be hypocritical".

> But a state of the Paris Commune type, a Soviet state, openly tells people the *truth* and declares that it is the dictatorship of the proletariat and the poorest peasantry; and by this truth it rallies to its side scores and scores of millions of new citizens who are kept down under a democratic republic, but who are drawn by the Soviets into political life, into *democracy*, into the administration of the state.[52]

The defence of "democracy" which Kautsky's critique embodied was part of a broader anti-revolutionary political position among reformist socialists in reaction to the Russian Revolution. In Russia, it was the Mensheviks and Socialist Revolutionaries who opposed Soviet power on the basis of "democracy", an argument then taken up by their international co-thinkers. Bukharin directly addressed this slogan, saying it was a necessary camouflage for those who "cannot possibly say frankly and openly, 'we want the whip and the stick for the workers'". Clamouring for the enfranchisement of the bourgeoisie and the rejection of the unabashed "dictatorship" of the workers represented an effort "to transform the class government of workers and peasants into a class government of the bourgeoisie under the pretext of admitting

51. Lenin 1942, p.28.
52. Lenin 1942, p.81.

all sections".[53] Engels had predicted that "democracy" would be the last refuge of reactionaries opposing the rule of the workers, and he was right.[54]

So the question of the proletarian dictatorship was that it was the rule of the exploited majority over the exploiters. As the first state genuinely of the workers, it did not need to obscure its true purpose under hypocritical phrases. In this sense it was important to defend its dictatorship rather than concede to "democracy", which is to say, to enfranchise the capitalists and their political representatives, which could only mean a step away from a workers' state. At the same time, the workers' dictatorship was a "higher form of democracy" precisely because it was a state where the workers were genuinely in power and excluded the capitalists.

Draper and Luxemburg

Draper identifies Luxemburg's critique of the Bolsheviks in her unpublished pamphlet *The Russian Revolution* as in keeping with Marx and Engels' perspective on the dictatorship of the proletariat.[55] The problem with using this pamphlet as a statement of Luxemburg's final views on the subject was that Luxemburg herself never believed it to be so. She had limited access to Bolshevik texts and as we shall see, changed her views in the process of the revolution in Germany itself.[56]

In *The Russian Revolution* Luxemburg argues "that the basic error of the Lenin-Trotsky theory is that they too, just like Kautsky, oppose dictatorship to democracy". The evidence for this statement revolves around the section of Trotsky's *From October to Brest Litovsk* where he explains why it was right to dissolve the Constituent Assembly, which had been elected by universal suffrage across much of Russia. Trotsky says:

> The open and direct struggle for power enables the labouring

---

53. Bukharin 1920, p.31.
54. Engels 1942.
55. Draper 1987, p.115.
56. Luxemburg directly references Trotsky's short history of the Russia revolution at the start of the section on "The Constituent Assembly" and also "Lenin's speech on discipline and corruption" later on, but notably not *State and Revolution*. Luxemburg 1961, pp.57, 72.

masses to acquire in a short time a wealth of political experience and thus rapidly to pass from one stage to another in the process of their mental evolution. The ponderous mechanism of democratic institutions cannot keep pace with this evolution – and this in proportion to the vastness of the country and the imperfection of the technical apparatus at its disposal.[57]

Luxemburg criticises this challenge to "democratic institutions" by highlighting examples of how parliaments in the French and English revolutions were impacted by "the living movement of the masses, their unending pressure", despite the formal, structural limitations of the elected bodies. Luxemburg goes on to say that "the more democratic the institutions, the livelier and stronger the pulse-beat of the political life of the masses, the more direct and complete is their influence – despite rigid party banners, outgrown tickets (electoral lists) etc". Luxemburg argued that the dissolution of the Constituent Assembly and the disenfranchisement of the bourgeoisie and their supporters in Russia represented "the elimination of democracy as such, [and] is worse than the disease it is supposed to cure".[58] Luxemburg, make no mistake, was for the dictatorship of the proletariat:

> [B]ut this dictatorship consists in the *manner of applying democracy*, not in its *elimination*, in energetic, resolute attacks upon the well-entrenched rights and privileges of bourgeois society, without which a socialist transformation cannot be accomplished. But this dictatorship must be the work of the class and not of a little leading minority in the name of the class – that is, it must proceed step by step out of the active participation of the masses...[59]

What both Trotsky and Luxemburg missed in these works is the perspective clearly outlined by Lenin and other Bolsheviks about the workers' state and the soviets as a higher form of democracy than

---

57. Trotsky 1919.
58. Luxemburg 1961, p.62.
59. Luxemburg 1961, pp.77–78.

parliamentary democracy, and also what *class power* the different institutions represented. Trotsky discusses the functioning of the soviets only in passing. He also does not describe any other element of workers' power, such as the factory committees or the trade unions. Luxemburg in her pamphlet only discusses the soviets as bodies that exclude those who do not labour from voting. Luxemburg, who suffered from a lack of information in her prison cell, treats the dissolution of the Constituent Assembly in the same terms as Kautsky, which is to say, representing the annulment of "democracy" in Russia. She does not indicate any appreciation of how precisely it was soviet power which created the most "democratic institutions" enabling "the more direct and complete" influence of the workers, nor does she recognise the most significant thing, which is for which *class* do they represent state power.

Notably Luxemburg herself would later oppose the right wing of the Independent Social Democratic Party (USPD) in Germany, which, like Kautsky, argued for the co-existence of a bourgeois parliament alongside the workers' councils. Luxemburg rightly recognised that one or the other must win out as representative of hostile class interests – the dictatorship of the capitalists or of the workers. The program of the Communist Party of Germany (KPD), drafted by Luxemburg in December 1918, was as clear as day on the question of the "dictatorship of the proletariat" and rejected parliamentary democracy as its form:

> The imperialist capitalist class, as last offspring of the caste of exploiters, outdoes all its predecessors in brutality, in open cynicism and treachery. It defends its holiest of holies, its profit and its privilege of exploitation, with tooth and nail, with the methods of cold evil which it demonstrated to the world in the entire history of colonial politics and in the recent World War. It will mobilize heaven and hell against the proletariat…it will turn the country into a smoking heap of rubble rather than voluntarily give up wage slavery.
>
> All this resistance must be broken step by step, with an iron fist and ruthless energy. The violence of the bourgeois

counterrevolution must be confronted with the revolutionary violence of the proletariat...

> Such arming of the solid mass of labouring people with all political power for the tasks of the revolution – that is the *dictatorship of the proletariat and therefore true democracy*. Not where the wage slave sits next to the capitalist, the rural proletarian next to the Junker in fraudulent equality to engage in parliamentary debate over questions of life or death, but where the million-headed proletarian mass seizes the entire power of the state in its calloused fist – like the god Thor his hammer – using it to smash the head of the ruling classes: that alone is democracy, that alone is not a betrayal of the people. [emphasis added][60]

This passage outlines the exact same justification for the necessity of the dictatorship of the proletariat as has already been reviewed in Lenin and Marx. The necessity of dictatorship flowed from the necessity of revolution itself, which is the forcible seizure of state power as the only way to overthrow the capitalists, whose resistance must be "broken" with "an iron fist and ruthless energy".

In discussing the supposedly "democratic" version of Luxemburg's dictatorship of the proletariat, it is worth looking at what her contemporary, Clara Zetkin, had to say. Zetkin was not imprisoned and seems to have been able to more easily access information on the contemporary debate on the dictatorship of the proletariat. She wrote an article in 1918 that responded to Martov's and Kautsky's attacks on the Bolsheviks, entitled *Through Dictatorship to Democracy*.[61] Zetkin had a better perception of the class significance of the soviets *vis-à-vis* parliamentary democracy, pointing out that:

> Had they accepted parliamentarism, the Bolsheviks would have

---

60. Luxemburg 1971.
61. The article on the Marxists Internet Archive is dated to 1919. Since it is a reply to two articles written by Martov and Kautsky in 1918, and it also speaks of the Left Socialist-Revolutionaries as if they were still part of the Soviet government, I think it is more likely to have been written prior to July 1918.

accepted an institution which, however important, is of very limited value; an institution which even in times of peaceful evolution has proved obviously inadequate to the needs of the proletarian struggle for emancipation... parliament is one of those state institutions which a victorious proletariat cannot simply take over and use for its own purposes. The new revolutionary wine must not be poured into old bottles. From this outlook, "Bolshevism" was assuredly justified in replacing the Constituent Assembly by the soviets, in replacing the activity of a determinative and legislative assembly, by the activity of organisations upon the broadest possible democratic basis, and simultaneously legislative, administrative, and executive.[62]

Zetkin was unequivocal, describing dictatorship as "stark, coercive dominion" and insisted that "who wills the ends must not shrink from the means. A proletarian revolution aiming at socialism cannot be effected without dictatorship".

A revolutionary heritage

In order to make his argument that Lenin and the early Comintern advocated some form of "specifically organised dictatorial regime" Draper ignores the early writings of leading Bolsheviks, which attempted to proselytise the lessons of the Russian Revolution to an international audience. A clear understanding of the dictatorship of the proletariat as the rule of the entire working class, and a massive expansion of democracy whose repression was directed against the capitalists is a clear feature of early Comintern staples like Radek's *Socialism from Science to Action* (1918), Bukharin's *Program of the World Revolution* (1918), Zinoviev's *To the IWW* (1920), and Lenin's works *State and Revolution* (1917), *The Proletarian Revolution* (1918) and *Left-Wing Communism* (1920). It was also spelt out in detail in Lenin's theses on *Bourgeois Democracy and Proletarian Dictatorship*, which were adopted at the founding Congress of the Comintern in March 1919. Lenin's 1906 observations on revolutionary dictatorship were confirmed: rule over

---

62. Zetkin 1926.

the capitalists based on force, and not on "law", with the new workers' state emerging out of "revolutionary seizure from below" which replaced the institutions of the capitalist state. These works did not contradict Marx and Engels' views on the dictatorship of the proletariat as a synonym for the workers' state but expanded them with fresh revolutionary experience.

Following the failed Left Socialist Revolutionary revolt against the Brest Litovsk treaty with Germany in July 1918, which coincided with the uprising of the 30,000-strong Czech Legion in Siberia, the Bolsheviks ruled alone and faced off against increasing pressures from within and without. In this increasingly desperate situation, and after several terrorist attacks against their leading members, including Lenin, the Bolsheviks turned towards outright red terror to break any opposition. It was only sometime after establishing their sole rule *in fact* that the Bolsheviks began to justify it *in theory*. This is important because it is typically asserted that the Bolsheviks always generalised the measures they were forced into in Russia into universally applicable lessons for the international revolutionary movement. In fact, it's clear that this warped theorisation of the dictatorship of the proletariat took time to develop under counter-revolutionary pressures, and was not an immediate leap, or a product of inherent problems in the ideology of the Bolsheviks.

Draper ignores the earlier foundational works of the Comintern, instead focusing on Bolshevik replies to Kautsky's 1919 book *Terrorism and Communism*. Even here, most of Draper's critique is based on wilful misinterpretation of what leading Bolsheviks such as Bukharin, Kamenev and Radek actually said.[63] While these writers, most clearly Trotsky, did defend the concept of the dictatorship of the Communist Party in Russia, they did so by eliding the difference between the rule of the party and the entire working class, *not* by arguing that the working class was incapable of self-emancipation.[64] This was certainly wrong, but indicative of the difficulties the Bolsheviks found themselves in, rather than a case of a "dictatorial" theory coming into full bloom.

---

63. Draper 1987, pp.137–38.
64. Trotsky 2007, p.104.

Conclusion

Draper's work on the dictatorship of the proletariat in Marx and Engels is extremely valuable. Volume 3 of KMTR is a masterful collation of the context and circumstances behind every reference made to the phrase "dictatorship of the proletariat", and indeed dictatorship in general, in their writings. However, his later work, *From Marx to Lenin*, shows that Draper was fiercely opposed to how the early Comintern, including Lenin, used this concept. Reviewing the concept with reference to Lenin and the early Comintern shows up weaknesses in Draper's interpretation, not just with respect to the successors of Marx and Engels, but also in his interpretation of "dictatorship" for Marx and Engels.

The "dictatorship of the proletariat" today is perceived by many socialists as a millstone around their necks to be explained away. This article has sought to explain why it was not just a coincidental element of Marxist thought. Rather it fully accorded with an understanding of the state as arising out of indissoluble class conflicts, that exists to maintain the power of the ruling class over the oppressed classes.

Even one hundred years after the Russian Revolution, the same fundamental issues remain. Is it possible for the working class to come to power without an act of "revolutionary seizure" whereby they smash the existing state institutions and replace them with their own, more democratic institutions of workers' power? Is it possible for such a workers' state to arise and to hold on without understanding the source of its power as being the force that it wields "dictatorially" against the old oppressors? An overview of the "dictatorship of the proletariat" from the founders of historical materialism to the period of the early Comintern vindicates Lenin's statement that it remains "essential to the victory of any revolutionary class".

References

Bukharin, Nikolai 1920 [1918], *Program of the World Revolution*, Socialist Labour Press. https://www.marxists.org/archive/bukharin/works/1918/worldrev/index.html

Cliff, Tony 1950, "On the Class Nature of the People's Democracies", July. https://www.marxists.org/archive/cliff/works/1950/07/index.htm

Draper, Hal 1987, *The "Dictatorship of the Proletariat" from Marx to Lenin*, Monthly Review Press.

Draper, Hal 2011, *Karl Marx's Theory of Revolution, Volume 3: The "Dictatorship of the Proletariat"*, Aakar Books.

Engels, Frederick 1942 [1884], "Letter to August Bebel", 11–12 December 1884, in *Gesamtausgabe*, International Publishers. https://www.marxists.org/archive/marx/works/1884/letters/84_12_11.htm

Engels, Frederick 1947 [1875], "Letter to August Bebel", March 18–28 1875, in Marx, *Critique of the Gotha Program*, Foreign Languages Publishing House. https://www.marxists.org/archive/marx/works/1875/letters/75_03_18.htm

Kautsky, Karl 1919 [1918], HJ Stenning (trans.), *The Dictatorship of the Proletariat*, National Labour Press.

Lenin, Vladimir 1942 [1918], *The Proletarian Revolution and the Renegade Kautsky*, Lawrence and Wishart. https://www.marxists.org/archive/lenin/works/1918/prrk/

Lenin, Vladimir 1964 [1917], "The Dual Power", in *Lenin Collected Works*, Volume 24, pp.38–41, Progress Publishers. https://www.marxists.org/archive/lenin/works/1917/apr/09.htm

Lenin, Vladimir 1965a [1906], "The Victory of the Cadets and the Tasks of the Workers' Party", in *Collected Works*, Volume 10, pp.199–276, Progress Publishers. https://www.marxists.org/archive/lenin/works/1906/victory/digress.htm#v10pp65-242

Lenin, Vladimir 1965b [1920], "A Contribution to the History of the Question of the Dictatorship", in *Collected Works*, Volume 31, pp.340–61, Progress Publishers. https://www.marxists.org/archive/lenin/works/1920/oct/20.htm

Lenin, Vladimir 1972 [1918], *The Immediate Tasks of Soviet Government*, in *Collected Works*, Volume 27, pages 235-77, Progress Publishers. https://www.marxists.org/archive/lenin/works/1918/mar/x03.htm

Lenin, Vladimir 1977 [1905], *Two Tactics of Social Democracy in the Democratic Revolution*, in *Collected Works*, Volume 9, pp.15-140, Progress Publishers. https://www.marxists.org/archive/lenin/works/1905/tactics/index.htm

Luxemburg, Rosa 1961 (1918), *The Russian Revolution and Leninism or Marxism?*, University of Michigan Press.

Luxemburg, Rosa 1971 [1918], Dick Howard (ed.), Martin Nicolaus [trans.], "What does the Spartacus League Want?", in *Selected Political Writings of Rosa Luxemburg*, Monthly Review Press. https://www.marxists.org/archive/luxemburg/1918/12/14.htm

Marx, Karl 1947 [1875], *Critique of the Gotha Program*, Foreign Languages Publishing House. https://www.marxists.org/archive/marx/works/1875/gotha/

Marx, Karl and Engels, Frederick 1999 [1848], *Manifesto of the Communist Party*, International Publishers. https://www.marxists.org/archive/marx/works/1848/communist-manifesto/

Radek, Karl 1921 [1920], Patrick Lavin (trans.), *Proletarian Dictatorship and Terrorism*, Marxian Educational Society. https://www.marxists.org/archive/radek/1920/dictterr/index.htm

Riddell, John 1987 (ed.), *Founding the Communist International. Proceedings and Documents of the First Congress, March 1919*, Anchor Foundation.

Trotsky, Leon 1919 [1918], *History of the Russian Revolution to Brest Litovsk*, George Allen and Unwin. https://www.marxists.org/archive/trotsky/1918/hrr/ch03.htm

Trotsky, Leon 2007 [1920], *Terrorism and Communism*, Verso. https://www.marxists.org/archive/trotsky/1920/terrcomm/index.htm

Zetkin, Clara 1926 [1918], Eden and Cedar Paul (trans.), *Through Dictatorship to Democracy*, Socialist Labour Press. https://www.marxists.org/archive/zetkin/1919/xx/dictdem.htm

JORDAN HUMPHREYS

Review: Indigenous people vs "settler" migrants?

Jordan Humphreys is a socialist activist in Sydney and has written extensively on Indigenous oppression and working-class history.

Nandita Sharma, *Home Rule: National Sovereignty and the Separation of Natives and Migrants*, Duke University Press, 2020.

NANDITA SHARMA HAS WRITTEN A VERY USEFUL BOOK that rightly polemicises against those on the progressive left who counterpose the rights of Indigenous people to those of migrants. As Sharma explains, it has become quite common in left-wing activist and academic circles to argue that migrants are "settlers" or even "colonisers", immigration is "conquest", and that Indigenous people need to be "centred" at the expense of migrants. Migrant populations, including those that have suffered – and continue to suffer – from racism are often portrayed as a privileged layer who benefit from the racism directed towards Indigenous people.

This is a profoundly conservative world view that expresses some of the worst, and most self-defeating, aspects of privilege theory politics. To start with, as Sharma writes, it downplays the racist treatment of migrants:

> Portraying all non-Indigenous people as "settlers" assumes that no clear distinction was made between Whites and non-Whites

> in the "White Settler" colonial projects, nor that any distinction is made between those racialized as White and those racialized as not White in today's White National-Native projects. Instead, those whom imperial states (and later nation-states) clearly racialized as undesirable and inferior (e.g., Trask's "Asians" in Hawai'i) are now represented as having been a party to the very projects they were expressly – and juridically – excluded from. Indeed, in the effort to render the experiences of Indigenous National-Natives and Migrants as *incommensurable*, the violence done to those who were made into Migrants is rendered as politically unimportant. (p.254)

One particularly terrible example that Sharma cites are the arguments of Bonita Lawrence, a Métis scholar, and Enakshi Dua, a self-identified "Asian settler colonist". Lawrence and Dua argue that in Canada, all

> people of color are settlers. Broad differences exist between those brought as slaves, currently working as migrant laborers, refugees without legal documentation, or émigrés who have obtained citizenship. Yet people of color live on land that is appropriated and contested, where Aboriginal peoples are denied nationhood and access to their own lands. (p.252)

That's right folks…even slaves were privileged settlers!

Lawrence and Dua also assert that campaigns by migrants against racism actually contribute "to the active colonization of Aboriginal peoples" and that "anti-racism is premised on an ongoing colonial project" and accepts "a colonizing social formation" (p.252).

These arguments are not confined to obscure academic journals. Here in Australia there have been multiple examples of people on the progressive left dismissing the struggles of racially oppressed non-Indigenous groups on the basis that they are somehow less legitimate than the struggles of Indigenous people.

In 2020 for instance a group of Sudanese high school students, inspired by the Black Lives Matter rebellion in the US, tried to organise a solidarity rally in Melbourne. They were instantly denounced on the internet as "settler" Africans. It was asserted that they had no right to organise such a rally as their experience of racism was supposedly fundamentally different from that of both Indigenous people and African Americans. This totally ignored the fact that Sudanese people in Melbourne had been the target of racist police harassment and hysterical right-wing media campaigns for years.

Similarly, during the campaign against the right-wing Reclaim Australia movement there were significant sections of the Sydney left who argued that unless Indigenous issues were the dominant theme of the rallies they were essentially reinforcing racism. This was despite the fact that Reclaim Australia's central focus was on opposing a supposed Islamic takeover of Australian society. In fact Reclaim Australia raised no racist demands about Indigenous people (although undoubtedly there were people in it who had racist ideas about Indigenous rights) and even flew the Aboriginal flag at their rallies. The idea that Muslims should have a central role in combating a movement dedicated to deporting them en masse from the country was never raised.

As Sharma explains, the counterposition between Indigenous struggles and other anti-racist struggles is rubbish. Often it is based on the idea that Indigenous struggles are radically anti-nationalist, while, as Lawrence and Dua argue, the struggles of other racially oppressed groups are "premised on an ongoing colonial project". This ignores the fact that most Indigenous struggles *also* accept the existence of capitalist states and national sovereignty. As Sharma puts it, "while sometimes deploying radical, anticolonial discourse, Indigenous National-Native nationalist projects do not disrupt a postcolonial world of separate and national territorial sovereigns", in fact they "reproduce it" (p.251).

In order to back up this argument, most of Sharma's book is a history of the formation and development of nationalism and nation states throughout the nineteenth and twentieth centuries. As the European empires colonised much of the world they divided their colonised subjects into "Indigenous-Natives" and "Migrant-Natives", "with the former regarded as more native than the latter". This division would also shape the politics of the national liberation movements that arose in opposition to the European empires:

> Both categories were codified in imperial law so that the two categories of colonized Natives were governed by different laws. These laws, which included differential allocations of land, political rights, and power for people in the two groups, materialized the differences between Indigenous-Natives and Migrant-Natives. Indigenous-Natives were granted formal access to territories and political rights on it through "Native authorities". Migrant-Natives were not. Such imperial distinctions profoundly reshaped politics in the colonies and informed how national liberation movements imagined which people were the People of the nation. (p.8)

As Sharma explains, national liberation movements "took the imperial idea of indigeneity as a stable and static group and retooled it to fit the nations they were in the process of creating" (p.8). As national liberation movements across Asia, Africa and the Middle East drove out the imperial powers and achieved at least nominal national independence, they also created their own form of national identity that reproduced divisions between "natives" and "migrants".

This had a devastating impact on those deemed to be migrants, as Sharma details. In Burma, Buddhist nationalists have unleashed waves of violence and forced expulsions of Rohingya people who have been "made Migrants both in national law and in everyday life". Conflicts in Africa, and in particular Darfur, have been framed as a "racialized conflict between 'Black African' National-Natives and 'light-skinned Arab' Migrants", feeding into Islamophobia. The infamous 1994 Rwandan genocide had its roots in "the self-identification of Hutus as the National-Natives of Rwanda and the categorization of Tutsis as colonizing Migrants" who need to be violently removed from a nation that they apparently did not "belong" to (pp.9–10).

In those countries with settler colonial origins like Australia, Canada, the United States of America, New Zealand etc, the situation is different from that in the post-independence nations, but the politics of separating "natives" from "migrants" is also evident. In these countries there are two separate groups claiming to be the real "natives": the Indigenous populations and the descendants of mainly European settlers. The Indigenous population is of course the oppressed group in this conflict, and socialists support the struggle of Indigenous people against the racism of the capitalist state in these countries. It has also primarily been the capitalist nation state that oppresses Indigenous people that has also oppressed migrant populations. However, as Sharma explains:

> [M]any Indigenous National-Natives, since at least the late 1980s, have come to view all Migrants (White and non-White) as barriers to their own claims to national sovereignty. Indeed, a growing chorus of Indigenous National-Native opinion asserts that all Migrants are "settler colonists". Some Indigenous National-Natives have even said that "the label settler is too historically and politically sterile" and that all Migrants are nothing less than "occupiers" (Ward 2016). As the "White" in White Settler colonialism is omitted and replaced by a generic discussion of "settler colonialism", negatively racialized people (i.e., Black, Latinx, or, perhaps especially, Asian people) – each of whom was expressly excluded from the White Settler colonial project – are increasingly depicted as colonizers of Indigenous National-Natives. (p.11)

Sharma here is not saying that "White people demanding the expulsion of Migrants in the name of being the 'indigenous people of Europe'" are equivalent to "various Indian or Aboriginal claims to national sovereignty in the United States, Canada, or Australia", nor that such divisions lead to genocide in this situation. However, as she writes (the term autochthonous here meaning ideologies based on a concept of Nativeness):

> [T]here are important similarities in the different uses of autochthonous discourses – and these are not merely semantic. All autochthonous discourses portray Nativeness as an essential,

> unpolitical characteristic of some people. Authochthony is further understood as a concept helping us better understand social relations. However, Nativeness is neither an essence nor an analytic tool. It is, instead, a racialized idea and political category allowing some to make claims against others. All autochthonous discourses are also relational. They produce Migrants as the negative others of National-Natives. By articulating Nativeness with "nationness" and claiming that only National-Natives have rightful political claims to power, autochthonous discourses count on the subordination of Migrants. (p.271)

While many Indigenous people claim that their concepts of self-determination or sovereignty are simply a return to pre-colonial Indigenous cultures, Sharma shows that in reality much of the political framework around Indigenous sovereignty borrows heavily from mainstream nationalist ideas. This shouldn't be particularly surprising for people from the socialist left. After all, as the most famous modern socialist writer on nationalism, Benedict Anderson, explained, all nationalisms, including those of the oppressed, are invented in response to the already established system of nation-states. The idea that they are fully formed, pre-existing, national identities inherited from a distant past is part of the mythic ideology of all nation-state projects, and all movements seeking to become nation-states.[1]

As Sharma makes clear in a reply to a recent critique of her book, this doesn't mean that Indigenous nationalism is just the same as the mainstream nationalism of countries like Australia. However the pitfalls of Indigenous nationalism can't be ignored.[2] In her book Sharma explores a number of negative examples of Indigenous nationalism.

In 1981 the Mohawks of Kahnawà:ke (in Canada's province of Quebec) adopted the Kahnawà:ke Mohawk Law and Moratorium on Mixed Marriages. This law meant that "any Mohawk who married a non-native lost the right to residency, land allotment, land holding, voting, and office-holding in Kahnawà:ke". The Membership

---

1. Anderson 1991.
2. Sharma 2021.

Department of the Kahnawà:ke's Mohawk Band Council further stipulated that "any Mohawk who married a non-native would leave the community". The Band Council defined a Mohawk as someone "whose name appeared on the Band list and Reinstatement list and who had 50% or more blood quantum". In 1981 several forced expulsions based on this law took place, then after a long hiatus they began again in February 2020, when letters were sent to 26 so-called "no-Mohawks" informing them that they had to leave the area.[3]

A similar situation has arisen regarding the Cherokee Nation's decision to exclude Cherokee Freedmen, the descendants of Black people who were slaves of the Cherokees and were brought with them on the Trail of Tears to lands later claimed as Cherokee national territory. For over one hundred years the Cherokee Freedmen were considered apart of the Cherokee Nation following the abolition of slavery in 1865. In the 1980s an attempt to remove the Cherokee Freedmen from the Cherokee Nation was struck down by a court ruling. In response Chadwick Smith, the principal chief of the Cherokees, "called a special election to amend the tribal constitution to exclude all those unable to prove descent from ancestors enrolled as 'Cherokees by blood'". Smith made it very clear that he believed "the sovereignty of the Cherokee Nation was at stake" and "that his action was primarily directed at expelling the approximately 2,800 Cherokee Freedmen" (pp.256–9).

These might seem like extreme examples, but they flow from the acceptance of the nation-state model as one that should be pursued by Indigenous people, albeit in a particular form, in order to apparently achieve sovereignty and liberation. Even when such exclusions aren't a prominent part of Indigenous nationalist projects, the reality is that all such projects involve coming to terms with the established capitalist state that controls the national territory and entering into an agreement with it, rather than struggling to overthrow it. It is this framework

---

3. To give a sense of how backward a lot of the debates about membership of Indigenous communities have become, compare the decisions of the Mohawks with the position of left-wing Native American activist and anthropologist Archie Phinney, who wrote in 1943 that "It would be a serious loss to the Indian cause if a half-blood or one-fourth blood exclusion rule should be adopted". Phinney 2003 [1943], p.40.

which underpins the counterposition between the rights of migrants and Indigenous people on the contemporary progressive left. To the problems that Sharma identifies with Indigenous nationalist projects I would add that understanding the class dynamics within Indigenous populations is absolutely essential. The narrow framing of Indigenous struggles as movements for the creation of sovereign political bodies, like the First Nations Assembly in Canada, has primarily benefited a small, privileged elite of middle-class and even capitalist Indigenous people rather than Indigenous populations as a whole. This layer has been increasingly promoted by the rest of the ruling class and the capitalist state in former colonial settler countries.

In Australia for instance the Morrison government's Indigenous Procurement Policy saw 10,920 government contracts, valued at $1.09 billion, awarded to 943 Indigenous businesses in 2020–21. This is set to increase in coming years, with Morrison announcing a target of 3 percent of the value of Commonwealth contracts to be awarded to Indigenous businesses from 2022 onwards. It is also notable that it is often government departments traditionally associated with the hard right of politics that have had some of the biggest contracts with Indigenous businesses. The largest number of contracts is with the Department of Defence, which signed 6,476 contracts (valued at $610 million) in 2020–2021 There is also significant ruling-class support behind some kind of national Indigenous political body, such as an Indigenous Voice to Parliament, a project backed by the Business Council of Australia.[4]

This follows the path already pursued in Canada and New Zealand, where significant Indigenous middle classes have been created that have become a conservatising force as the political bodies they have established have been incorporated into the pre-existing capitalist state.

Sharma's criticism of the counterposition between the rights of Indigenous people and migrants is useful, but I would go further. The whole framework of settler colonial theory, and its premise that in countries like Australia the key power dynamic is essentially that

---

4. National Indigenous Australians Agency 2021.

between "settlers" and "non-settlers", leads to total confusion. As I've explained in a previous issue of this journal:

> It is particularly disorienting to argue that the relationship between Australian capitalism and Indigenous people today is "colonial" in nature, with its implication that all of "settler society" is bound up in a colonial exploitation of the Indigenous population. This is to attribute the continuation of Indigenous oppression to the population as a whole rather than Australian capitalism and those who run it.[5]

It also ignores the long history of sympathy for and solidarity with Indigenous struggles by the labour movement and the socialist left in Australia, about which I've also written in previous issues of this journal.[6] This is because settler colonial theory is profoundly shaped by the rise of identity politics and privilege theory which seeks, as another contributor to this journal put it, the "elevation of select identity groups to moral and political pre-eminence, while implicitly or explicitly subordinating others".[7] So something that would have strengthened Sharma's argument would have been a consideration of how the rise of identity politics has negatively impacted on the socialist left's understanding of issues of oppression.

The only serious alternative to the politics of ranking different oppressed groups against each other is revolutionary socialist politics rooted in solidarity and working-class self-emancipation. Recently I came across the February 1921 front cover of *The Crusader*, the newspaper of the African Blood Brotherhood. The Brotherhood was an organisation of radical Black activists in America who after a few years joined the Communist Party. The front cover of this issue of *The Crusader* celebrated the national liberation movement in Ireland, declaring:

> The Irish fight for liberty is the greatest Epic of Modern History. It is a struggle that should have the sympathy and

---

5. Humphreys 2021a.
6. Humphreys 2021b and 2022.
7. Garnham 2021.

active support of every lover of liberty – of every member of an oppressed group. The Negro in particular should be interested in the Irish struggle, for while it is patent that Ireland can never escape from the menace of "the overshadowing empire" so long as England is able to maintain her grip on the riches and manpower of India and Africa, it is also clear that those suffering together under the heel of British imperialism must learn to CO-ORDINATE THEIR EFFORTS before they can HOPE TO BE FREE.

Clearly these revolutionaries didn't think that the role of radicals was to diminish the struggles of other oppressed and exploited groups, nor to venerate their own struggle as the one for everyone else to bow down to in moralistic reverence.

An issue that I wouldn't agree with Sharma about is the acceptance that the "Commons" is an alternative to the nation-state model. I'm a pretty classical Marxist, workers' state with workers' control, kind of person, and the Commons is all a bit too vague and prefigurative for my liking. However the thrust of what Sharma is arguing is right. Revolutionaries ultimately should be looking to a world based on human emancipation from national borders, and while we can support the right to self-determination for oppressed groups, that doesn't mean we have to be uncritical of these movements, particularly considering the more than half a century of negative experiences we can now draw on from China to India and beyond.

I'm reminded of something that the great Irish civil rights leader and socialist Eamonn McCann said at the Marxism conference in 2015. He explained that while socialists of course make a distinction between the nationalism of the oppressed and the oppressor, we should never forget that at the end of the day we are internationalists, not nationalists. When a young comrade asked him what his greatest regret in life was, McCann replied that it was not arguing more seriously and confidently with those activists who went from the civil rights movement into the Irish Republican Army. Within a few years many of them would be dead, and those who survived would see their national movement become a hollow shell of the hopes, dreams and desires that had once animated them to join it.

Real solidarity with oppressed people means being willing to *critically* engage in struggles and debate out the complex issues.

References

Anderson, Benedict 1991, *Imagined Communities: Reflections on the Origin and Spread of Nationalism*, Verso.

Garnham, Sarah 2021, "The failure of identity politics: A Marxist analysis," *Marxist Left Review*, 22, Winter. https://marxistleftreview.org/articles/the-failure-of-identity-politics-a-marxist-analysis/

Humphreys, Jordan 2021a, "Capitalism, colonialism and class: A Marxist explanation of Indigenous oppression today", *Marxist Left Review*, 21, Summer. https://marxistleftreview.org/articles/indigenous_oppression/

Humphreys, Jordan 2021b, "Aboriginal unionists in the 1890s shearers' strikes: a forgotten history", *Marxist Left Review*, 22, Winter. https://marxistleftreview.org/articles/aboriginal-unionists-in-the-1890s-shearers-strikes-a-forgotten-history/

Humphreys, Jordan 2022, "Red and black: How Australian communists fought for Indigenous liberation", *Marxist Left Review*, 23, Summer. https://marxistleftreview.org/articles/red-and-black-how-australian-communists-fought-for-indigenous-liberation/

National Indigenous Australians Agency 2021, *Indigenous Procurement Policy*. https://www.niaa.gov.au/indigenous-affairs/economic-development/indigenous-procurement-policy-ipp#data

Phinney, Archie 2003 [1943], "Problem of the 'White Indians' of the United States", *Wicazo Sa Review*, Vol. 18, No. 2, *The Politics of Sovereignty* (Autumn), pp.37–40.

Sharma, Nandita 2021, "Decolonization without National Sovereignty: a response to Neil Braganza", *Spectre*. https://spectrejournal.com/a-response-to-neil-braganzas-review/

LIZ ROSS

Review: Nuclear secrets and racist lies

> **Liz Ross** has written extensively on a range of issues including women's and gay liberation, the environment and the Australian union movement. Her most recent book is *Stuff the Accord! Pay Up! Workers' resistance to the ALP-ACTU Accord* (2020).

Elizabeth Tynan, *The Secret of Emu Field*, NewSouth, 2022

The bomb caught us then at Twelve Mile... "Something **wrong!**"... bluish smoke rolled over...filled up the hills, the holes – rolled along the ground – to the tree tops... Right over the top of us...[1]

IN 1953 INDIGENOUS ACTIVIST JESSIE LENNON, HER FAMILY and many others were suddenly exposed to fallout from the Totem I nuclear blast, part of British nuclear testing in central Australia. In her book, *I'm the one that know this country,* she recalls the horror, the bewilderment, the sicknesses, miscarriages and cancers that followed – and the anger and activism in the fight for compensation. Elizabeth Tynan follows up this story and many others in *The Secret of Emu Field*. Here she forensically and damningly documents the secrecy, the inadequate warnings, the total lack of care for the local Indigenous groups after the explosion, the lack of responsibility for civilian and military staff working at the test sites and the overall reckless testing of atomic weaponry, all for Britain's imperial ambitions to become the third nuclear superpower.

---

1. Lennon, p.88–9. Emphasis in the original.

"The wrenching irony and tragedy of Totem", as Tynan reveals of the Emu Field detonations, "for both the Aboriginal people and the military personnel caught up in the tests were that the harm was caused in pursuit of technology that was soon to become obsolete" (p.63).[2]

Tynan's brief covers the three British nuclear test sites, Monte Bello Islands, Emu Field and Maralinga, where various weapons components and bombs were tested in central Australia and off Western Australia's coast, between 1952 and 1963. *Emu Field* is her second book covering the Totem I and II blasts. The first, *Atomic Thunder* (2016), dissects the better-known Maralinga Buffalo and Antler tests and a third, about Monte Bello and the Hurricane and Mosaic explosions, is still to come.

World War II saw the horror of atomic bomb devastation in Japan's Hiroshima and Nagasaki. Enough you would think to end nuclear warfare forever, but for the world's imperialist powers – the USA and the USSR – it was the start of a Cold War nuclear arms race. Britain, though nearly bankrupt, was desperate to restore its position among the powerful nations, planning a nuclear future as early as August 1945. Foreign secretary Ernest Bevin said, "We've got to have this thing… whatever it costs… We've got to have the bloody Union Jack on top of it".[3] However, despite its wartime nuclear collaboration with America, Britain found itself shut out of any future joint projects, forcing it to look to its former empire for cooperation.[4]

When Canada rejected their overtures for testing grounds, Britain turned to Australia in 1950, attracted by the "vast, empty spaces" and availability of uranium. The Australian government welcomed the request (p.216). As *The Rockhampton Morning Bulletin* editorialised on 15 October 1953, "Almost overnight we have emerged as a prospective major supplier of the precious and coveted ore, source of the military

---

2. The tests at Emu Field were for fission bombs that split uranium or plutonium, as with the bombs at Hiroshima and Nagasaki. In July 1954 the UK Cabinet decided to develop fusion or H-bombs, which forced elements like hydrogen to fuse and resulted in more powerful explosions.
3. Quoted in Tynan 2016, p.115.
4. The McMahon Act of 1946 excluded Britain and other countries from nuclear cooperation, over a British spy scandal. The British thought it was a commercial decision to corner a lucrative market in nuclear weaponry and energy. The Act was amended in 1958 to let the British back in. Tynan 2016, p.98.

power in the present and of industrial power in the not distant future" (quoted on p.235).[5]

The deal was secretly signed on 16 September 1950, with the Australians expecting an equal partnership. The British, however, proved reluctant or bluntly refused to share information, providing bland statements covering up the real purpose of the projects[6] (p.94). A secrecy that has continued.

The Australian government was just as determined to keep a lid on information reaching the general public and the press, enacting extra laws which severely limited access to all sites.[7] Prime Minister Robert Menzies only notified Cabinet after he'd agreed to the UK's request, while limiting any involvement or information sharing for the project to a few ministers and defence chiefs.

So close to the bombing of Japan, however, Cold War warrior Menzies had to both assure Australians of the inherent safety of the tests and of the necessity to thwart the so-called Communist threat.[8] In one of his weekly *Man to Man* radio talks, he explained:

> There is tremendous public interest in Atomic Bombs... Unfortunately there are scare stories, wild allegations and between you and me, a good deal of nonsense... But we must face the facts. And they are that the threat to the world's peace does not come from the Americans or the British, but from aggressive Communist-Imperialism. In this dreadful state of affairs, superiority in atomic weapons is vital. To that superiority Australia must contribute as best she can. (quoted on p.200)

---

5. Reynolds 2000 expands on the expected industrial bonanza the Australian ruling class planned for.
6. The official British description provided to the Australians was that Emu Field tests would "determine certain characteristics of fissile material", with no other detail provided.
7. The top-secret Woomera Rocket Range's prohibited area was extended to Emu Field in March 1953, just months before the October test. Secretive D-notices which restricted press reportage were established for the first time by Menzies. Sydney's *Daily Mirror*, an anti-Liberal publication, was one of the few mainstream papers that consistently questioned the tests.
8. In 1953 the Communist Party of Australia was already campaigning against the British tests and H-bombs.

Despite his bluster, Menzies was well aware that atomic testing on Australian soil would be controversial. After formally agreeing to the tests, he asked British Prime Minister Clement Attlee not to announce the deal until after May 1951, the date of the upcoming Australian election. Labour's Attlee agreed and Menzies won.

Done on the cheap, involving drastic compromises with safety, Emu Field's Totem I and II devices tested options for mass-produced, smaller fission weapons. The explosions and a series of so-called minor tests left a radioactive time-bomb which the British walked away from, just as they did after the later Pacific tests.[9] Limited compensation and clean-up costs were extracted from the UK, but only after increased pressure from Australia arising from damning exposés in the late 1970s and the 1984 Royal Commission.

Even then, the clean-ups of all three testing sites were cursory at best, straight-out dishonest in most cases, continuing the enduring lies of those in charge.[10] At Emu Field the area was barely touched, though some equipment was removed at the time, including a tank used on-site to measure exposure to radiation. Still radioactive, it was sent to the Puckapunyal army base then shipped to Vietnam for the war there. In the latest decontamination work, undertaken in the 1990s, the pitiful $600,000 budget was underspent. Hundreds of thousands of radioactive trinitite glass fragments, buried vehicles and other decaying structures litter the area still.[11] There are almost no living creatures to be seen to this day.

Official statements repeatedly claimed there were no Indigenous Australians in the testing zones. This was a lie. Both governments were very well aware of their presence and as early as March 1953 had developed covering statements if questioned. For example: "...our reply should be that the Australian Government have satisfied themselves that no aborigine will come to harm" (p.60). They certainly knew about earlier Aboriginal opposition to setting up the Woomera Rocket Testing Range in 1946. Once again, as Tynan writes in her earlier book,

---

9. Maclellan 2017.
10. Although some expressed regret afterwards, they suffered no penalties.
11. Trinitite contains trapped radioactive materials including plutonium (pp.84–5). The "minor" Kitten tests at Emu Field caused chemical and radioactive contamination.

Atomic Thunder, many hundreds of Indigenous people lost access to their homelands and traditional ways of life, "swept away from the desert test sites like detritus".[12]

At a time when Indigenous Australians didn't have the vote and were counted amongst the flora and fauna of the country, little care was shown to the local groups. And of those found in the area before or after the tests, some were forced to go to Yalata, a virtual prison camp, while others were removed with no regard for where they went.

Many died from the blasts. But among the survivors, some became lifelong activists. One Yankunytjatjara man, Yami Lester, went down this path after being blinded, speaking up for his people and his land. He was ridiculed by Ernest Titterton, one of the key Australian scientists overseeing the project, who called the allegations a scare campaign. His dismissed their concerns in racist terms, arguing that, "if you investigate black mists you're going to get into an area where mystique is the central feature" (pp.132–4). Until his death he refused to acknowledge any harm done.

It wasn't just that their current lives were destroyed, the Indigenous population lost much of their past. Priceless artefacts in the region, recording an early "Stonehenge" structure and evidence of a long-standing civilisation (estimated today as at least 50,000 years of continuous occupation) were destroyed as the sites were prepared for the blasts, or by the tests themselves. All of this was known to those in charge beforehand.

In a somewhat hollow victory, the lands of Emu Field (1996) and Maralinga (1984) were grudgingly handed back to the Tjarutja owners, more to shed the government's responsibility than as a genuine land rights settlement.[13] Visits to the area require permission from the local custodians, but also from the Defence Department, as they are within the Woomera Prohibited zone, where dangerous weaponry is still tested.

There were no nuclear tests in the area from 1963, not just because the British decamped, but also due to the growing opposition to atomic weapons. Just a year into the tests, public opinion was turning, and by

---

12. Tynan 2016, p.34.
13. Green 2014.

March 1956 a Gallup poll showed that the majority of Australians were against the tests. Politically the situation was changing too, as bipartisan support collapsed and in June 1956 the ALP Caucus belatedly voted to oppose future tests.

Internationally there was pressure for a nuclear disarmament treaty, with the development in 1954 and 1955 of a widely supported International Peace Campaign. In Australia the Communist Party, in line with the Soviet Union's "peaceful coexistence" policy, also agitated against nuclear weapons.

The strength of the anti-nuclear campaigns meant the Australian ruling class was never able to develop a nuclear industry, much to the frustration of the country's warmongers and nuclear power proponents. However with the current nuclear submarine project and a renewed push for so-called clean nuclear power, we cannot rest in our opposition.

Knowing who our enemies are is crucial for our continuing battles. While critical of the Australian ruling class, many, including Tynan, see Australia as a lapdog, vassal or "atomic banana republic", mindlessly led by great and powerful friends, the UK or US. This leads her to using such concepts as "nuclear colonialism",[14] seeing Australia as a colonial outpost rather than as the imperialist, capitalist state it has been for most of its existence. For the alternative, Marxist understanding of Australia's capitalist imperialist role, two books by Tom O'Lincoln[15] spell out this important distinction.

Menzies, as well as being the "lickspittle Empire loyalist" he undoubtedly was (p.372), saw the potential of a nuclear weapons and power-based economy to fuel ambitious post-war reconstruction plans. Projects such as the Snowy Mountains Scheme, the Woomera Rocket Range, ramping up investment in education and expanded resource exploration were all part of an integrated charging-up of Australian capitalism.[16]

---

14. Tynan 2016, p.23, references Jennifer Viereck's definition of nuclear colonialism as "the taking (or destruction) of other people's natural resources, lands and wellbeing for one's own, in the furtherance of nuclear development".
15. O'Lincoln 2011 and 2014.
16. See Reynolds 2000.

This book is an essential part of an expanding body of work, art, music, documentaries, scientific research, personal memoirs and so on, that adds up to a totally damning picture of Australian and British complicity, cover-ups and dangerous recklessness that has resulted in the destruction of Indigenous Australian and military and civilian personnel's lives, leaving a toxic legacy for us all. In Alistair Hulett's moving song he concludes, in words just as applicable to Emu Field:

> *Out on the plains of Maralinga*
> *What happened there was a bloody disgrace*
> *Out on the plains of Maralinga*
> *It was total disregard for the whole human race.*[17]

References

Green, Jim 2014, "The nuclear war against Australia's Aboriginal people", *The Ecologist*, 14 July. https://theecologist.org/2014/jul/14/nuclear-war-against-australias-aboriginal-people

Hulett, Alistair 1992, "The plains of Maralinga", from the album *Dance of the Underclass*, Red Rattler Records. https://www.youtube.com/watch?v=V9BxpFy_1kM

Lennon, Jessie 2011, *I'm the one that know this country!*, Aboriginal Studies Press [2nd edition].

Maclellan, Nic 2017, *Grappling with the bomb. Britain's Pacific H-bomb tests.* ANU Press, Pacific Series.

O'Lincoln, Tom 2011, *Australia's Pacific war. Challenging a national myth*, Interventions.

O'Lincoln, Tom 2014, *The neighbour from hell. Two centuries of Australian imperialism*, Interventions.

Reynolds, Wayne, 2000, *Australia's Bid for the Atomic Bomb*, Melbourne University Press.

Tynan, Elizabeth 2016, *Atomic Thunder: the Maralinga Story*, NewSouth.

---

17. Hulett 1992.

ALEXIS VASSILEY

Review: *Breaking Things at Work*

Alexis Vassiley is a socialist based in Western Australia who has been active in anti-racist and anti-fascist campaigns, and has contributed to the *Labour History* journal.

Gavin Mueller, *Breaking Things at Work: the Luddites Were Right About Why You Hate Your Job*, Verso, 2021.

BREAKING THINGS AT WORK ANALYSES EPISODES of working-class struggle throughout history in the service of a radical left approach to technology and automation. Many on the left see technology as at worst neutral – the technology itself isn't the problem, it's who controls it. Others say that technology "is a boon to socialism" as it creates the conditions of radical transformation – the "fully automated luxury communism" thesis.[1]

Mueller disagrees – arguing that "technology often plays a detrimental role in working life, and in struggles for a better one" (p.4). His approach views technological change in the context of class struggle and capitalist social relations. We need to ask for what purpose are bosses introducing a particular technology, how does it affect workers' work lives as well as broader society, and what struggles does it provoke.

The US mining unions' response to vast post-war automation is set out in the chapter "Against Automation". Mining workers struck for months in 1949 and 1950 to respond to the introduction of equipment

---

1. Bastani 2019.

called "the continuous miner" or "the man killer". Raya Dunayevskaya of the Johnson-Forest Tendency (and formerly Trotsky's secretary) argued that your attitude to automation depended on your "relationship to the machine". Capitalists, management and union officials alike sang its praises, while workers' bodies suffered its effects. She quoted an autoworker: "All Automation has meant to us is unemployment and overwork. *Both at the same time*" (p.69). Meanwhile *Fortune* magazine called John L Lewis, head of the United Mine Workers, "the best salesman the machinery industry ever had" (pp.66-7). Dunayevskaya "mercilessly criticized the 'labor bureaucracy' as 'brainwashed', as they took management's side against their own workers while their power base was cut out" (p.69) – the mining workforce was cut in half.

One (all too short) section notes that Black Panther leaders Eldridge Cleaver and Huey Newton took up the question of automation and technological change and its negative impact on Blacks in America (p.82). Black workers in Detroit in the 1960s referred to the increased productivity that had come with new machinery speeding up their work as "niggermation" as they suffered incredibly high rates of injury and death – a casualty rate higher than the Vietnam War (p.83).

In the 1980s, the introduction of computers sparked debate and resistance. One pseudonymous writer argued for sabotage, noting in an IT workers' magazine that "rather than freeing clerks from the gaze of their supervisors, the management statistics programs that many new systems provide will allow the careful scrutiny of each worker's output regardless of where the work is done" (p.104).

Automation is a subject full of wild predictions, often a fact- and history- free wonderland. Some, like Kai-Fu Lee, formerly of Google China, predict the total replacement of knowledge work. Others don't go this far, but buy into the mythologising of technology's "magic", divorced from the human labour, at all levels, that powers it. Yet automation and artificial intelligence (AI) is not about replacing the working class, but better exploiting it. Technology reshapes work and controls workers, augmenting exploitation[2] (and often not even increasing productivity, as Marxist economist Michael Roberts notes[3]).

2. This term is from Moore and Woodcock (eds) 2021.
3. Roberts 2022.

As a Data and Society report states, "automated and AI technologies tend to mask the human labor that allows them to be fully integrated into a social context while profoundly changing the conditions and quality of labor that is at stake" (p.115).

Jeff Bezos calls Amazon Mechanical Turk workers "artificial artificial intelligence".[4] It is telling: the original Mechanical Turk, or Automaton chess player, was an eighteenth century hoax where a puppet designed to look like a machine supposedly played chess. A human chess master was hidden inside. The reality behind the hype is that "ghost work" – hidden from consumers and paid at a pittance in piece rates – is what powers AI. One company, Samasource, specifically targets slum dwellers for the mindless work of feeding information to machine learning algorithms. Its former CEO disgustingly justified the low wages by not wanting to "distort local labour markets" in Kenyan slums (p.118). Technology is made to seem like an autonomous agent operating apart from human intervention. This fetishisation of technology serves multiple purposes. It wows consumers and venture capitalists. It helps give corporations some distance from the negative impacts they cause. And it can make workers more fearful for their livelihoods.

Class struggle in a context of changing work arrangements and more technology at work is not new. Textile workers in England in the early 1800s had their lives transformed by new machines which massively increased productivity: "wages plummeted and hunger began to set in" (p.9). Under the name of a mythical "King Ludd" – hence, Luddites – they fought back: "At the height of their activity in Nottingham, from November 1811 to February 1812, disciplined bands of masked Luddites attacked and destroyed frames almost every night. Mill owners were terrified. Wages rose" (p.10). Spies, crackdowns, repression and executions crushed a movement that Eric Hobsbawm described as "collective bargaining by riot". Today, the term Luddite is not connected with collective struggle, but rather, misleadingly, with technophobia. History, as Mueller observes, "has not been kind to the Luddites" (p.11).

---

4. Jones 2021, p.31.

The introduction of the "Taylor system" in a Massachusetts factory in 1911 sparked a walk-off. Today, workers in a hospital smash up robots meant to replace them with baseball bats, while Amazon workers fight back in workplaces where Dickensian conditions are enforced with cutting-edge technology and surveillance.

That workers take centre stage is key to the book's strengths. Support for workers' struggles is part of this. So is the centrality of the working class to capitalist production, and the effect of new technologies on workers' conditions, livelihoods, and health.

Mueller situates his politics within the Marxist tradition:

> Marxism is a theory of struggle. ... Technology is an important site of these struggles: not only is militant opposition to technology a historical fact, but it can suggest a more liberatory politics of work and technology – one that is more easily supported by Marx's work than are contemporary post-work utopias. (p.29)

In an interesting section in chapter 1, the author sympathetically surveys some of Marx's own writings on technology, finding a certain ambivalence but not a technological determinist. While Mueller identifies with workerism, a current foreign to this journal, (and is overly sympathetic to hacking), the politics of *Breaking Things at Work* are refreshingly good.

The book's arguments have implications both for the approach to technology in the here and now, and in the future. "[T]he radical left can and should put forth a decelerationist politics: a politics of slowing down change, undermining technological progress, and limiting capital's rapacity, while developing organization and cultivating militancy" (pp. 127–8), Mueller argues. The term decelerationism may seem jarring. And to talk about "Luddism" as a political current is over-egging it. But it is right to say that struggles "against" technology are progressive. Looking further forward, socialists often argue that under socialism workers would simply take over the global supply chains and use all of capitalism's technology.[5] This is too simplistic.

---

5. See for example, Hillier 2022.

Technology is designed for labour exploitation and capital accumulation (and war) under capitalism, and can't always be disentangled from the social relations it was produced under. As Mueller points out, we need to pay attention to the way work is organised and the working conditions. We should reject production for production's sake and efficiency as a goal in itself. Chapter 2 sets out the debates within the Bolshevik Party on these questions, but this is not fleshed out.

In a short book of 130 pages, Gavin Mueller draws together the work of many writers, and offers vignettes of numerous vastly different struggles. The historical approach employed is useful, as indeed it is whenever something is portrayed as new and shiny. The book is not without its limitations. It can be meandering, and often covers topics in insufficient depth. But it's insightful and thought-provoking – definitely worth a read for those interested in questions of technology and automation.

References

Bastani, Aaron 2019, *Fully Automated Luxury Communism*, Verso.

Hillier, Ben 2022, "What would be different about a socialist economy?", *Red Flag*, 24 July. https://redflag.org.au/article/what-would-be-different-about-socialist-economy

Jones, Phil 2021, *Work Without the Worker: Labour in the Age of Platform Capitalism*, Verso.

Moore, Phoebe V and Jamie Woodcock (eds) 2021, *Augmented Exploitation: Artificial Intelligence, Automation and Work*, Pluto Press.

Roberts, Michael 2022, "The Future of Work 3 – Automation", 4 July. https://thenextrecession.wordpress.com/2022/07/04/the-future-of-work-3-automation/